C000081277

THE EVIL
THAT MEN DO

Brian Masters

BLACK SWAN

THE EVIL THAT MEN DO
A BLACK SWAN BOOK : 9780552143073

Originally published in Great Britain by Doubleday
a division of Transworld Publishers Ltd

PRINTING HISTORY
Doubleday edition published 1996
Black Swan edition published 1997

Copyright © Brian Masters 1996

The right of Brian Masters to be identified
as the author of this work has been asserted in accordance
with sections 77 and 78 of the Copyright Designs and
Patents Act 1988

Condition of Sale
This book is sold subject to the condition that it shall not,
by way of trade or otherwise, be lent, re-sold, hired out or
otherwise circulated in any form of binding or cover other
than that in which it is published and without a similar
condition including this condition being imposed on the
subsequent purchaser.

Set in 11-on-12pt Melior by
Hewer Text Composition Services, Edinburgh

Black Swan Books are published by Transworld Publishers Ltd,
61–63 Uxbridge Road, London W5 5SA,
in Australia by Transworld Publishers (Australia) Pty Ltd,
15–25 Helles Avenue, Moorebank, NSW 2170
and in New Zealand by Transworld Publishers (NZ) Ltd,
3 William Pickering Drive, Albany, Auckland.

Fifth Printing

The Random House Group Limited supports The Forest Stewardship
Council® (FSC®), the leading international forest-certification organisation.
Our books carrying the FSC label are printed on FSC®-certified paper.
FSC is the only forest-certification scheme supported by the leading
environmental organisations, including Greenpeace. Our
paper procurement policy can be found at
www.randomhouse.co.uk/environment

Printed and bound in Great Britain by Clays Ltd, St Ives plc

Brian Masters began his career with five critical studies in French Literature, and proceeded to write the first full history of all the dukedoms in Great Britain. His subjects for biography have ranged from John Aspinall to E. F. Benson, from Marie Corelli to Georgiana, Duchess of Devonshire. He has rescued twentieth-century society hostesses from the footnotes into a book of their own, and traced the origins of the ruling family of Udaipur in India. His groundbreaking study of mass murderer Dennis Nilson, *Killing for Company*, won the CWA Gold Dagger for non-fiction in 1985, after which he found himself invited to lecture on murderers as well as dukes, gorillas and hostesses. He is also the author of the highly acclaimed *The Shrine of Jeffrey Dahmer* and has recently translated Voltaire's *Treatise on Tolerance*. Although he writes widely for a number of publications, Masters is best known for his features in the *Mail on Sunday*'s magazine *Night and Day*. His latest work, '*She Must Have Known*': *The Trial of Rosemary West*, is now available as a Doubleday hardback.

Also by Brian Masters

Molière
Sartre
Saint-Exupéry
Rabelais
Camus
Wynyard Hall and the Londonderry Family
Dreams about H.M. The Queen
The Dukes
Now Barabbas was a Rotter –
The Extraordinary Life of Marie Corelli
The Mistresses of Charles II
Georgiana, Duchess of Devonshire
Great Hostesses
Killing for Company – The Case of Dennis Nilsen
The Swinging Sixties
The Passion of John Aspinall
Maharana – The Udaipur Dynasty
Gary
The Life of E.F. Benson
Voltaire's Treatise on Tolerance
(edited and translated)
The Shrine of Jeffrey Dahmer
Masters on Murder
'She Must Have Known':
The Trial of Rosemary West

For Marie-Anne and Michel

CONTENTS

FOREWORD

The reader deserves a warning. The subject of this book is really too large, too disparate and elusive for any digest to be successful. It has worried philosophers and perplexed playwrights for centuries, and it is one of the few problems which is both incapable of resolution and has attracted the same commentaries and wisdoms in the fourth century BC as on the cusp of the twenty-first century AD. We seem never to learn, but never to abandon the attempt at learning, for the subject is essentially ourselves.

Why are some of us good-natured and do nice things, and others apparently wicked and destructive? There are a dizzying number of possible answers, none of them entirely satisfactory alone. I hope I may at least help show how they are connected and suggest a possible synthesis. That is my excuse for making yet another attempt at learning and adding another book to the frustrating pile. I do not pretend this effort adds new insights into the eternal mystery of human character, only that it may unravel some of the old.

I have been led to this endeavour by work in the past which has forced me to consider and comprehend some of the blackest individual acts of severely disturbed people – repetitive and compulsive murderers. In so doing, I have clung to the notion that their behaviour, though part of the human potential and not therefore alien to it, was rare, and I longed one day to write about saints, wholly good and cherishable people who would redress the balance of my skewed study. Well, they have had to fight to make their way, cropping up occasionally throughout the book

9

and dominating the final chapter, but I am glad they are here. As I did not know how the book would turn out when I started, I should have despaired had the saints been unable to make themselves heard at all.

Because the subject is necessarily circular, readers will find themselves revisiting familiar thoughts under different guises, and will often feel they are treading the same path over again. I ask them to bear with me, for it is this very familiarity, this sudden re-recognition of an old friend, which helps to fix the subject and prevent its unnerving evaporation into ephemeral theory. I hope that, by the end of the journey, they will feel the train was worth boarding in the first place.

Brian Masters,
London and Castries, 1995

1

THE ASHES IN THE BREAD

The mighty Basilica at Padua is infused with a very special atmosphere. You are aware of it as soon as you pass through the great mediaeval door and enter, blinking, into the high, cool gloom, after the battering heat outside. It is not just the size of the building which impresses, nor its sudden silence broken only by shuffling feet and the odd fluttering of a stray pigeon. You know immediately that you have come to see somebody, or rather that somebody is there waiting for you, and as your eyes grow accustomed to the stark change in light, you notice that the focus of people gathering, quietly praying, or merely walking, is way down towards the end. And there, drawn by curiosity and by something more – a certain indefinable but potent and even rather worrying (because unanticipated) call to friendship – you must yourself go.

This pervasive sensation of personality strikes even those indolent tourists who wander in to see what's on offer and are surprised to find they no longer feel like wandering out quite so indifferently; or those students of art who come to gaze upon the magnificent bronze bas-reliefs by Donatello which adorn the rear of the altar, and who linger afterwards for another reason. For there on the left is another altar, parallel to the nave, with rows of pews before it which are never wholly empty of people. And behind the altar, in an elevated position, is the tomb of a man who died more than seven and a half centuries ago but whose funeral is, in a sense, still going on. For his friends have never ceased to lament him, and their descendants, or proxies, do so today.

The tomb is not set in the wall, but stands imposingly before it, enabling you to walk round and behind it. It is impossible to resist this walk. There you will find an endless stream of people who, one after the other, or sometimes half a dozen at a time, reach up and place the palm of their right hand on the hard stone. There they stand for perhaps thirty seconds before moving on to make way for the next person. Some bow their heads and mumble in prayer, but most are silent and many are tentative, for they may not have known when they first entered the basilica that this was what they were destined to do. I have seen many a proud unbeliever place his hand on the slab and be visibly subdued. Whether they do so in obedience to the herd, or from reticent, uncertain respect, or out of sheer adventure, I know not. There are doubtless a variety of reasons which draw the hand to St Anthony's side, chief among them, of course, the simple gesture of the faithful. Speaking for myself, as a non-Christian, I only know that the first time I went to that tomb I was invaded by a feeling of beneficence, by the knowledge of intense goodness.

I have also been to Dachau and Auschwitz. There one is assailed by an atmosphere of unspeakable wickedness. It makes one giddy, fearful, and ashamed. The walls reek of disgusting memories, 'of how people had to defecate standing upright as a solid mass in sealed carriages; of how babies slithered about in the resulting muck; of how women near childbirth were herded in gas chambers to the music of Viennese waltzes; of how a young girl was praised for her beauty and, told to turn about and walk away, was shot in the back; of how men dug great pits, and then waited on the edge of them for the machine-guns to topple them over.'[1]

The liberators of Belsen came across little children 'resting their heads against the stinking corpses of their mothers, too nearly dead themselves to cry'.[2]

To recognise that the thousands of pilgrims who grow warm in the presence of Anthony and the thousands of Nazi guards who treated their fellow men and women as vermin are interchangeable, that they are all part of mankind and its myriad potential, that they feel the same pain and suffer the same deprivations and disappointments, that they are all, in short, vessels of both good and bad behaviour, must give one pause. Indeed, there are many who will resist the juxtaposition and find it insulting. For them, Anthony was a saint and the Nazi guard a monster, and on such certainties, they say, must rest our moral sanity. But would they be so sure if the good behaviour they applaud were directed towards, say, a child molester, or the bad behaviour they deplore were visited upon a spider? Why must it be less wicked to torture a sentient being to death if that sentient being is not human? Can morality be circumscribed, limited, diluted in such manner? Can we be *relatively* good and *relatively* bad, or is there an absolute measure which allows us to condemn the man who clubs a cat to bloody extinction, with as much indignation as we condemn the SS guard with his indiscriminate gun?

These are difficult questions, to which almost any answer carries inherent dangers and contradictions. Moral absolutes are usually improperly understood and may release all that is bad and destructive in human nature. On the other hand, moral relativity may also sanction vicious cruelty towards those perceived as below the line, be they Jews, blacks, Vietnamese, Palestinians or animals. The best, or most 'saintly' people, do not grade their moral behaviour in this way, and men and women as disparate as Albert Schweitzer, Grand Duchess Ella, Aelred of Rievaulx and Audrey Hepburn demonstrated their goodness of heart with consistency. We must try to understand why they were impelled to behave well, while others have wallowed, with parallel consistency, in evil. That the task is packed with difficulty may be illustrated by the very sentence I have just written, for it carries within it at least three questionable assumptions: a) that there are 'impulses' to behaviour, rather than 'choices' between behaviours, b) that we are consistent one way or the other, for good or bad, and c) that there is such a thing as 'evil' at all, instead of a sequence of harmful actions by rotten people. All of this we shall have to examine, but for the moment we may perhaps posit one uncontroversial certainty, namely that St Anthony of Padua and Adolf Eichmann each started life as a helpless and harmless babe-in-arms, dependent for his present and future upon what was done to and for him. Neither, at the beginning, was an agent for good or bad, but a mere mewling infant.

Even this seemingly obvious statement has, however, been disputed by moral philosophers. Does the concept of an innate human nature make any sense? There are those who maintain that man is inherently good and learns how to behave badly, others who aver the contrary, that wickedness is our natural lot, and that we can conquer it only by constant attention. The first view is that of the Renaissance humanist, of Montaigne and of Rabelais, whose faith in 'human nature' was so joyful that he could mock the wicked in the sure knowledge that mankind was irresistibly drawn towards the good. It is also, in some degree, the view of the Enlightenment, as represented by Locke's *tabula rasa*, the notion that each person was a blank page of innocence on which experience would write its message and draw his character, though this does not so much suggest inherent goodness as inherent nothingness. Rousseau's flamboyant depiction of the 'noble savage', the naturally decent fellow of the woods corrupted by society and organised civilisation, is confused because Rousseau claims both that man is naturally good and that man brings evil into the world.

His disciples, however, were not confused, and they celebrated his vision as the honouring of innate benefi-cence and balance. This gave rise to the so-called Romantic Fallacy, which I shall consider later. Not many years after Rousseau's promulgation of the noble savage idea, there walked out of the woods a living specimen who, it was hoped, would prove the point. It happened at the village of Saint-Sernin in southern France on January 9, 1800. A strange creature from the forest was caught scavenging for food, and though it appeared to be a wild animal, it walked erect. As soon as those who captured the creature realised it was human, a boy of about twelve years in fact, they attempted to care for him.

The Wild Boy of Aveyron, as he became known, was virtually naked and very dirty, with no apparent awareness that he was human, no modesty, and no ability to relate in any way to his captors. He could not speak, was intolerant of confinement, and defecated in a standing position, without warning or embarrassment. When his rescuers tried to clothe him, he tore the garments off and ripped them to pieces. Offered white bread, he spat it out immediately, and seemed familiar only with potatoes. He bit anyone who approached too close. It was time to alert the scientists. Here, apparently, was the noble savage in person.

Over the next months, attempts were made to bring the boy back into the human race. (When he was found he wore the remnants of a tattered shirt, which indicated that he had been lost or abandoned some years before.) He had the benefit of a patient tutor and a woman who grew to love him with a mother's devotion, yet he never learnt to speak or to return affection. With some optimism, he was given the name Victor, but the experiments to which this poor wretch was subjected met with repeated defeat, while he longed to return to his freedom and his woods. His only pleasure was sipping a slow glass of water as he stared through the imprisoning window at the sky and the moon, erstwhile companions of his solitary life. He did not, could not, understand civilisation.

Most importantly, did Victor bring from his natural state of innocence an inherent goodness which would put his civilised captors to shame? Invited to dinner at the salon of Madame Récamier, he stole everything small enough to grab, and clambered up a tree, which left the astonished guests resentful that Rousseau was not alive to see his theories disproved. But were they disproved? Theft is a transgression against a specific

15

moral rule, but does not, in itself, denote badness if the rule has no significance for the thief. What was infinitely more telling was that Victor was never able to see the world through the eyes of anyone but himself. He had no capacity for empathy and lacked the simplest moral tools which would have equipped him to modify his behaviour according to how it might affect those around him. He certainly learnt how people could hurt, for his tutor, having bestowed love, would unwarrantably remove it to see how the boy reacted (which was, of course, with terrified disappointment). But he never learnt to recognise that other people existed except as satisfiers of his needs. They did not have their own fears and pains – they were objects to him. The Wild Boy of Aveyron did not prove that the primitive state was one of essential goodness, but he did prove that it was irremediably selfish, or self-centred. Which is not to say that it was not also innocent (literally *harmless*): the boy showed no malice or cruelty, did not seek revenge, did not direct hostility against individuals. He was not so much immoral as pre-moral.

The opposite view, then, that human nature is innately bad, is not sustained by the Aveyron story. The boy was indifferent to morality, not determined to undermine it, and since bad behaviour must by definition be purposeful, the natural state would seem to be free of deliberate wickedness. Yet there persists the notion that natural self-regarding impulses, if not regulated, will inevitably lead to bad behaviour, that badness is somehow easy and virtue hard, or 'unnatural'. Baudelaire carried this idea to its ultimate expression by declaring that virtue was 'artificial' and therefore not-in-nature,[3] and Iris Murdoch has spent a lifetime searching for the goodness in man by creating characters who perversely declare there is none. 'Our vices are general, dull, the ordinary rotten mud of human meanness and cowardice and cruelty and egoism, and even when they're extreme they're all the same,' says the dying Guy Openshaw in *Nuns and Soldiers*. 'Only in our virtues are we original, because virtue is difficult, and we have to try, to invent, to work through our nature against our nature.'[4]

By this reckoning, human nature is not so much bad as disastrously *weak*, non-resilient and easily corrupted. I shall return to this crucial idea later, with reference to Murdoch as well as examples drawn from life rather than fiction, but for the moment it is important to keep the idea clear in mind when we hear the implacable laments of those who would have humankind steeped in pollution. 'Hell hath no limits,' says Mephistopheles, 'nor is circumscribed in one self place; for where we are is Hell, and where Hell is there must we ever be.'[5] This grim landscape, from which no escape to clearer air is foreseen, was matched by the more gloomy of the existentialists in the twentieth century; indeed, Sartre's play in which he famously identifies Hell with Other People is entitled *No Escape* or *No Exit* (*Huis Clos* in the original). The conviction that badness is endemic in human nature is one which allows all manner of determinists, from religious dogmatists to Freudian excavators and, nowadays, genetic calculators, to imprison the human spirit. It may well be that we have nobody to blame for bad behaviour but ourselves (or our fate or our nature), but that is a far cry from saying that we are doomed to behave in no other way. Charles Morgan put it with beguiling eloquence when he wrote, 'Evil isn't an army that besieges a city from outside the walls. It is a native of the city. It is the mutiny of the garrison, the poison in the water, the ashes in the bread.'[6] While acknowledging that badness is within, Morgan somehow contrives to reassure us that it can be confronted and disarmed by the very act of recognition.

There is one circumstance in which it is uncomfortably difficult to refute the assertion that human beings are naturally bad, and that is when they have the *sanction* to behave badly. The ghastly manifestation of Nazi concentration camps only fifty years ago, still within the lifetime of many of us, was testimony to what ordinary folk – greengrocers and bus drivers before the war –

can do when they believe they have official permission or instructions to smother inhibition. Lest we thought only Germans were prone to the particular weakness of obedience, an experiment was conducted on Americans by Stanley Milgram in 1963 with notorious results. It is well known even to people who have never read his report or are unacquainted with the earlier, unpublicised experiment by A. H. Buss.

Milgram asked for volunteers to help ascertain the effect of punishment upon learning. They were shown a 'learner' strapped to a chair with an electrode attached to his wrist. He was to be given some words to learn by heart, and each time he made a mistake he would receive an electric shock which would increase in intensity. The forty volunteers were told they were his 'teachers', and they would have the switches with which to administer the shocks. Each switch was labelled to indicate how severe was the punishment to be inflicted, so the 'teachers' would know exactly what they were doing. Except that they were being deceived. There were no electric shocks, and the 'learner' was an actor who could simulate pain and terror according to the level of supposed ordeal undergone, from grunting at 75 volts, to an agonised scream at 285 volts and imminent death at 450 volts. The undeclared experiment was upon the 'teachers', to determine how far they would go in following instructions despite the certain knowledge they were causing visible suffering to a human being, and at what point their conscience would intervene to refuse compliance.

The results were horrifying. Two-thirds of the 'teachers' obeyed most of the instructions and many went to the final hurdle of shooting 450 volts into a man already in acute distress. One of the actors was told to reveal that he had a heart condition and was a trifle worried about submitting himself to the experiment. He was reassured, as part of the charade, that the experiment might be painful but would cause no lasting harm to his heart. The actor begged to be set free after 150 volts, and complained about his heart when the voltage increased. Nevertheless, 26 of the 40 experimenters went so far as to administer the maximum shock of 450 volts.[7]

It is pointless resisting the inference from this terrible exercise (and everyone involved was depressed by it), namely that the human soul is not pure, that the capacity for evil deeds lurks, often unsuspected, within all of us. Fortunately, the capacity to resist evil impulses is also in evidence, for many of those who obeyed suffered visibly from having to stifle conscience, but this is, alas, significantly weaker. One of the purposes of this book will be to seek whether there are ways in which the good element may be better nourished than the bad, so that a repeat of Milgram's experiment might in theory achieve more cheerful results.

Nobody should pretend that any one person has a monopoly of good or bad characteristics. Even Jesus lost his temper, and Goebbels was a devoted father. There are legions of detailed examples of how good and bad may co-exist in a single personality, some of them astonishing. The case of Dr H.H. Crippen, convicted of the murder of his wife in 1910, is a case to the point. Nearly a century later, his name still conjures images of cold-hearted slaughter and pitiless dismemberment, all for the freedom to elope with a mistress, Ethel Le Neve. The case is famous also for Crippen's arrest, on board the SS *Montrose*, following a radio message from the captain; it was the first time wireless had been instrumental in catching a criminal. There was a moment in his trial when Dr Pepper, of the Royal College of Surgeons, having described the large piece of flesh excavated from beneath the Crippens' house, composed of skin, fat and muscle from the thigh and lower part of the buttock of a woman, then produced some skin. The hideous moment in which the pieces of his dead wife's skin were handed round in a soup plate for inspection left him, alone of all the people in that crowded Court, quite unmoved.[8] An irredeemable monster, therefore, a quiet little man with a black soul?

19

Not a bit of it. 'Just as the Crown, with all its resources, had not been able to produce a single person who could say otherwise than that in every relationship of life Crippen had always behaved with kindness, consideration, and unselfishness, so every one who came in contact with him from his trial to his death – and some of them were fairly hardened prison officials – looked upon him not only with respect, but with something like affection.'

These unexpected observations belong to Filson Young, who edited a transcript of Crippen's trial in 1920, the introduction to which afforded him the opportunity for reflections which were by no means popular. 'The region of human morality is not a flat plain,' he wrote. 'There are hills and valleys in it, deep levels and high levels; there are also certain wild, isolated crags, terrible in their desolation.' Young warned his readers not to neglect the complexity of human nature, the co-existence within any one person of good and bad influences, often leading to a collision of contradictory characteristics, then went on, very boldly, to *praise* Dr Crippen: 'the very crime itself brought out in him high human qualities'. The unwelcome point, he wrote, was 'never to forget the dual nature of human character and the mystery in virtue of which acts of great moral obliquity may march with conduct above the ordinary standards'.[9]

I have myself had reason to contemplate a similarly disquieting example of this duality. Dennis Nilsen was convicted on six counts of murder and two of attempted murder in 1983, though he is known to have killed between twelve and fifteen men. He throttled them when they were drunk or asleep, kept their bodies for months, and finally dismembered them and burnt them on a huge bonfire in the back garden. Or so it was with the first nine victims, for he then lived in a ground-floor flat. Later, he moved to an attic, with no floorboards beneath which to secrete what he facetiously called 'a new kind of flat-mate', and no garden. He felt, he told me, that he could do no mischief there, that the restrictions of his new abode would prevent his ever being consumed by the black dog of his murderous impulses again. Alas, was not to be, and three more men ended their lives in that attic, their heads boiled on the stove, the flesh cut into pieces and flushed down the toilet.

But in the first week of residence, Nilsen had come across a young man slumped against a wall in the West End of London, obviously drunk. He was precisely the kind of young man who had fallen prey to Nilsen before – almost destitute, friendless, in need of help. A police car pulled up, and policemen were about to cart the man away. Nilsen intervened, assured the police that he knew the vagrant and would take care of him, they need not worry (he had once been a policeman himself). He took the man home and put him to bed, making sure that he slept on his front so that he would do himself no harm should he vomit during the night. The next morning he gave the man a hearty cooked breakfast, talked to him, encouraged him, and sent him on his way. 'I felt elated that day,' he told me.

He could not remember the man's name, but with questions placed in the right corners the police were able to track him down. They asked him if he recalled having been taken home by a man with a slight Scottish accent some three years before. He did, and with no knowledge of whom he was talking about, or the charges which Nilsen faced, he said, 'Yeah, that man rescued me. He was a real saint.'

The word comes as a shock to those addicted to thinking in one dimension. Nilsen had befriended another young man, Carl Stottor, who was very unhappy over a broken love affair and was talking of suicide. Nilsen told him he was far too young to be talking in such a way, that he had the whole of life in front of him. They chatted for two hours, and went home, holding hands in the taxi. During the night, Nilsen tried three times to strangle Carl, finally holding him under water in the bathtub until the bubbles of air ceased. He then dragged the body to the bed. Nilsen's dog, knowing the difference between a corpse and a whisker of life, licked Carl's leg,

21

Nilsen, who could have despatched him in
ed on the fire, fetched extra blankets, rubbed
to encourage circulation. Once again, all
details were corroborated by Carl's own memory
of the event. Years later he told me that the experience
had profoundly unsettled his moral compass. 'I don't
know if that man was my murderer or my saviour,' he
said, 'because he was both.'

Ted Bundy is probably the most notorious repetitive
killer in the United States. He confessed (obliquely) to
twenty-three murders of young women, though he is
thought to have killed many more. Handsome, plausible, persuasive, Bundy conducted his own defence,
but was eventually convicted on the evidence of his
teeth-marks in the flesh of a victim. He was executed
in 1989. And what of his previous history? In 1969,
he had received a commendation from the Seattle
Police Department for having pursued and captured
a purse-snatcher and returned the purse to its owner.
In 1970, he saved the life of a drowning three-year-old
by plunging fully clothed into a lake and bringing the
child to shore. At university he was a volunteer on the
Crisis Clinic hotline, helping people in trouble, soothing
fears, building confidence.[10]

So random and contingent does the explosion of bad
behaviour appear to be that it may well hinge upon a
word or a gesture. It has been said that if Beethoven had
not turned to music he might have become homicidal.
And Thomas Keneally's justly famous book *Schindler's
Ark*, now very faithfully translated into a cinema film by
Steven Spielberg under the title *Schindler's List*, reveals
how haphazard or fortuitous goodness can be. Oskar
Schindler was not a nice man. Unfaithful to both wife and
mistress, vain, self-satisfied and a fairly commonplace
opportunist with the necessary ruthlessness to get what
he wanted, he flourished under the Nazi regime and
felt ideologically bound to it. Nevertheless, he saved
over 1,000 Jews from certain death, at considerable risk
to himself, and magnificently restored their dignity. It

was at one precise moment, sitting on horseback on a hill overlooking the Cracow ghetto as Jews were being rounded up or shot in their beds, that Oskar's moral feeling woke up. The moment might have passed without touching him, and the salvation of Schindler's Jews might never have occurred.

Even more pertinently, Keneally makes it clear that Oskar has much in common with the friend he covertly despises, the camp commander Amon Goeth, a positively fiendish man who kills between puffs on his cigar. 'Just the same, the reflection can hardly be avoided that Amon was Oskar's dark brother, was the berserk and fanatic executioner Oskar might, by some unhappy reversal of his appetites, have become.'[11]

The truth is at once simple and subtle. 'Il y a dans tout homme, à toute heure, deux postulations simultanées,' wrote Baudelaire, 'l'une vers Dieu, l'autre vers Satan.'[12] The characters of Dr Jekyll and Mr Hyde have entered the subconscious of the English-speaking world, their names quoted by millions who have never read Robert Louis Stevenson's book but understand, to some extent at least, its burden; Jekyll and Hyde are the same person and always have been, though they seem to be unrecognisable to each other, the one decent and good, the other so bereft of feeling that he can crash into a little girl and leave her screaming on the pavement. So, implies Stevenson, can we all. Another famous and unread book is Mary Shelley's *Frankenstein*, published in 1818, in which the monster created by Dr Frankenstein is depicted as issuing from him, from his brain, from his thoughts, and is therefore part of him, his brother. The creature represents the inadmissible dark side of his creator and, oddly enough, it is the creature who recognises this first.

Literature abounds in other examples. James Hogg's *Confessions of a Justified Sinner* shows Wringhim being corrupted by a stranger who leads him on to murder; only gradually do we realise that the stranger is Wringhim's hidden self, his personal devil. Hermann

Hesse's *Steppenwolf* offers a man who acknowledges the irreconcilable duality of his nature, Apollonian and controlled on one side, Dionysian, savage and raw on the other. This perception of duality ascends to a Gnostic sect nearly two thousand years ago, the Manichees (followers of the Persian sage Mani), from whom we derive the adjective 'Manichaean', an epithet frequently applied to conflicts between opposites. According to this doctrine, Good and Evil are equal forces in the world, competing for influence; hence the disturbances they cause in every man's moral dilemmas. Jung's idea of the 'shadow', the unrealised potential in each individual, is a Manichaean echo – the shadow being the dark brother, split off, rejected or repressed.

Again, this notion of darkness and a denied fraternity answers to a powerful secret knowledge of self which most people will not face, which is why those books about murder which attempt to explain or comprehend rather than parade the ghastliness as something alien and at a safe remove are not popular. One does not have to reach into literature or philosophy to find this fear expressed. Nilsen himself remarked upon it.

> The population at large is neither 'ordinary' or 'normal' [he wrote]. They seem to be bound together by a collective ignorance of themselves and what they are. They have, every one of them, got their deep dark thoughts with many a skeleton rattling in their secret cupboards. Their fascination with 'types' (rare types) like myself plagues them with the mystery of why and how a living person can actually do things which may be only those dark images and acts secretly within them. I believe they can identify with these 'dark images and acts' and loathe anything which reminds them of this dark side of themselves. This usual reaction is a flood of popular self-righteous condemnation but a willingness to, with friends and acquaintances, talk over and over again the appropriate bits of the case.[13]

Nilsen is right. There is a reluctance on the part of all but professional philosophers to contemplate one's shadow, and it is a reluctance based on fear. We are afraid of the devil within because we doubt our ability to control his appetites once they have been acknowledged and heard. That is why it is easier to talk of these daemonic forces as if they can only be seen objectively, outside ourselves, since it is unimaginable they should be harboured more intimately. Talking at length in pub and club and at dinner tables about the latest gruesome murder is a way of recognising this devil by proxy: we actually welcome a new murder as an avenue towards disguised introspection, disguised even from ourselves.

Subconsciously, we are perfectly well aware of the constant inner conflict between control and liberation, conformity and eccentricity, restraint and release. (By 'constant' I do not mean at every minute of every day, but at various crises throughout life.) Taken to extremes, control may lead to paralysis, liberation to excess, and the strain of this tension between the opposites of our dual nature may prove so burdensome that we seek to stifle it, and largely succeed. When a fresh mass murderer turns up in the press, he allows our smothered inner debate the respectability, relatively danger-free, of an objective airing.

The aesthetic, calming pleasure of Apollonian control and the wild, ungovernable terror of Dionysian excess, polar opposites in the human experience, may be seen in the contrasting talents of Alec Guinness and Maria Callas. Sir Alec is the perfect exemplar of the disciplined artist, his every portrayal a masterpiece of miniaturist architecture, building a character with a hundred telling details, leaving nothing to chance, the actor as master craftsman. His performances are cosy and comforting, even when they depict unsavoury characters (such as Fagin), because they objectify human experience, control and dominate it. Maria Callas, on the other hand, was frightening. She let loose the untamed daemon, the dark shadow within, unsettling our civilised blanket on the truth. Before her, *prima donnas* would plonk themselves in the centre of the stage and bellow their melodies out front. Callas prowled around the stage like a tigress, clung to the drapes if she felt like it, or sang into her armpits. When, in the second act of *Tosca*, after the long scene with her enemy Scarpia, she spied the knife on the table, we saw what she was thinking and we trembled for her. It was a moment when Dionysus became visible and his power over Tosca as we watched her surrender was such that a wave of fear swept over the audience.

No wonder we do not wish to confront our daemons. And no wonder, too, that the ancient Greek dramatists saw the theatre as a way of confronting them by proxy, just as today we talk about the serial killer in order to avoid recognising him. Maria Callas was the supreme modern exponent of *catharsis*, the purging of dangerous passions by depicting them fictionally. She was the actress as servant of the people.

Without actors to represent the conflict in our dual nature for us, we have to resolve it both alone, in our individual relationships, and in society, and that is when the subtle evaluation of choices comes into service. Ethics are nothing less than the balancing of influence between intelligence and impulse, Apollo and Dionysus, and as such, morality should not be seen as a necessarily inimical constraint, but as a *reconciler*. Moral codes resolve the battle for advantage between good and bad behaviour, and are therefore necessary to human happiness. Without them, we should disintegrate into perpetually vacillating egos, at war with ourselves (and some paranoid schizophrenics do just that).

It is not easy to behave well. It requires effort, struggle, mastery. As the Iris Murdoch character said above, vice is the simple option, whereas virtue denotes difficulty and sweat. 'Nature does not give a man virtue,' wrote Seneca, 'the process of becoming a good man is an art.'[14] The ancient Chinese sage Hung Ching expressed much the same idea: 'The nature of the man is evil – his goodness is only acquired by training.'[15] St Paul's exhortation, 'Do

26

not let evil conquer you, but use good to defeat evil,'[16] at least recognises the struggle. There is a sense in which virtue without struggle is mere apathetic complacence, a kind of empty smile; and another, more controversial, sense in which the struggle itself *is* the virtue, whether or not it achieves benign results. The young Milwaukee necrophile, Jeffrey Dahmer, who killed seventeen men, 'defleshed' (his word) their remains and consumed parts of them, indisputably indulged in wicked acts. Yet there was a period, between the first and second murder, when he was locked in a struggle to defeat the evil forces within himself. His first victim died in 1978. From that moment, Dahmer knew of what he was capable, what lurid power lurked in his soul, and for nine years he fought to keep it at bay, to satisfy it with little substitute sacrifices. He turned to the Church for psychic help, for strength to supplement his own, but eventually, on the night in 1987 when he tore Stephen Tuomi's heart from his chest, the devils triumphed. Nevertheless, even Dahmer could be regarded as a virtuous man. As I wrote at the time, 'One way to measure a man's morality is by the degree of effort he invests in the struggle against immorality; the repeated sinner may well have repeatedly tried to resist sin.'[17]

Stern, scolding 'moralists' (as opposed to moral philosophers) may well find the above paragraph offensive, in so far as it dares attribute any worth at all to a man convicted of murder. They should ask themselves how often they have fallen short of standards they profess to uphold. According to Professor Kohlberg at Harvard, we nearly all do. Kohlberg put forward a theory to explain variations in moral judgement, according to which there are six stages of moral development in ascending levels of goodness. The most basic stage is the avoidance of an action for fear of the punishment it might induce, and is thereby entirely self-regarding. The second stage recognises reciprocity, that there are the competing needs of other people which should be taken into account. Stage three embraces actions which are likely to earn social approval, and stage four moves on to those which express one's duty towards society. Stage five places the needs of society above individual convenience, while the final stage raises the demands of conscience and ethical choice to the paramount position.

Kohlberg concluded that only 6% of the population ever reached the final level of moral development, which must imply that a worrying 94% do not match their behaviour to their conscience. Only a pitiful 20% reach stage five, that of respecting the rights of others. In Stanley Milgram's obedience test mentioned earlier, three out of four of those who refused to administer the electric shocks were adjudged to have reached stage six of moral development.[18]

One of the most insidious forms of moral depravity does not find a niche in Kohlberg's scale, unless it be stage one masquerading as stage six. As we have matured our moral understanding, so too have we evolved a sneaky method of side-stepping it through the subtle snares of hypocrisy. The hypocrite may undermine all our attempts to measure goodness and badness, by presenting a false face which nonetheless convinces.

And thus I clothe my naked villainy
With odd old ends stol'n forth of Holy Writ:
And seem a saint, when most I play the devil.[19]

So the crafty Richard III. From Molière's *Tartuffe* to the bourgeois manipulators who abound in Alan Ayckbourn's plays, writers have counted it among their first duties to warn us of this wriggler at our feet. He is the dark shadow, the bad brother, counterfeiting the good and making the task of distinguishing good yet harder than it might already be. Scornfully, he places in question the whole enterprise of virtue. 'All that so-called morality', says Cato in Murdoch's *Henry and Cato*, 'is simply smirking at yourself in a mirror and thinking how good you are. Morality is nothing but self-esteem, nothing else, simply affectations of virtue and spiritual charm.'[20] Or, more bluntly, 'all altruism feeds the fat ego'.[21] This is a typically pessimistic view (not shared by the gloriously biophilic author), but it would be foolish not to give it the weight it deserves, for there are indeed many overtly good people whose true character is deplorable. José Maria Escriva, founder of Opus Dei in 1928 and currently a hot favourite for sainthood, is obviously one, and some (notably Germaine Greer) say Mother Teresa of Calcutta is another.

If we have learnt anything thus far, it is that there are enormous gradations of moral worth between the saint and the sinner, between St Anthony and Adolf Eichmann, and that just as few of us achieve the ethical purity of the first as plumb the noisome depths of the second. Humility must be our guide in attempting to unravel why there should be such a thick terminal moraine of bad behaviour clogging up the moral evolution of our species. It is not good enough simply to point the finger at bad behaviour, lock up the transgressors and take refuge in our comfortable superiority. 'We have somehow to understand, without accepting, what goes on in the hearts of the wicked.'[22] To which I would add, that it is equally urgent to enquire what makes a person behave well. As Dr Lydgate says in *Middlemarch*, 'I wonder what it is makes us care for one another?'

In the course of this enquiry, we shall look at explanations from genetic determinism, anthropology, ethology and environmental influences, but when all is said and done, the mystery of choice must remain. Bessie Gilmore, the mother of Gary Gilmore, whose life of crime and death by firing squad in 1978 was chronicled by Norman Mailer in *The Executioner's Song*, was perplexed. She had brought up her two eldest sons together. Frank turned out to be a peaceable and inoffensive man. She said, 'One son picked up the gun. The other did not pick up the gun. Why?'[23]

Why did Oskar Schindler turn towards the good at his moment of moral anxiety, when Adolf Eichmann, who transported Jews to their deaths, given a parallel opportunity, turned to the bad?

The moment of choice came when Eichmann for the very first time visited the extermination camps and saw what happened to the Jews. He nearly fainted. But instead of heeding his emotional reaction, he pushed it down to go on with the task that he had been assigned and that he embraced as his own obligation. This was Eichmann's point of no return. There and then he abdicated from reacting as a human being.[24]

Even his evil must be grasped and understood. For to do otherwise is to sink into that same blind certainty which steeled his heart for the utmost cruelty. We cannot afford to see good and evil as irreconcilable opposites, for then we risk shaping our behaviour according to the worst, not the best. As Anthony Storr has written, 'When men divide the world into good and evil, into sheep and goats, what happens to the goats is usually horrible.'[25]

2

FOREGONE CONCLUSIONS

Evil is an occult word meaning little more in reality than conduct which is so bad that it is better left unexamined. In short, to label somebody or some act 'evil' is a substitute for thought, and as such, uniquely dangerous. What we should be asking is whence we derive our good behaviour, and whence our bad.

There are those who maintain that mankind is innately bad, and must be taught how to become good. These include sages such as Seneca, already mentioned; anthropologists who subscribe to the view that the human species is descended from a killer ape and that murder courses naturally through our veins; and psychologists who believe our natural instincts have to be thwarted by acquired restraints, leading to constant frustration. They are all rather pessimistic accounts of human nature, which promise a bleak future for our species.

Ranged against them are the optimists, who insist we are descended from peace-loving vegetarians; that social or environmental influences have conspired to deflect us from our true nature; that bad behaviour is aberrant, the result of chemical imbalances in the brain or disorders of personality. (For them, the Wild Boy of Aveyron must have been mentally peculiar before he was abandoned in the forest – indeed, that was probably *why* he was abandoned.) If we can manage to avoid all the malign influences which bombard us, and revert to our aboriginal selves, the world will be a more harmonious place.

The pessimists nearly always win, because they have the most seductive arguments, there being a paradoxical desire in most people to think the worst of our species. Well, the evidence for an in-built taint is certainly overwhelming, and it is no surprise that the doctrine of Original Sin should have taken such a hold in the Western world. I shall look first, then, at the idea of man's inherent badness, and consider the opposite proposition, that man is inherently good, in later chapters.

There are several variations of the determinist premiss that our natures are shaped in advance. It may be held that we are bad because we are aggressive, or because we are imprisoned by our genes and chemicals, or because we are descended from Adam. Let us briefly look at each position in turn.

'Nature herself, I fear, implants in men some instinct towards inhumanity,' wrote Montaigne some four centuries ago.[1] Nowadays we might rephrase the remark, and say that man is innately *aggressive*. It would be difficult to find anyone who would seriously disagree with such an assessment, but confusion occasionally arises as to the meaning of 'aggression'. Some people seem to think it virtually synonymous with 'hostility' or 'violence', and talk as if aggression were the monopoly of football hooligans and habitual murderers.

This is seriously misleading. Properly understood, aggression is a life-force with manifold beneficent effects. It is the source of ambition and enterprise, of mastery over the environment, of that independence upon which individual survival depends, of leadership, amicable competition, artistic creation, even of love (in so far as an utterly apathetic and inert person would hardly succeed in having his love noticed). A better word for this innate, healthy and wholly necessary instinct might be self-assertion, as Adler recognised, leading to self-fulfilment. Mrs Thatcher was aggressive, but nobody has suggested, as far as I am aware, that she was cruel. Jesus was aggressive, in his determination to have his message heard.

Useful aggression has been the hallmark of our astonishing success as a species. Anthony Storr put it succinctly in his observation that 'if man were not aggressive, he would not be man at all.'[2] It has permitted us to space territory between us for the better stability of equals not squabbling over the same few inches, and we know all too well how important this spacing is when it is under threat: jostling, overcrowded cities in which the impulse for independent space is thwarted may result in self-assertion turning sour, becoming distorted by frustration; in such circumstances aggression might well turn to hostility. I feel it on an underground train if a stranger, faced with a row of empty seats, chooses to sit next to me and unnecessarily diminish the space between us. The implication of the saying that an Englishman's home is his castle (applicable, I have no doubt, also to a Chinaman or a Bolivian) is that he is happy within his own space, and would be threatened were it invaded. He owes his home to benign self-affirmation.

It is well known that this kind of defensive aggression has been observed by ethologists amongst all manner of species when protecting their territory against intrusion. It is, of course, instinctive and anterior to the thoughtful social organisation of men, as was wonderfully demonstrated by the experiment with sticklebacks conducted by the pioneering ethologist Niko Tinbergen. By placing two male sticklebacks in the same tank and artificially manipulating their respective territories, so that what seemed to one stickleback to be his space suddenly became the space of the other, he noticed that their defensive-aggressive behaviour immediately switched. The one who thought he was in *his* territory reacted with overtly angry behaviour towards the other, while the one who appeared to have strayed into foreign territory attempted to retreat.[3] The point of the experiment was to show that there was no enmity between the two creatures; on the contrary, their aggression was conducive to harmony, as each 'knew' (in some undiscoverable way) that he should stick to his own patch. It also showed, perhaps, that their solution of the problem with which they were confronted actually avoided battle. Whether

33

or not human ideas of morality may derive from the instinctive regulations of our animal ancestry is a subject to which I shall return later.

To widen the notion still further, there is a sense in which aggression is an inevitable expression of our simply being. It is allied to the force which causes the stalk to reach for the sky, its flower to bloom in time for the bees, the bees to devote all their energies to manufacturing their honey and small mammals to scooping it out. It is the very energy of life, up and out and yonder, and by this reckoning our evolutionary programming renders us aggressive – that is, growing, moving forward and surviving – willy nilly. The force of Darwin's natural selection is, after all, not a matter of choice. Even to say it is irresistible is wrong, for that allows the notion of resistance to slip in unheralded. It simply *is*.

Thus far, it is clear that aggression *per se* is not 'bad' in any strict sense. When, however, we come to consider the innate aggressiveness of the male, the argument that it, also, is conducive to good is more awkward and difficult to sustain. Feminists intent upon establishing equality of the sexes resist the idea that it is inherent in the very nature of maleness to pursue and penetrate, while the appropriate parallel behaviour of the female is to yield and submit, yet almost every observation in the wild confirms it (a notable exception being the praying mantis female, who bites her mate's head off during copulation and proceeds to gobble him up).[4] Moreover, when this balance of aggressiveness and submission is upset, the resulting confusion produces neurosis of one kind or another. One may be pretty sure that the abnormally unassertive male and the abnormally dominant female, in human beings at least, are each insecure and more liable than their orthodox counterparts to behave badly as a result. To this extent, then, the male is bound by his maleness to be the more aggressive and, once again, that aggressiveness is beneficial both to himself and his partner as well as, in the grander sense, to the continuation of the species.

This is not to say the female is never aggressive in nature, only that her aggressive responses are provoked by different stimuli for different reasons. The female will be aggressive, not to encourage copulation, but to protect her young, and we are quick to condemn a mother who does not exhibit this kind of protective aggression, and instead neglects her offspring, as a 'bad' mother.

Incidentally, that the females of other species sometimes indulge in competitive singing or squeaking in order to attract a mate may sometimes expose the assiduous ethologist to unenviable risk, as happened to Professor Harold Evans in Colorado. 'Even the simple wing sounds of midges and mosquitoes play a role in bringing the sexes together,' he said. 'In this case it is the female that attracts the male by the hum of her wings, a fact quickly apparent to singers who hit a G in the vicinity of a swarm and end up with a mouthful of male mosquitoes.'[5]

Aggressiveness in males may also reveal itself in display, as with the well-known examples of the peacock's glorious plumage and the baboon's glowing bottom. So far as I know, nobody has ever been able to work out why the human male has such a disproportionately large penis in comparison with every other mammal (apart from the Bonobo chimp perhaps), though it has been suggested that this, too, might be for display – not, as one might expect, to entice the female, but to impress other males.[6] It might be an assertion of status to ward off competition, or a threat. Graffiti are generally drawn by men to be seen by other men, as phallic art across the centuries convincingly demonstrates. It is certainly true that men refer to their penis as a 'weapon', that they sometimes slap their mates across the face with it and are inordinately proud of showing it off.

Aggressiveness in itself, then, is not a danger to society. It neither incites anti-social behaviour nor defies moral norms. It simply sounds as if it is reprehensible, due to a confusion of meaning which makes 'aggressive' appear synonymous with bellicose, belligerent, antagonistic. More correct and less ambiguous words for the same quality might be dogged, single-minded, resolute. With such epithets in mind, it is not difficult to find examples of benign aggressiveness throughout history, the most obvious being Sir Winston Churchill. His response to the threatened invasion of Britain in 1940 was so classic an instance of the territorial imperative at work that he came to represent the entire country (not just politically, but emotionally); to bare the teeth for all of us.

More recently, the career of businessman Richard Branson perfectly illustrates the positive power of benign personal aggressiveness. The son of a barrister and stipendiary magistrate, and grandson of a privy councillor and High Court judge, Richard was born in 1950 to a comfortable but not very noticeable life. The fact that he edited the school magazine was also hardly remarkable – hundreds of others may lay claim to as much, and most of them are now nonentities, their bright assertiveness fizzled out or stifled by the commonplace. What made Richard's forward thrust so astonishing was its relentless appetite for new challenges, and the enduring nature of his achievements. At the age of nineteen he set up the Student Advisory Centre, now a much-valued nationwide organisation called Help. At the same time he began his business empire, starting with a mail-order company from home and building up to recording, music publishing, retailing in twenty-five countries, and finally Virgin Atlantic Airways in 1984. He is a director of companies in Russia as well as the United States, the founder of a charity, the holder of the world record for the fastest crossing of the Atlantic by a ship. In 1987 he was the first man to cross the Atlantic in a hot air balloon, and did the same across the Pacific in 1991, making the longest ever flight in a hot air balloon and at the fastest ever speed (6,700 miles at 200 mph).

Richard Branson has been lucky to the extent that nothing has tended to check his natural self-assertiveness.

Had he been stumped by bad heredity, hostile social circumstances, cruel upbringing, or a temperament prone to morosity and mental hesitancy, he would have turned out quite differently. Recent studies have tended to show that men become dangerous when their personal aggressiveness is unnaturally contained. 'Aggression is liable to turn into dangerous violence when it is repressed or disowned,' writes Anthony Storr. 'The man who is able to assert himself in a socially acceptable fashion is seldom vicious; it is the weak who are most likely to stab one in the back.'[7] Weak like Jeffrey Dahmer, across whose path to development and growth a crushing dam fell. Weak like John Reginald Christie, who, failing to impress with his personality or to achieve sexual arousal, killed his women and copulated with their corpses (he was hanged in 1953). Weak like hundreds of stabbers and slashers, who use the gleaming knife as a permanently erect, hard and penetrating substitute for a flaccid, unprepossessing penis.[8] It does not bear thinking how many slaughtered or disfigured women are the victims of a man's *lack* of healthy aggression. Pathetically, even during rape the weak man frequently demands that the victim should 'put it in' for him, thereby assisting in her own violation, since he is not capable of it by himself.[9]

So anxious can men become in the contemplation of their unassuaged aggressiveness that they will go to extreme lengths to prevent any other man from replacing them. That another man's aggression should be properly expressed appears to be intolerable to many men. It is well known that the vast majority of domestic murders are the result of sexual jealousy, wherein either the adulterous wife or her lover is killed (significantly, with a knife rather than the hands). Not so well known is the fact that there are still twenty-three countries in the world where female circumcision and infibulation are practised quite legally. Circumcision is a fearsome matter, requiring the removal of the clitoris or sometimes most of the external genitalia. Infibulation is almost worse, but reversible; it involves sewing up the lips of the vagina to make intercourse impossible. The vagina may be re-opened for conception and childbirth, and sutured again when no longer necessary for these purposes.[10] The mutilation would be risible were it not so awful. It is the man's doubts concerning the strength of his personal assertiveness to retain exclusive right to his property which are being thus revealed.

Sadistic cruelty towards the sexual partner is another manifestation of natural aggression distorted. Unsure whether the woman will fully appreciate and value the quality of the man's aggression, he needs to elicit visible and audible proof of it by taking pleasure in her pain. Her cries are confirmation of his worth. His self-esteem is so fragile that he must *invent* his aggression through her suffering, whereas true purposeful aggression needs no suffering to bolster it. The knowledge that man is the only animal capable of enjoying the suffering of another, whether of his own or a different species, is a very heavy burden, and I have found nobody able to explain why it should be so. Obviously, imagination is the most important ingredient, for you cannot enjoy another's pain unless you can imaginatively know what he or she is feeling. Otherwise there would not be much point, and the wails of the victim would be no more than irritating noise. Other animals, lacking that development of brain which permits the imagination to flourish, cannot be sadistic, and when a lion brings down a wildebeest, however bloody and stark it may appear to us, cruelty has nothing whatever to do with it. 'A leopard at the kill is no more violent or angry than an antelope is angry with the grass it eats.'[11] Natural aggression does not deal in fictions.

Nor does it recognise justice. There is a species of eagle which sometimes lays two eggs, both of which might hatch to produce chicks. The likely food supply will only support one chick, and so nature decrees that while the mother is away searching for food, the chicks, still sitting in their shells and unable to move closer than beak level, peck at each other until one of them expires.

On the other hand, when an exhausted stag with tears in its eyes yields to its pursuers, there is no solace in the contemplation of what is natural, for the human beings who torment it are doing so precisely for the delectation of the torment. Bear-baiters wanted to watch the bear suffer as it was torn to pieces, and cockfighters desire to hear the shrieks of the battered birds. You have only to look at the owners of pit-bull terriers to see what is the purpose of dogfighting. They are all, to a man, feeble brutes visibly ill at ease with their own lack of useful aggressiveness, who use the dogs as surrogates. Theirs is an imagination poisoned, and their sport a totem to what they feel to be their failure in manhood.

Cruelty to animals is just as wicked as cruelty towards other people, and sadism remains sadism whatever its object. We are not dealing here with a hierarchy of values, but with the disruption of naturally biophilous patterns of aggressive behaviour into destructive forms. All manner of excuses and justifications, from foxhunters and bullfighters alike, are concocted to avoid such conclusions as these, precisely because, I suspect, the bullfighters and foxhunters fear the conclusions may be correct.

(Paradoxically, the imaginative appreciation of others' pain is a necessary part of the development of sympathy, as we grow out of self-absorption into mutual co-operation through the gradual realisation that we can cause as well as receive pain, a realisation which could never occur without imagination. But that belongs to a later subject.)

Either humans do not feel ashamed of their sadistic impulses, or they fail to recognise them for what they are, since from the earliest literature to the present day unpleasant delight has been taken in depictions of cruelty to sentient life. I am not thinking only of depraved sex books which are no more than mas-turbatory aids for inadequate men (they are rarely used by women), nor of the lurid nonsense of the Marquis de Sade himself. The authors of signifi masterpieces, from Shakespeare downwards, have not been averse to the inclusion of vicious scenes, such as the blinding of Gloucester in *King Lear*. The most terrible scene I personally know is that in Homer's *Odyssey* where the Cyclops' eye is burnt out, a description in powerful, passionate words but, for me at least, unquotably nasty.

According to some anthropologists, we are nasty because we are descended from nasty creatures. Put in another way, both benign and distorted aggression are innate in human beings because human beings are the modern representatives of predatory apes, and we cannot escape our ancestry. The thesis was first put forward by Raymond Dart in a scientific journal in 1953 and taken up by Robert Ardrey in his landmark book *African Genesis*. It caused much controversy, as one might expect, for it proposed that mankind was in essence a killer race which emerged from peaceable anthropoid origins by developing an instinct for murder. The idea was that there had been a number of different ape-like strains, many millions of years before the development of the large brain (and its concomitant baggage of conscience), all of which were strictly vegetarian. Our ancestors, faced with a depletion in natural resources, had to learn to eat meat in order to survive. Hence they stood upright for the first time, the better to see prey at a distance, thus strengthening their legs for pursuit and freeing their hands for the use of weapons. To fashion and use those primitive weapons profitably, the brain had to become more efficient, inventive, and ultimately cunning. Hence modern man was the offspring of this creature, named *australopithecus africanus*, a carnivorous hunter and predator who surpassed his less adaptable rivals by honing aggressive techniques.[12] (The up-to-date view is that man is only a collateral relation of *australopithecus*, a species which came to a dead end.) Of the other related strains of ape, few survived, and today only the gorilla, chimpanzee and orang-utan represent their descendants.

The evidence consisted of the remains of an *australopithecus* surrounded by the bones of his prey, which he was alleged to have dragged back to his den for consumption.

The theory is nowadays disputed, for reasons we shall examine when we come to consider the apologists of a non-aggressive ancestor of mankind originally innocent of slaughter (see Chapter Three). But there are some who yet cling to the notion of our violent distant past to explain man's predilection for brutality, and if they are correct (conflicting theories crop up almost yearly) then aggression is as natural to us as it is to the lion; indeed, 'lion-hearted' is usually thought to be a complimentary epithet. This is a form of determinism. We are what we are and there is nothing we can do to make ourselves otherwise.

For the moment, it is worthwhile to consider two objections to the theory, one factual, the other a matter of interpretation. In the first place, it is now known that chimpanzees are not the harmless bands of co-operative families they were once thought to be. Observations in the wild have confirmed they can sometimes form themselves into rival groups which will fight to the death, suggesting their ancestry might also be tainted with aggression, and that aggression therefore pre-dated the emergence of proto-man from the other apes. Secondly, even if aggressive behaviour is inexorably our lot, the purpose of that aggressive behaviour was no more than the survival of the species, and was not therefore malign. Only if it could be shown that our hominoid ancestors had developed the distorted aggression which we call wilful cruelty could it be safely concluded that our character was determined long ago.

Some fanciful writers claim to have discovered just that: the first-known murder of one pre-human ape by another on the evidence of a skull with a dent in it, which they then presume has been caused by the wielding, at shoulder-level, of a weapon made from the shin of an antelope. The only possible response to this is that it is imaginative and provocative, but hardly conclusive. The reconstruction of an unknown encounter between two postulated individuals at a distance of several million years cannot be said to be reliable. There is as much, in the evidence, to suggest the antelope shin served as a walking-stick for a senile ape.

If anthropology works from the past forwards in order to show how man is shackled by his fate, modern psychology tends to reach identical conclusions by arguing from the present backwards. Freud, analysing modern neuroses rather than ancient bones, was also convinced that aggression was innate in mankind, and that it was the expression of man's ineradicable 'death-wish'. Like many of Freud's insights, this one has entered the language so completely that it is used by people as part of everyday speech, without any appreciation of what it means (other such words are 'displacement', 'regression', 'fixation', 'sublimation', and many more).

Freud's understanding of the death-wish is almost religious. Inanimate matter precedes the animate. As living organisms we will one day, in death, return to the inorganic condition from which we have temporarily emerged. It follows, according to Freud, that the inanimate state is not only antecedent but preferable, and that the purpose of all life is death, to sink back into that peaceful, untroubled, dark nothingness which life, with its bothersome stimuli, has interrupted (the idea that death is the purpose of life is originally Schopenhauer's). What happens with aggression is that the death-wish is neurotically turned *outwards*, that instead of seeking death for the self, the individual seeks the humiliation, destruction, even the death, of others.[13] This theory could well be applied to the crimes of Jeffrey Dahmer, who certainly seemed to be inanimate most of his life, spoke with a necrophilic monotone, and would clearly have liked to be dead. His victims piled up on a shrine in his bedroom, their skulls and skeletons tokens of his desire to find companionship in the comforting torpor of death. I feel sure Freud would have relished the Dahmer case.

He might also have had interesting things to say about the paintings of Francis Bacon, preoccupied as they are with disintegration, raw and decaying flesh, images of death and of an identity revealed in his self-portraits as fractured and putrid.

Most of Freud's astonishing intuitions have survived, but the death-wish explanation for aggression is now everywhere discredited. It is an illogical leap to posit that because the inorganic state precedes the organic it is therefore preferable to it; it is absurd to suggest we are better off if we are stimulated by nothing at all, in which case we might as well all die immediately; and there is no sensible way in which being aggressive towards others can replace being aggressive towards oneself, because they achieve different ends.

If Freud's understanding of aggression is grimly pessimistic, and the anthropologists' merely speculative, there is another route we can take to explore the nature of aggression, and that is by observing the behaviour of infants to see whether aggressiveness, either 'good' or 'bad', appears to be natural in them.

The great child psychoanalyst Melanie Klein thought that every child was born with a predisposition towards destructiveness which was so powerful that it frightened him, disturbing his first months of life with permanent anxiety. The child is worried lest its aggression might repel the mother or result in its own annihilation.[14] (To be fair, she also said the instinct for love was likewise innate.) Helpless and utterly dependent, the child knows, if it can 'know' anything, only that it has urgent needs and requirements which must be satisfied. The first object it encounters is the mother's breast, which it quickly discovers will provide the primary need. Very soon afterwards it discovers that the breast is intermittently withdrawn, is no longer available, and this produces the fresh sensation of frustration. Klein suggested that the alternation of satisfaction and frustration issuing from the same object gave that object the simultaneous qualities of 'good' and 'bad', between

43

which the child only later manages to make a distinction. Until he can, he is nervous, and his aggression is more likely to declare itself.

That may be a rather theoretic way of approaching the problem, but it is confirmed by common sense. Obviously, the child and the mother are to some extent in conflict, the one imperious in his demands, the other wishing to regulate how those demands are satisfied. The point has been well put by Professor Steve Jones:

> There is a natural tendency to assume that the bonds between mother and child are driven by mutual devotion. However, to the cold eye of the biologist the transaction between generations is also based on conflict. There are many chances for mother and child to exploit each other. It is in the child's interest to gain as much attention as possible from its mother. The mother's concern is to provide as little as will allow her offspring to survive. If she is too generous to one child, the next may suffer.[15]

It is at this crucial early stage that so many mistakes are made. A mother may not recognise that her child's apparent selfishness is a natural self-affirmation which she should encourage. She may deny the child attention in order to 'teach it a lesson' and strengthen its incipient ability to cope with adversity. Or she may over-indulge it and become its servant. If either course is followed to an extreme, the child is likely to grow into a severely disturbed adult, with a very confused idea of moral values. In the first instance, other people will be seen by him as enemies; in the second, as providers. In neither will they exist as people with needs of their own.

Victor, the Wild Boy of Aveyron we met in Chapter One, was never able to escape the imprisonment of self. His captors despaired of teaching him anything which might temper that relentless egotism which made him indifferent to any world but that of his own narrow requirements for food and comfort. 'I am sorry to see the natural man so egotistical,' wrote the contemporary philosopher and anthropologist J.J. Virey.[16] It was noticed that, like a domestic dog or cat, Victor could be both untroubled by cold weather and take pleasure in warming himself by the fire.

There was one occasion when he did appear to gain some insight beyond himself. One of Victor's domestic duties was to lay the table for his carers, Monsieur and Madame Guérin. He continued to do so even when Monsieur was taken away to hospital, thereby causing Madame additional distress which she could not explain to him. When Monsieur died, and Victor again laid his place at table, Madame collapsed in wretchedness of grief. Something told Victor that he was indirectly responsible for this, and he did not lay Monsieur's place at table again. Whether the boy really did appreciate Madame Guérin's unhappiness and try to alleviate it, or whether he merely did not want her to be angry with *him*, nobody can tell.

So, that the infant's universe is self-centred is only to be expected, and that his aggressive drives should be directed towards keeping himself in the centre is natural. At the very beginning, a child cannot differentiate between people and objects; they are all satisfiers of needs, furniture in his indistinct world. His need to explore and develop will seek to use all these things as fodder for his curiosity, and many a parent has been disappointed to find that a new toy has been immediately taken to pieces. In the normal course, he will grow out of this self-centredness, mature, and recognise reciprocity of effect and his responsibility for the well-being of others. If he does not, it is a sign that his moral development has atrophied.

I knew a boy once, whom I officially fostered for two and a half years, who continued to take gifts immediately to pieces when he was in his adolescence. To him, they were not witnesses of affection, but props in his private world, for him to do with as he wished. He had been brought up by a grandmother who had never demanded anything of him, never scolded if he stayed out all night, never made him go to school, never objected when he piled his unwanted food on to her plate. Her negating kindness had kept him in infancy, a moral ghost, frightened and dangerous.[17] Even more starkly, when Jeffrey Dahmer was approaching puberty, he still did not consider animals as beings with life in them, but as objects to be dissected to see how they worked.

Absolute licence engenders anarchy, and the early learning of moral boundaries must necessarily involve some frustration of will. Ashley Montagu thought that *all* aggressive behaviour was the result of frustration and that *none* of it could rationally be called innate; he said Freud was simply wrong.[18] Of course, frustration must play a part in allowing self-assertion to degenerate into hostility, as there are so many things a child must not do or touch or meddle with, for its own safety. But the balance is not loaded. The child, too, will do what it can to frustrate the intentions of the adult.

Consider the case of eight-year-old Peter, a boy undergoing therapeutic treatment. He was already a master at deflecting the wishes of adults, especially if an attempt to influence him was being made. He asserted himself *solely* by frustrating the efforts of others. Elizabeth Burford points out that this is analogous to those afflicted with *anorexia nervosa*, who will affirm their identity and will by rejecting the very food that would save them and strengthen that will. It is aggressiveness let rip. Miss Burford goes on:

> He illustrated his attitude to those in authority by drawing a picture of the therapist and his mother falling off a cliff-face whilst he stood triumphantly on the cliff-top watching their descent. Most of Peter's energy was directed at undoing what others were attempting.[19]

With the proper, delicate amount of opposition applied, aggression can be channelled to positive advantage, enabling the child to learn about independence without enslaving others. In this way, the infant becomes gradually less aggressive as he discovers he has gradually less need to be. A psychoanalyst who takes a patient backwards through time to his earliest days will invariably find a greater degree of frustrated aggression expressed as he gets closer to the beginning.

The murder of two-year-old James Bulger by two ten-year-olds in Liverpool in February 1993 was shocking in its detail and its apparent callousness. The infant was abducted from a shopping mall, marched through the streets for two and a half miles, then bludgeoned to death with bricks and an iron bar and his body left on a railway line to be cut in half by a train. The callousness was, however, only apparent, and it was quite wrong for Jon Venables and Robert Thompson to be tried in an adult court as if they had adult perceptions of moral responsibility. Their moral understanding was still in the stage of development, and in their case it had obviously been retarded by inadequate parenting. They were not vicious louts, but two little boys who had not yet learnt a) that they did not have a right to satisfy their curiosity in whatever circumstances, and b) that the way to rid themselves of an irritation was not to use their aggression upon it. They were at the stage of wondering what-would-happen-if, which is the way any child explores and discovers the parameters which must govern its life, but they had been given insufficient direction. When they walked off with the infant James, they had no murderous intentions. By the time they had gone so far that they did not know what to do with him, he had become an object to be disposed of. They had the moral sense of much younger persons, whose aggressive impulses were their only guides to deal with a situation they found infringing.

Martyn Harris recalls having plugged a hamster into a light socket to see what would happen, and his four-year-old son displayed similar curiosity by trying to smash a family tortoise to see how it worked. He calls this 'a simple confusion of categories, between animal and toy' and points out that it is possible to be in possession of the relevant information yet still have no understanding of its import.[20]

Occasionally, such people never develop into full moral agents and remain child-like in their ownership of aggression well into adulthood. They are then usually termed psychopaths and are utterly unresponsive to moral chastisement because they simply do not understand it. We shall have cause to examine the (thankfully rare) phenomenon of the psychopath in a later chapter; for the moment it is important to recognise that he is essentially immature, that his actions bear comparison with the totally untutored infant. Cleckley stated that the psychopath was ignorant of what life meant to others, that he was pathologically egocentric.[21] So, if it is not pressing the point too far, is the newborn child.

It would be right, then, to conclude from this that a disposition to be aggressive is innate, and to that extent predetermined in human nature. It would be wrong, however, to equate this with a disposition to be hostile, to be bad and to do wrong. Aggressiveness, properly nurtured, need not be malevolent. 'Species incapable of mutual attack do not, apparently, ever find the occasion to become friends,' writes Mary Midgley.[22] Human nature is not stained.

But is it, nonetheless, programmed in other, ineluctable ways? Or if not, is it so fragile that it can be readily shaped by extraneous influences? I have argued so far that robust, assertive human behaviour, sometimes called aggressive, is not inevitably bad, and agree with Edmund in *King Lear* that we are not 'villains by necessity'. There are strong arguments against this happy conclusion, and when argument fails, there is always religion. Different expressions of a determinist view of human nature may be found among the geneticists, inheritors of Darwin's revolutionary insight; among behaviourists, who think we can all be managed, like Pavlov's dogs; and by some Christians. But the best among them temper their excesses with humility, and recognise that the true state of affairs is likely to be a fusion of all these methods of coming to grips with the human experience.

Charles Darwin's *The Origin of Species by Means of Natural Selection* was published in 1859. It is probably one of half a dozen books in the history of literature which have profoundly altered the way mankind understands the world, and especially his place within it. For the first time, men were invited to consider the possibility that they were not, after all, central and supreme in the living world and utterly different in value from all other creatures, but one among many in the vast brotherhood of life. Darwin was the first to tell a shocked and incredulous world that human beings were descended from apes, and his explanation of the descent by natural selection did not diminish the shock.

Natural selection meant the gradual and constructive adaptation of different species to the conditions in which they were each bound to exist, the better to secure their survival in those conditions and the continuation of the species. The adaptations were achieved by genetic mutation. A perfect example in recent times is offered by the peppered moth, which was once very common in the north of England. The colour of this moth had been evolved by its genes to provide camouflage from predators when it lodged on the trunk of a tree. Then came the Industrial Revolution of the nineteenth century, and the tree trunks of Lancashire suddenly grew black with the soot from a thousand factories. On such a tree the peppered moth stood out a mile even to a short-sighted bird. At which point natural selection took over to produce a new strain of the same moth, but black in colour, which was much more likely to survive than its unfortunately conspicuous brother.

The same process has been at work in distinguishing human beings from their brothers according to the prevailing conditions of their habitat. For example, northern Asians have very narrow eyes to protect the

49

eyeball both from sun-glare bouncing off snow and from bitterly cold winds. In the same way, Indians who live high in the Andes where the air is very thin have evolved large chests to gather and hold as much oxygen as they can. Eskimos are small and squat to conserve body heat, while those who live in the Sahara desert are tall and slim in order to lose it.[23]

It is now more correct to regard these mutations as less purposeful than accidental, a sequence of random swaps, some of which work, some of which do not, the best of which eventually prevail. As Steve Jones has put it, 'we are the products of evolution, a set of successful mistakes'.[24] Sometimes a mutation will result in a genetic flaw which is less successful, such as Down's Syndrome, hermaphroditism, or the horrifying disfigurement of John Merrick, the Elephant Man.

Darwin almost stumbled when he came to face the implication that if our minds were the product of natural selection, so too might be the functions of those minds and the ideas contained within them. Our metaphysical conceits as well as our moral codes have evolved along with our bipedal stance and our general lack of hairiness.

If one considers other species whose minds have become more sophisticated with the generations, then the idea that ours has changed in a similar way seems less preposterous. Birds 'know' where they should be going during migration, and how to get there, whether by reading the stars or bombarding the ground below with echoes. Salmon know which river is theirs, and a baby cuckoo, with no parent to guide him, knows where he should go because his genes tell him; in a sense, it is the gene which 'knows'. Is it possible that our distinction between 'good' and 'bad' – our moral knowledge in fact – is likewise an accident of genetic mutation which has come from nowhere and been preserved by the process of natural selection as a quite useful thing in the battle for survival?

Another corollary. Since most mutations cause visible flaws in human beings born with physical defects, is it not possible that some people might be born with a flaw in that gene which is responsible for behaviour and its effects, a gene responsible for responsibility, in other words? Could it be that bad people have bits in their gene cupboard which are missing or have been sliced off?

These are ideas which frighten the most eminent geneticists. Natural selection is merely a mechanism, they say, and not a force for good. 'To depend on DNA to define morals is a dangerous thing to do ... where biology stops and principles begin should never be forgotten ... Although biology may tell us a lot about where we come from, it says nothing about what we are.'[25] But the same author (Professor Jones) is obliged to concede that traits of personality may have a genetic component, which should make him less sure about the source of principle, for the tendency to behave with regard or disregard to moral principles is, after all, a trait of personality.[26]

Richard Dawkins's seminal book *The Selfish Gene* made the distinction between the gene which is a 'replicator' and the individual human being (or ant, or elephant) which is a 'vehicle'. The vehicle is ephemeral, the replicator which passes from one vehicle to another is immortal:

> Individuals are not stable things, they are fleeting. Chromosomes too are shuffled into oblivion, like hands of cards soon after they are dealt. But the cards themselves survive the shuffling. The cards are the genes. The genes are not destroyed by crossing over, they merely change partners and march on. Of course they march on. That is their business. They are the replicators and we are their survival machines. When we have served our purpose we are cast aside. But genes are denizens of geological time: genes are forever.[27]

51

Dawkins nevertheless managed to avoid the implication that genes for making moral decisions should be regarded as the seat of those moral decisions, instead of the vehicle, the human being, who is merely their temporary home. 'By dictating the way survival machines and their nervous systems are built, genes exert ultimate power over behaviour. But the moment-to-moment decisions about what to do next are taken by the nervous system. Genes are the primary policy-makers; brains are the executives.'[28] Precisely. The man who behaves badly is himself merely the doer, the instrument of bad behaviour; the sources of that behaviour, by Dawkins's own definitions, are the man's genetic dispositions, the policy-makers.

The world of sociobiology is periodically in turmoil over these abstruse matters. Nobody wants to allow determinism of such an overweening kind, even if the arguments point uncomfortably in that direction. If altruism and wickedness are determined by little things we carry in our cells, then we ourselves are not autonomous; we are powerless. Darwin's legacy is so unsettling that his lessons are constantly being evaded in order to place men back in the central position they so crave. 'While sociobiology is therefore useful for understanding the evolutionary context of human social behaviour,' writes the professor of physiology at the University of California in Los Angeles, 'this approach should still not be pushed too far. The goal of all human activity cannot be reduced to the leaving of descendants.'[29] That, alas, is the whole point of natural selection. If it applies to the kangaroo and the water-rat, why should it not also apply to mankind?

Scientists are perhaps wary of some of the more loopy Darwinian offshoots of the nineteenth century, and understandably do not wish to repeat them. We hear little talk now of 'phrenologists', who were held in some regard from 1870 onwards. They studied people's heads in the belief that chronic criminality would reveal itself in cranial bumps. The shape of the skull, the lay of the jaw, the length of the nose were held to indicate congenital propensities towards either violence or peaceableness. A man's character resided in his physiognomy.

The lineal descendants of phrenology are the neuro-biologists, who no longer look at the skull, but at the chemical activity going on inside it. Their work is strictly scientific (i.e. they only want to know how it works, not to influence it), but its implications are once more deterministic. It appears that the source of our emotional responses is an area at the base of the brain called the hypothalamus. It is this which causes us to 'freeze' in fear at the sight of a threatening tiger, to increase our blood pressure and glucose, to excite our rage and willingness to fight, and especially to weaken our sensory perceptions so that, if we do get bitten, we do not feel it. The hypothalamus also makes our hair (literally) stand on end, just as it does to a cat confronted by an intruder. Experiments have shown that interference with this area of the brain will manufacture anger when there is no sufficient cause for it. In theory, a person can be made to behave 'out of character'.

Then there is the matter of the hormones. One in particular, testosterone, is in plentiful supply within the male, notably less abundant in the female. An over-supply of testosterone can provoke excessive anger or displays of lust, to the point, again, of making a person seem 'out of character'.

Third, it is possible artificially to stimulate the brain into increasing or decreasing its electrical rhythms so as to control its influence upon behaviour. There is a machine, the electroencephalogram, which measures and records this electrical activity so as to allow doctors to decree how it might be altered. I once accompanied one of the world's greatest contemporary pianists, the late John Ogdon, when it was decided that he would have to undergo electrical interference with his brain. He had been behaving irrationally for some time, cutting marks in his temples with a razorblade, attacking his wife Brenda suddenly and purposelessly but with unaccustomed violence, at other times placid and compliant. It was his unpredictability which worried the doctors (and, at the piano, delighted the world), and so they tried to eradicate it, to make John more malleable and safe. They tinkered with his internal wiring and he became a much calmer man. But that intoxicating panache which had won him the Tchaikovsky prize in Moscow was thereafter rare, subject to artificially induced mood.

The point of the story is to question whether brain states have a direct correlation with mental states at all. Doctors remark that some aggressive psychopaths (only some, mind you, between a quarter and a third) show abnormally slow brain rhythms, analogous to that of a child, and they conclude that the psychopaths suffer from cortical immaturity.[30] All that means is that their brains do not work as well as other people's. It says nothing about their decisions to behave well or ill. We do not say that we have made up our brains to do something, but that we have made up our minds. John Ogdon played music with his mind, not his brain. The determinists may well be right to suggest that if the brain has an imperfectly functioning hypothalamus or a chemical imbalance then it will function imperfectly. I do not think it can be said that a man is robbed of his character, self, personality, because his brain is faulty.

Mary Midgley makes the useful analogy between the brain and a carburettor, which does not know how to enter races, let alone win them. 'Winners need carburettors, and thinkers (including neurologists) need brain cells.'[31]

There are plenty of examples of mass murderers whose brain function has been impaired by accidental injury (Henry Lee Lucas, Bobby Long, Charles Manson), but it is an unwarranted leap, I suggest, welcomed by those of a determinist attitude, to conclude that they are murderers *because of* the brain injury. The expression of personality is frequently affected by damage to the frontal lobes, in so far as inhibition is weakened and all manner of vulgar and salacious thoughts come tumbling out, but the personality is intact and the lewd ideas were already there before; they had only been successfully repressed. Bobby Long's murderous personality *pre-existed* his road accident and was given freer rein by it.

The best example is one in reverse, given by Dr Oliver Sacks. He calls the patient Donald. Donald murdered his girlfriend while under the influence of a drug. So brutal and disgusting were the injuries to the poor girl that they could never be revealed in open court. The manner of death was discussed *in camera*, without Donald's presence. He himself had no recollection of the crime at all. He was afflicted by what is called organic amnesia, in other words he was not repressing an unpleasant memory, there was simply no memory there to repress. It had disappeared.

Donald spent four years in a psychiatric hospital for the criminally insane, where he looked after the garden and achieved a calm stability entirely at odds with the apparently manic crime which had placed him there. Nobody disliked him. The time came for him to be allowed out on parole, and on one such outing his bicycle was nearly involved in a head-on collision with an oncoming car. Donald swerved, lost control, was thrown and landed on his head.

His frontal lobes had been severely damaged, and Donald lay in a coma for two weeks. Then he began to recover, and as he did so, he kept crying 'Oh God' and 'No', as if tormented. What had happened was that Donald now saw every detail of a crime which he did not know had happened. He did not so much recover memory as discover it, and the images were frightful. He was forced to live, in his head, an event which terrified him, and twice almost drove him to suicide. These were not fantasies he was seeing; they coincided in every particular with forensic descriptions which had not been mentioned in court, or revealed to Donald himself. After four years of tranquillity, Donald was faced with a murder he did not know he had committed.[32]

What had happened? No-one would suggest that the

head injury had created a new person. The condition of Donald's brain did not control the nature of his character; it was his narrative which did that – his personal history. The brain state merely enabled that personal history to be apprehended after a period when it had eluded apprehension. Once again, the determinist option, the notion that we are predestined to conduct ourselves in ways over which we have no control, does not survive scrutiny.

There is no more overbearing determinism than that which underpins Christian faith, certainly since the teachings of St Augustine. He it is who first landed us with the concept of Original Sin, according to which, the moment Adam and Eve ate the apple, corruption entered into them and all their posterity for evermore. None of us can do good because we want to, since we are all condemned by the mistake of our original forebears to do bad. Only by God's grace (for which read whim) can any of us be virtuous. Without it, we are damned and irremediably evil. Even babes in arms are to be regarded as limbs of Satan, destined for eternal torment unless God chooses to rescue them. Hence, there is no point in complaining or trying to do anything about it. Our character is our noose. No wonder Iago is so gloomy in Verdi's opera *Otello*, based upon Shakespeare's play, wherein he sings, 'Dalle vita d'un germe o d'un atomo vile son nato. Son scellerato perchè son uomo, e sente il fango originario in me.'[33]

Twice the indignant Bertrand Russell referred to 'this ferocious doctrine',[34] which was adopted and refined by Luther and Calvin. Luther went so far as to aver that salvation was an undeserved gift which no amount of decent behaviour could earn, a prescription for despair if ever there was one. The seventeenth-century Puritan Dr John Dod was a keen disciple. He taught that children were born with a spark of evil in them which had to be beaten out like a forest fire lest it should 'rage over and burn down the whole house'.[35] The idea that adults have to be protected from children is especially obnoxious, and no matter how subtly modern Christians disclaim the doctrine, it lies at the heart of their religion and occasionally erupts in ugly manifestations even now.

One such was the Bulger trial, to which reference has already been made. When the two little boys were first arrested, crowds assembled outside the police station and hurled themselves at the van which contained them. Had they been able to get their hands upon the children, they would have torn them limb from limb. In the courtroom eight months later, there was a whiff of Salem in the air as these two dumpling boys, who looked as if they should be playing conkers, were ceremonially saddled with the burden of adult guilt. Nobody quite said so, but Robert Thompson and Jon Venables were being regarded as the enemy, the tainted apple, the source of all our pain and trouble. Sentencing them, the judge declared that they had been found guilty of a crime of 'unparalleled evil'. Neither boy had the faintest idea what 'evil' meant.

I shall have cause to consider the Christian idea of sinfulness in another context later, but for the moment it is enough to note that, at its most rigid, the inhuman pessimism of orthodox Christianity renders it one of the most determinist and hopeless theories humankind has ever had to face. In its Augustinian form, it more or less instructed that decent conduct was a waste of effort and that all men were base. It is difficult to see why anyone should ever bother to do good if perpetual torment is the inevitable reward.

Until very recently, another modern theory which appeared to say the contrary, namely that human nature was malleable, not fixed, held considerable sway. But in a disguised form, behaviourism was yet another determinist doctrine which proposed that, while a propensity to good or bad behaviour was not innate in human nature, it could be fashioned by external circumstances. 'Give me the baby and my world to bring it up in,' wrote one John B. Watson, 'and I'll make it climb and use its hands. I'll make it a thief, a gunman, or a dope-fiend. The possibility of shaping in any direction is almost endless.'[36]

57

Proper behaviourists were never quite as flippant as this, of course – the remarks of Mr Watson may serve to illustrate the perils of enthusiasm. But he is not all that far from the truth of a theory which purported to apply Darwinian principles of evolution and natural selection to the behaviour of men. If conduct was not genetically programmed, it was nonetheless alterable according to the different influences which might act upon it, and it would, through a process of sequential alterations in response to different stimuli, select and adapt and evolve.

The senior priest of behaviourism, B.F. Skinner, based his thought upon the observation that behaviour which was conducive to pleasure would be repeated, and that which led to painful results was likely to be avoided in future. (This sounds very much like the Greek philosopher of the fourth century BC, Epicurus, who boiled moral philosophy down to the precept that pleasure was the Chief Good and pain the Chief Evil.) Hence, by stages, particular patterns of behaviour would evolve, build upon one another, and construct an individual who would act for the better satisfaction of his psychic comfort. The development of fetishes shows how this mechanism works. An adolescent may experience his first sexual desire in the presence of a woman, say, who wears green nail varnish and allows her hands to caress him. Knowing that the proximity of this woman is both wrong and dangerous, he fixes his attention on her nails rather than her body, and ever after associates arousal with green nail varnish, to such an extent that he finds it difficult or impossible to achieve arousal in any other way. The part is substitute for the whole, the symbol for the real thing, and the boy's behaviour pattern is twisted out of gear ever after.

A particularly gruesome example of fetishism was afforded by Jeffrey Dahmer, whose first intimate, tactile experience of another human being had been on the operating table when he was four years old. (His parents had not been very demonstrative, and his contact with them had been somewhat distant.) When the boy underwent a double hernia operation, the surgeon's hands entered his body and touched his intestines. The association of the hidden inner parts of the intestinal tract with intimacy and invasion was never to leave him, and when, more than twenty years later, he had homosexual encounters in Milwaukee, he would drug his partner and place his ear to the man's stomach, listening to the music of digestion. When he turned to murder, it was in the stomachs of the corpses that he made the first incision, and in their intestines that he plunged his hands.[37]

Dahmer's fetishism indicates how a behaviour pattern can go wrong, that a stage in the development of behaviour may be frozen. The healthy evolution of behaviour should, on the contrary, proceed from one stage to the next, the outcome of each stage influencing progress towards the next.

It is immediately clear from this how circumstances, influences, stimuli, *may determine* behaviour. Skinner himself wrote, 'That the person is unfree is an essential assumption for a scientific view of human behaviour.'[38] The determinism may impinge from without, rather than passing down with the genes or the soul, but it is just as powerful. It allows social conditions, family influence, wealth, opportunity, political climate, education and a host of other extraneous considerations to design a person, and it takes us back to Locke's *tabula rasa*, the blank slate on which experience writes the tale. Zola's vivid and depressing masterpiece *Germinal* shows how individuals born into conditions of intense social deprivation are robbed of their freedom to develop by stages into wholesome human beings, and laments the sewing of crime in 'ce crâne d'enfant'. Zola was a behaviourist before his time.

He might have been wrong, however. A study of Danish children adopted at birth showed that their characters and propensity for good or bad deeds (crime, in fact) followed more closely that of their natural fathers, whom they had never met, than that of their adoptive fathers, whose influence upon them had been quotidian.[39] That would seem to indicate that environment is at least of questionable import. But what is most objectionable in the behaviourist viewpoint is the idea that the individual will only respond to influence and stimuli *in such a way as to extract the most benefit for himself*. There is no room for altruism, no room for disinterested action, no space for the development of relative moral values which might point to less personal benefit but greater spiritual worth. If the Darwinians celebrate the selfishness of the species, the geneticists the selfishness of a ruthless gene, Christians the selfishness of God (in our image), Freudians the selfishness of the ego, the behaviourists surpass them all by attributing the purpose of conduct to the satisfaction of conduct itself. This is worse because it is wilful. All action is designed to promote the well-being of the actor.

The danger with all these deterministic approaches is that they breed abandonment of effort, abnegation, surrender and inaction. They are all excuses for doing nothing, and as such engender a horrid fatalism within the breast. This need not be so. As Mary Midgley has pointed out, there is the world of difference between determinism, properly understood, and fatalism. Determinism should be a description of the way things work, whereas fatalism is the superstition that things work that way in order to do us down.

We can still be cheerful. First, determinist descriptions rarely allow for the unexpected, yet life is built upon it, the very process of genetic mutation being essentially random. Steve Jones insists upon the *unpredictability* of natural selection and genetic switching, the very opposite, in fact, of a determinist rigidity, and puts the matter with characteristic flair:

No dinosaur could have guessed that descendants of the shrew-like creatures playing at its feet would soon replace it: and the chimpanzees who outnumbered humans a hundred thousand years ago would be depressed to see that their relatives are now so abundant while their descendants are an endangered species. Evolution always builds on its weaknesses, rather than making a fresh start. The lack of a grand plan is what makes life so adaptable and humans – the greatest opportunists of all – so successful. Life's utilitarian approach also means that speculating about the future of evolution is a risky thing to do as it is difficult to guess what a pragmatist will do next.[40]

In just such a way have our greatest heroes and most admirable saints escaped from the imprisonment of the expected, and soared to heights of imaginative humanity that no determinist could have predicted. These people are as exciting as the adaptable gene, as aggressive as the god-free and neurosis-free ego, as refreshing as the actor without a script. And they are emphatically not collapsed in self-regard.

They confound the determinists.

3

BEASTLY BEHAVIOUR

The intellectual and spiritual crisis created by Darwin's unprecedented insights led many to the conclusion that, if life were naught but a constant fight to the death, there could be no room for moral distinctions of any kind. It was 'every man for himself, and the weaker shall fall'. Something of this attitude lingers to the present day, dressed up in modern scientific jargon, and occasionally springs forth unadorned. 'We must teach our children altruism,' says Dawkins, 'for we cannot expect it to be part of their biological nature.'[1]

Less scrupulous readers than Richard Dawkins have tended towards a facile understanding of Darwin's work which either misinterprets the points he wished to make, or fails to spot the direction in which he was moving. Much has been made of the Struggle for Existence as a paradigm for inevitable selfishness, yet Darwin explicitly stated that he intended the concept 'in a large and metaphorical sense, including dependence of one being upon another, and including (which is more important) not only the life of the individual, but success in leaving progeny'. He gives as illustration the plant struggling for existence at the edge of the desert, and proclaims it could more properly be said, and more positively put, that it is dependent on the moisture. Also, as the mistletoe is disseminated by birds, its existence must depend upon them and it must 'struggle' with other plants to attract the birds without which it would die. 'In these several senses, which pass into each other, I use for convenience sake the general term of struggle for existence.'[2]

Further on, he specifies that each species may take

the best possible advantage of the instincts of other species with which it comes into contact, stopping short of the suggestion that it might pursue a course of action designed for the direct benefit of another species altogether. At the same time, however, Darwin saw that instincts must change and evolve by natural selection in much the same way as corporeal structures change and evolve, which is a step towards the idea that moral perceptions, in so far as they are 'instinctive', have evolved from the behaviour of animals. Twelve years later, in *The Descent of Man*, he was bolder. 'We have seen that the senses and intuitions, the various emotions and faculties, such as love, memory, attention and curiosity, imitation, reason, etc., of which man boasts, may be found in an incipient or even sometimes in a well-developed condition, in the lower animals.' Or, 'There is no fundamental difference between man and the higher animals in their mental faculties. The difference in mind between man and the higher animals, great as it is, certainly is one of degree and not of kind.'[3]

In the years since, moral philosophers, sociobiologists, ethologists and simple observers have built upon Darwin's ideas to such an extent that there is now a very respectable army of thinkers to maintain that the genesis of our moral understanding, and the very source of our goodness, lie in pre-existent animal behaviour. E.O. Wilson, for instance, has stated that human nature exercises constraints upon the way we behave no less than ant-nature works upon ant-behaviour. Accepted constraints (i.e. moralities) are not unique to mankind; their precursors are everywhere to be seen.

While we must always be aware of the dangers of anthropomorphism, that is of attributing human motives to the actions of animals quite otherwise programmed, or of making Fido see the world through our eyes, there are now manifold examples of animal conduct which, if we must not call it 'good' or 'kind', we can term 'beneficial' and 'conducive to well-being'. The point is that 'goodness' and 'kindness' have *evolved* from 'conducive to well-being', that they are abstractions which influence our lives because we are the distant offspring of much less sophisticated creatures who were already moving in that direction. According to such a view, our goodness is inherited from the animal world.

Birds which nest on the ground are especially vulnerable to predators, and they have had to evolve a 'morality' in order to protect their young. At the sight of a hungry fox, the mother will emerge from the nest and make herself conspicuously visible, holding out one wing as if it were wounded and limping along in an obviously painful manner. The purpose is to lure the fox away from the chicks by offering it a larger and easier meal, then taking flight just in time to escape the fox when it is ready to pounce. There is nothing specialist about this observation; it has been seen by millions in televised wildlife programmes. The effect is to save the lives of the chicks by taking a considerable personal risk. Whether the bird is 'thinking' what to do is not the point – it is behaviour which pre-dates thinking.

Other manifestations of altruistic behaviour, encompassing suicide, self-sacrifice, giving and even rescuing, have been observed. Social insects routinely commit suicide for the greater good of the community. A worker bee is sterile and therefore has no need to ensure the survival of its own genes. To quote Professor Dawkins's happy analogy, 'the death of a single sterile worker bee is no more serious to its genes than is the shedding of a leaf in autumn to the genes of a tree'.[4] Similarly, some species of caterpillar (which are *not* sterile) sacrifice themselves and their genes to warn other caterpillars of the danger which lurks.

Necessarily more impressive is like behaviour among the higher mammals. 'If a chimpanzee is eating and he sees another chimpanzee begging for food he feels compelled to give some of his food away, even though he shows clear signs of anger and irritation.'[5] Threatened baboons have been seen to carry off a wounded member of the tribe rather than leave it to the mercies of a predator, and to rescue a baby clinging to the corpse of its dead mother.[6] Eugène Marais watched an entire drama unfold as a group of baboons were caught unawares by a leopard, who had shown up rather earlier in the day than he would normally have been expected, before the group could retreat to its protected den; two of their number peeled off and made for an escarpment overlooking the leopard, waited for the right moment, and then fell upon it in the almost certain 'knowledge' that they would be sacrificed.[7]

The dominant stallion in a herd of Mongolian wild horses will always bring up the rear and will turn to attack a pack of harassing dogs even though he is certain to be torn to pieces.

The wild dogs themselves have their own pattern of service to one another. They have been known to feed sick and injured adults and go in for babysitting, when they will bring a snack to the babysitter. Other species adopt orphans.

The most maligned creature (by us, that is) must be the wolf, and yet we could copy his habits with profit. He is amongst the most loyal of beasts, monogamous, affectionate, respectful towards his kind, only killing prey in order to eat, sharing, and strongly inhibited against attacking females and young. Indeed, neglect or abuse of the young is impossible for a wolf. So is lack of dignity in treatment of the old. Affection and mutually benign ties are the norm for them, and they are expressed in delicately nuanced social manners, forms of greeting and reassurance obviously designed to ensure harmony and display love.

There have been cases of whales rescuing infants or weak members in danger of drowning, holding them with their weight and pushing them up to the surface for air. One extraordinary example was that of a dolphin which, in exactly the same way, spotted a human swimmer in difficulties and brought him to the surface. How it was that the dolphin knew the man was in danger, and why it was that a dolphin should feel the need (impulse? desire?)

to save him has not been explained, but it is hardly fanciful to interpret such an action as the embryonic seed of moral intervention. Konrad Lorenz has written of his admiration 'for those physiological mechanisms which enforce, in animals, selfless behaviour aimed towards the good of the community, and which work in the same way as the moral law in human beings.'[8]

In the light of which, it is possible to see the sacrifice of Father Maximilian Kolbe in 1941 as an expression of his animal inheritance. The story is astonishing and comforting, from whatever angle it is approached, and as an instance of pure goodness it stands high. Kolbe was a Roman Catholic priest, of the Franciscan order, and a Pole. When the Nazi terror was unleashed, he knew his duty lay in helping as many unfortunate Jews as he could, notwithstanding the possibly horrific consequences for himself. Kolbe was an impressively stoical man who appeared not to notice when he was beaten by SS guards, one of whom thrust his crucifix in his face yelling, 'Do you believe in this?' and struck him across the jaw every time he answered 'Yes.' His penetrating gaze made the guilty feel exposed and avert their eyes. Eventually, he found himself in Hell itself, the notorious camp at Auschwitz. Even there, he continued to preach Mass and hear confessions in the full knowledge that such activities were punishable by summary execution.

There was a particularly despicable rule at Auschwitz, according to which ten random prisoners must die for every one that escaped. It was intended precisely to undermine that sense of community and mutual responsibility which lay deeper than and was antecedent to civilisation itself, for no fugitive could ever escape the knowledge that he had condemned ten of his fellows to death by his self-regarding act. It was as if the Nazis knew that these bonds of dignity were strong because they had their roots in instinct, and they were determined to smash them. They sought to unhinge men from their instinctual past. Punishment was correspondingly awful. The ten would be shut into airless concrete bunkers underground, there to starve to death very slowly.

On the last day of July, 1941, the sirens sounded to announce the escape of a prisoner. Inevitably, the following morning ragged and dispirited prisoners were made to line up and, many trembling with fear, await their destiny. The deputy camp commandant and the Gestapo chief, Fritsch and Palitsch, walked slowly down the ranks, picking out their victims with brutal relish. When they came to the last, and selected a young man called Francis Gajowniczek, he burst into tears. 'Oh please, please,' he gasped, 'my wife, my poor children, please spare me, I'm not old, I'm young. I can work, work hard for you. I don't want to die.' Racked with sobs, he was reduced to the most pitiable indignity. Fritsch and Palitsch were unmoved, rather contemptuous.

Prisoner 16670 Kolbe had been standing in the second line. He now stepped forward without permission, walked up to Fritsch and stood to attention before him. 'Halt!' shouted the commandant as his guards moved threateningly towards the small priest with his horn-rimmed spectacles. 'What do you want?'

Father Kolbe pointed to Francis. 'Herr Commandant, I would like to take the place of this man. I would like to die in his place.' Fritsch was thrown off balance. 'Who is this man?' he said to Palitsch. 'What's it all about?' Palitsch did not have to answer. Kolbe said, very quietly, 'I am a Catholic priest and I want to take his place. He has a wife and family.' Fritsch yelled back, 'Are you crazy? An idiot?' and one of the SS men went to strike the priest for his effrontery. Palitsch restrained him.

Kolbe went on, 'I would like to die in his place. I'm of no use to anyone any more. This man is young and strong. He has a wife and family. I have no-one.' Fritsch stared at him, but the calm gaze of Father Kolbe was too powerful and he had to drop his eyes. 'Accepted,' he barked. 'Don't look at us, look at the floor,' screamed an SS officer. Gajowniczek rejoined the ranks, and Kolbe was placed with the condemned men. He was forty-seven years old.[9]

Thirty years later Father Kolbe was canonised by another Pole, Pope John Paul II, in the presence of Francis Gajowniczek. The Pope visited the cell where Kolbe had died, finally injected with phenol, and declared himself moved. It was said the spirit of God had inhabited the man, which is why he is now revered as a saint of the Holy Church. But it could also be said that Maximilian Kolbe was inhabited by the history of his species, that he was obedient to the bright bond of tribal loyalty which resides deep without our bones and is too often smothered by the accretions of human subtlety. In a very real sense, it is true to say that Maximilan Kolbe behaved like an animal, while his executioners behaved like humans.

Lest admirers of Father Kolbe's goodness be offended by its being ascribed to instinct, I should declare that, of course, there are important differences between the instinct which dictates that a baboon should sacrifice its life for its fellows and the priest's selfless martyrdom, but the differences are, as Darwin said above, those of degree rather than kind. There are grades between the two, yet the source of each is identical, the priest having answered an urge beyond rational explanation. What constitutes the difference is the human being's awareness of the consequences of his act, his ability to see an image of it (i.e. to imagine it), to plan it in advance and contemplate it in retrospect. We do not know how the baboon reaches the decision to be a martyr, but we may be sure he has not thought about it in moments of tranquillity.

The leaf-cutter ant appears to demonstrate the ability to make plans, but his activities are a perfect example of unreflective instinct. He collects bits of leaf, stem and flowers, mixes them with saliva and faeces, and covers the floor of his underground home with the resulting muck – a kind of sticky carpet. What the ants are doing is getting a field ready for sowing, for in this paste they then drop seeds of their favourite fungus which will grow into the leaf-ant equivalent of caviar. They are fastidious, too, carefully pulling out any other stray fungus which tries to grow on their field. All this activity is clearly sequential – the leaves are collected *for a purpose*, as the ants are not interested in eating them, but in using them, and in some weird way they 'know' what the leaves are for and what treats will eventually be their reward for preparing them so carefully. But they cannot do anything else. The instinct is imperious.

Recent studies have shown, however, that there are some instinctual drives which can be adapted to fit new circumstances, in which case the instinct is shown to be malleable and, to some measure, experimental. Darwin himself noted a woodpecking finch in the Galapagos which fed on insects found within tree bark, but was not equipped with a beak long enough or hard enough to extract them. So he used a cactus thorn, held in his beak, and lo! he was a woodpecker. This, too, was done by instinct, but there had to be a time when the instinct was 'invented', when the first finch picked up the first cactus thorn. There is an element of planning and foresight in this, but it is impossible to say what, in the process of natural selection and gradual adaptation, is doing the planning or seeing the results ahead.

This process is observable on a domestic level, as any British person lucky enough to have milk bottles delivered to his door will confirm. Until about thirty years ago, milk bottles were safe from the attention of birds. They were hard and forbidding, and as they did not exist in the birds' natural décor, it was only to be expected they would not know what to do with them. One day (or one year – nobody can be precise), a bird worked out how to peck through the cap on the top of the bottle, and within a very short time all the birds of that species had inherited the knack. A new instinct had been created, and so successful was it that stronger milk-bottle caps had to be manufactured to deal with it.

These are instincts with practical uses. We are still chasms away from that instinct which engenders moral decisions and prompted the self-sacrifice of Father Kolbe, the instinct which can contemplate itself and project into the future, but I believe it is possible to see it adumbrated in minor but moving form in the behaviour of some animals. I have had to spend a lot of time at John Aspinall's private zoo at Howletts, near Canterbury, for a biography I wrote of him which dealt especially with his relationship with the animals. To that end, I thought I should learn to emulate that relationship in order to understand it; I passed hours in the company of one gorilla, Djala, and watched the others very closely. Three incidents stand out in my mind as stunning examples of moral decision.

In the early days, before the zoo was open to the public, Aspinall used to go for walks in his parkland with his wife, children, guests, and a band of three or four adolescent and mature gorillas. On one occasion, Aspinall's son Damien, then four years old, was engrossed in something under a bush and became separated from the rest. With the adults busy in conversation and the gorillas in play and exploration, nobody noticed that Damien had got left behind, until one gorilla, a childless female called Mounda, detached herself from the group. She retraced her steps, found the little boy two hundred yards away, crying, and fetched him back to join the others. He was, for Mounda, a member of the group; she would not have done the same for a hare or a rabbit.

It is important to note that these were not domesticated animals, household pets, but were living as a proper band in their own enclosure, so successfully content in their gorilla identity that they have since grown into the colony with the highest record of breeding in captivity in the world (at the time of writing there have been forty births). In my own sessions with Djala, he would most like a prolonged good-natured fight, in which he would knock me over, I would punch him, tickle his belly when he was down, protect myself as best I could when he hurled himself at me. It was perfectly obvious that he was several times stronger than I was, with his great shoulder muscles and arms like tree trunks, but I wondered how this could be obvious to him, and why I emerged with only a few light bruises.

Later, I understood. A film was taken of Aspinall playing with the huge adult silverback male, Djoum, during which the animal took some gentle swipes at his friend with a mighty fist. When the film was shown in slow motion, it became clear what was really happening. Instead of hitting Aspinall with the full force of his punch, Djoum brushed him with the back of his hand. Recognising well enough the awesomeness of his strength beside that of a middle-aged human, the gorilla purposefully restrained himself and made the decision to hold his power back lest it be harmful. In playing with his own family, all of them far tougher than John Aspinall, he had no need for such restraint and let rip with obvious glee. With Aspinall, instinct informed his behaviour in such a way as to render it harmless. In some way he must have been able to 'imagine' what it was like to be as weak and feeble as a human being and use that knowledge to frame a 'moral' decision.

The most astonishing incident was the third, some years later, when Damien had married and his wife had given birth to a little girl. It was Damien's habit, as it was his father's, to enter the gorilla enclosure regularly, staying there with the silverback, three adult females, and up to eight assorted adolescents and infants. The whole band not only tolerated these intrusions, but welcomed them. When the baby was two months old, Damien and his wife took her in with them and presented her to the adult females. It was no surprise that they treated the human baby with curiosity, tenderness, and what looked like admiration, passing her from one to the other for inspection. What was amazing was the way in which they held her.

Gorilla babies are tough, and can withstand being dragged around the floor without injury, or clinging to the mother's back when she darts around the enclosure and hurls herself at a rope. Moreover, after about one month of life they develop thick, muscular necks, so that the mother need not worry if the head should hang unsupported. A human baby, on the other hand, has a proportionately large head and narrow, fragile neck for much longer. The female gorilla, when she received the little girl in her arms, did something quite extraordinary. She placed her big hand behind the baby's head in order to support it, more or less exactly as the human mother would have done. How her instincts should so immediately have adapted to take account of the new circumstance is a mystery, but it is not fanciful to suggest that she was moved by the gorilla equivalent of a desire to do the right thing, to govern her behaviour in such a way as to achieve a good rather than a harmful effect.

What this may intimate is a pre-human glimmer of what we now call conscience. If one takes knowledge to be the understanding of which actions are likely to be conducive to good, and conscience the selection of and preference for those actions, then the gorilla's conscience must be antecedent to knowledge, for nobody would suggest that she knew, in any cognitive sense, that the human baby's head should be supported. But she chose to support it, because she also knew, in a deeper instinctual sense, that it would be harmful not to. There is something magical about conscience, viewed from this prospect, because it is beginning to look as if it could be as old, venerable and mysterious as our remote ancestors' bones and their genes still coursing within us. Conscience is perhaps pre-human, its preferences echoing back long before thinking men began to formulate and explain them. If this be true, then Maximilian Kolbe's heroic deed answered a call more ancient than any religion.

Human morality would therefore be a reflection of conduct we have inherited from our animal ancestry, which is very welcome news indeed, for it would mean that we have a natural disposition to behave well, in other words that we, as a species, are innately good. It has been convincingly argued that this disposition is, in itself, an example of natural selection working to ensure the survival of the species, for the original hominoid groups, who stood on their hind legs, thus becoming more mobile, travelling further afield in search of food, had to learn to co-operate with one another to make the group harmonious and thereby more efficient. Before this formation of co-operative groups, millions of years ago, the individual was, it is supposed, unassailable, and his selfishness necessary to his well-being. Morality began with the herd.

Bertrand Russell pointed out that the purpose of a moral code was 'to bring the interest of the community to bear upon the individual, and to produce an identity between his interest and that of his herd which would not otherwise exist'.[10] Bruce Chatwin has taken this idea further, and suggested that the original small communities of men were essentially defensive; that, harried and besieged by predators, they evolved 'all the voluntary graces that bring equipoise to society', by which he means charity, altruism, decency, and trying to do good. 'Might not all these have evolved as stratagems for survival,' he asks, 'hammered out against tremendous odds, to avert the threat of extinction? Would they, therefore, be any less instinctual or directionless? Would not a general theory of defence explain more readily why offensive wars are, in the long run, unfightable? Why the bullies never win?'[11]

There is now a huge literature on the theory of the 'territorial imperative', which holds that animals are loyal, above all else, to the territory which they inhabit, as a group, and to that section of the territory which is theirs by assignment or competition. We have already considered the example of the sticklebacks who will ritually defend a territory even when, by the intervention of human experiment, they are deceived. Stories of birdsong intended to mark out territory are too common to require repetition (and are delightfully copied by soldiers singing on the march or Welsh miners singing in honour of their communal bonds). We have only to observe how our dogs mark out their territory by lifting the leg far more often than ordinary needs would demand, and our cats by rubbing perfumes excreted from the side of the jaw. In some animals, the female will not deign to mate with a male unless he has a decent territory to offer her and can demonstrate his attachment to it by defending it loudly. (Again, there are human equivalents in the desirability of a man having a home to offer his bride, and his ceremonial carrying of her into it 'over the threshold'.) The bowerbird devotes more time and energy to creating and decorating his territory than to anything else in life, building a bower of such matchless beauty and impressiveness, carrying coloured stones from great distances to adorn it, that no female can resist. It is the territory that she is wedded to, more than its inhabitant.

When it comes to the territory held by the group in common, this must be defended by each individual subordinate, for the moment, to the interests of the whole community. It is for this reason that harmonious co-operation and kind behaviour can co-exist with hostility and even ferocity towards the intruder. It was Herbert Spencer in *The Principles of Ethics* (1892) who first formulated the amity–enmity complex to explain how it is that one may be good towards one's fellows and bad towards those excluded from the fellowship. Essentially, one's fellows are those who share the territory, and the rest are those who threaten it. Innate conscience requires love and decency to operate within the fellowship, but the same conscience demands that defensive wrath be displayed towards those who are not part of the herd and who impudently impinge upon it. This duality is observable in the conflicts between Montagus and Capulets in *Romeo and Juliet*, and their twentieth-century representatives the Jets and the Sharks in Leonard Bernstein's *West Side Story*; the Jets and the Sharks are New York gangs, admirably loyal towards one another within their group, and fiercely antagonistic towards members of the rival group. (Incidentally, the origin of the word 'rival' is in the riverbank which often marked the boundary of a territory.) It is equally observable in the seething conflicts between Israelis and

Arabs, precisely over a patch of territory called Palestine, and between opposing factions of Irishmen over another patch in the north of their island. Chatwin is right in so far as there is moral superiority in the 'natural' defensive mode and the 'unnatural' bullies or intruders never win because their moral ground is less secure, but each of the conflicts mentioned above is intractable because *all* parties, laying claim to the same patch, consider themselves defensive and honourable.

An animal in secure tenure of his territory will behave belligerently towards an intruder and chase him off. At the edge of his territory, where the intruder himself becomes a potential defender, the rules of engagement are somewhat less clear. Niko Tinbergen described what herring-gulls do in such a situation. Each defender, roused to the point of incipient explosion, gives threat to the other, looking fierce, flapping wings, uttering shrieks. But neither can attack because neither is, at the edge of their respective territories, in the wrong. Something has to happen, otherwise all their disciplined rage will overflow and do damage. So they both begin furiously to tear up grass.

Ethologists call this 'displacement activity', that is the diversion of energy into an activity unrelated to aggression or defence, undertaken for the specific purpose of avoiding conflict. Sticklebacks place themselves vertically adjacent and start boring into the sand with their heads, looking daggers at each other the while, rather than risk coming to blows. Many readers will recognise the situation and perhaps their solution to it. There is a furious row over rights and duties, let us say in the kitchen: the husband has disordered materials on the wife's territory, and she is furious. Voices are raised, ill-natured things are said, a fight seems likely. Just as the volcano is about to erupt violently, the wife throws herself into a chair, grabs a glossy magazine, and proceeds furiously to flick through the pages, not even pretending to look at any of them, as if the magazine were her enemy. She is behaving like a herring-gull, indulging in displacement activity in order to avoid dangerous conflict. Displacement activity is one way of doing the right thing, or at least of preventing oneself from doing the wrong one. It is another brick in the long, slow architecture of morality, and it is innate, not learned.

Another is the well-known 'appeasement gesture' which many animals perform ritually to prevent injury to the weaker among them. The gesture usually involves either literally turning away the threat by pointing the teeth or claws in a direction away from the opponent, or by submitting the weaker part of oneself towards the opponent. Two dogs meet in the park and squabble. The defeated presents the nape of his neck to the victor, who thereby is actually prevented from doing any harm. Or the dog may offer his hindquarters, another vulnerable and virtually indefensible area, to divert dangerous aggression; he is submitting, not for copulation, but for ritual harm-free dominion. My cats ritually lick each other's necks (and mine, too, I might add) in submission and appeasement, and lift their tails to expose the anal area when stroked.

There are many appeasement gestures we habitually indulge in, without perhaps realising it. When we shake hands, we reveal that we are unarmed. We indicate submission in a variety of ways, either gently by bowing the head slightly, or flamboyantly by sinking to the floor in a grand curtsey. Hindus touch the feet of their princes, and Englishmen kneel to be knighted. The origin of these gestures has been forgotten, and only their form remains, but as Storr rightly points out, 'submissively presenting hind quarters or licking a dominant animal's neck is not psychologically far removed from the familiar ritual of saluting a superior officer'.[12] The same author makes the observation that when a monkey wishes to be bold towards another who is threatening him, he will sometimes present himself submissively to a stronger male before he will have the courage to defend himself against the first, and suggests this is similar to the little boy enlisting the help of a bigger boy in the playground to see off his tormentor. Konrad Lorenz's detailed observation of the complex appeasement gestures of geese is particularly illuminating. What he calls a triumph ceremony involves all the hissing and swaying and threatening one would expect in a real conflict, but the fight has been completely submerged in memory and only the ceremony remains. Some Indian tribes in North and South America do exactly the same – pounding and stamping and shouting but never coming to blows.

The point in raising these matters is that they are the source of that bonding between members of a group which has given rise in human society to concepts such as loyalty and kindness. Appeasement gestures ensure harmony and identification as members of a group; they cement the bonds which are important if the group is to feel secure and unburdened by anarchy, and bond-behaviour ultimately leads to morality, that is suppressing individual expression for the benefit of the community. Religions are replete with the most glaring appeasement gestures, from the Catholic's kneeling before the altar and allowing himself to be fed by another's hand, to the Muslim's prostrating himself with forehead on the ground, exposing the nape of the neck to attack. All these bond the community and promote moral behaviour within it. They create fellowship and trust, without which it would be difficult to see why one should do good (i.e. benefit another as well as oneself) in the first place. Thus they are the breeding ground for decency.

The gentlemen's clubs of London are not unlike communities of greylag geese. They have their rituals and their ceremonies, and their bond-behaviour is deep and mysterious. When young, I used to think that one's relationships were divided into two groups: friends, of whom there might be three or four, to whom one would tell one's troubles and be utterly free in expression; and acquaintances, up to twenty folk one might take a meal and swap pleasantries with, but to whom one would reveal next to nothing. When I was admitted into the world of gentlemen's clubs, I realised there was a third category, not intimate and self-revelatory, nor superficial and glib, but somewhere in between on the level of confidence, and much more profound than either on the level of loyalty. You may never see a fellow member of a club outside its walls, yet your bonding with him is more certain, because more selfless, than that with a close friend. (I mean, of course, those of the London clubs which are gregarious, and exclude those others where one might go in order to fall asleep.) I know that I *cannot* behave badly towards a fellow club member, except in ritual banter (not because I am forbidden, but because it is impossible), whereas I am able so to do with a friend. I am told that similar bondings occur in the armed services and at some public schools.

Bond-behaviour makes possible that degree of self-sacrifice which would otherwise be absurd, and Father Kolbe's martyrdom occurred precisely because he had become part of the group in Auschwitz and responded instinctually as a group member. The fact that he was not Jewish is beside the point. The Nazis *created* bond-behaviour by their idiotic viciousness, and we may be certain they had never read any ethology.

There are many other examples, from the twelve apostles to recent hostages in Beirut. Aelred, the third abbot of Rievaulx Abbey in the thirteenth century, devoted his life to the celebration of bond-behaviour among his monks, with the result that there has scarcely ever been a more impressive tribe in the history of English monastical fraternities than at Rievaulx during his term, and the overwhelming sense of goodness which pervaded the place was due to Aelred's instinctive understanding of the value of appeasement gestures. St Theresa of Avila likewise established a group mentality which fostered decency and good-will, elevating moral candour to a point of ultimate principle. In each case, the evolution of goodness and benign conduct were made possible by an unwitting inheritance of the amity–enmity complex from our ape-like forebears. St Theresa might not have appreciated the implication, but it was almost certainly the invention of co-operation and kindly feeling as a means towards survival that effected the great (and still otherwise unexplained) leap from the large-brained ape to the subtle and conceptual human being. The apes developed love and conscience, and later we came along to discuss them.

There are other ways in which the animal kingdom manifests the beginnings of a moral dimension, though to discuss them in detail would take us away from the central route. Hunting dogs, for example, will not eat until their children have been sated – the future must come first. (On the other hand, lion cubs will have to wait until Mum and Dad have finished before they can catch the scraps of a meal – the explanation being that the lion has a longer life and must conserve energy, whereas the adult hunting dog is more vulnerable and is less likely to live long.) And examples abound of symbiotic relationships between different species, where one helps the other as a matter of course. That which has arisen between dog and man is a very recent one, in geological time, and probably started as a mutually beneficial team on the hunt, as it still is in Alaska, and, in mock form, in Wiltshire. Nobody can doubt the depth of loyalty which the dog bestows upon his human companion, or the total absence of guile in his devotion. It is a most upsetting sight occasionally to see the human return this goodness by visiting upon the obviously uncomprehending dog conduct of malice and cruelty. 'A dog is an image of God, better than us.'[13]

Less well-known symbiotic relationships occur between some large fish and smaller species, called cleaner-fish. The large fish opens his mouth and allows the cleaner-fish to swim inside, pick his teeth, and swim out again through his gills, which he also cleans. The cleaners are more or less the same size as the fish which the big one would normally eat, yet they are perfectly safe as the relationship serves them both.

Elephants are much more sensitive than was once thought. With an infrasonic language which carries seven miles, and thirty different vocalisations, they are also deeply communicative, co-operative and devoted. They are known to grieve when one of their number dies; in Aspinall's zoo at Port Lympne, the elephant group, when let out of their night quarters, *unfailingly* walk over to the spot where they know their senior male, Assam, is buried, and caress the earth with their trunks.

Still with John Aspinall, a remarkable story illustrates the probable presence of gratitude in a gorilla breast. One of the band at Howletts, a senior female called Founa, was dependable but rather aloof. Aspinall and the head gorilla keeper Peter knew well enough that she was fond of them, but she never showed it, carefully avoiding any demonstration of affection. One day it was discovered she had a rectal prolapse and had to be taken to London Zoo for an operation. Aspinall went to visit her every day while she was in the sanatorium, and she gurgled a welcome to show she was pleased to see him. Though she had a scar a foot long, Founa healed very quickly and was back at Howletts within a week. When Aspinall next went to see her, she held his hand firmly for half an hour and would not release it; it was the clearest sign that she was thanking him for having been there in her moment of terror and fright.

However, it must be admitted that there are some instincts which, when circumstances demand, clearly override the instinct for good. Migratory birds have been known to desert their hungry young and abandon them to certain death if the seasons cheat them and the urge to make the annual long journey is pressing; this is perhaps an instance of one good taking precedence over another. There are also many ways in which animals develop talents for deceit, dissemblance, treachery, none of which can be rightly considered 'bad' as far as the survival of their species demands, but which should give one pause before going too far in seeking animal origins for such overtly human abstractions. Whereas the previous chapter attempted to show that wickedness was not necessarily innate in humankind, this one must avoid the opposite trap of concluding that we owe all our capacity for goodness to the animal kingdom. Therein lies what came to be known in the nineteenth century as the Romantic Fallacy.

It is a seductive notion, nevertheless, and boasts an increasing number of adherents. After a long period when the theory was regarded as hopelessly naive, it now appears to some to be not so fallacious after all. Listen to Jean-Jacques Rousseau's famous celebration of the Noble Savage, 'at peace with Nature and in amity with his fellows':

> Men are wicked, as sad and repeated experience demonstrates. And yet, Mankind is naturally good. What, then, could have brought him to such a point of depravity, unless it be the changes in his constitution, the progress he has made, and the knowledge he has acquired? ... There is absolutely no fundamental perversity in the human heart.[14]

Though Rousseau based an entire moral and educational philosophy upon the premiss, he was by no means the first to propose it. One of the tenets of the Renaissance, which reached France from Italy more than two centuries before Rousseau, was the perfectibility of man when freed from the chains of prejudice and ignorance and allowed to be true to his natural state. The first great apostle of freedom, François Rabelais (whose wise giant Gargantua has given us an adjective describing appetites), had massive confidence in the natural goodness of man; if left to their own devices, he wrote, the instincts of men will guide them to the path of virtue, for they are inevitably attracted by the good. And at the very end of the twentieth century one may still find philosophers echoing a Rousseauesque doctrine; 'Man's good inclination is inborn', says M.A. Amiel, 'and his evil inclination only incidental.'[15]

At the root of this optimism is the idea that moral worth

increases in direct relation to men's closeness to the soil, that the peasant, the farmer, the herdsman, the country lad, are all part of the earth which gives them sustenance and to which they owe respect. They do not feel they must fight Nature, or one another, but assume their place as an integral element within Nature, and are thereby instantly and constantly at peace. They have sprung from the earth, live on it and in it, and will return to it in the proper course. The earth is home, comfort, solace and refuge. When the Aboriginals of Australia wanted to thank the earth for its gifts, they cut open a vein in their forearms and let the blood drip upon the ground.

We have all noticed how much more relaxed, less neurotic, are country dwellers compared with their urban cousins. Rousseau's identification of artificial city life as the source of man's illness seems vindicated by daily observation of the spites, contests, envies and grievances which beset those trapped in modern conurbations; for so many, their greatest ambition is to escape to the country where they can 'wind down', where they can feel wrapped up and protected by the natural world to which they rightly belong and from which they have been disastrously banished.

Studies of primitive peoples living in harmony with the earth have repeatedly demonstrated how pacific and placid their lives can be, how relatively free they are from trouble. When Eskimos were first encountered, for example, travellers were astonished at how gentle and shy they were, how timid and utterly foreign to the idea of hostility. When disputes arose between individuals, Eskimos dealt with them by ritualised song contests and drum duels, reminiscent of the appeasement gestures described earlier. (Alas, time moves on, and many of the Eskimo peoples, deprived of their isolation, have been corrupted by modern values and habits.) The apostles of man's supposed emergence from a tribe of fierce weapon-wielding hunters were somewhat put out by this evidence of primitive people living in peace, and ascribed the phenomenon to accident. 'What has been revealed is nothing more than that people living where nobody else wants to live may quite possibly suffer from non-aggressive dispositions,' wrote Robert Ardrey, adding, yet more provocatively, 'timid people tend to live at unfashionable addresses.'[16] Nearly thirty years later, Ardrey is largely discredited as a bombastic exaggerator with a turkey-carpet style, his loyalty to his thesis overriding awkward evidence.[17]

One of Ardrey's most impassioned opponents is the late Bruce Chatwin, whose experiences travelling in some of the world's most remote spaces, and his careful reflections thereupon, convinced him that the ancestors of man were nomadic, pastoral and peaceful. He points out that 'nomos' is Greek for 'pasture', and that a nomad was self-evidently someone who moved from pasture to pasture. Observing, further, that all the great monotheistic religions have sprung from a pastoral milieu, Chatwin advanced the theory that the nomads were the 'crankhandle' of history, and introduced in his own support the writings of the Arab philosopher Ib'n Khaldun. This wise man, himself a nomad, declared that 'the Desert people are closer to being good than settled peoples because they are closer to the First State and are more removed from all the evil habits that have infected the hearts of settlers', and Chatwin adds the comment that Ib'n Khaldun based his idea on an intuition – 'that men decline, morally and physically, as they drift towards cities'.[18]

Each reader will enlist his own examples of people who tend to illustrate the point, from the local village boy, tender-hearted and kind, who went to London to make his fortune and returned a corrupt soul, to the saints of the Roman Catholic Church, so many of whom tended sheep and roamed the hillsides. Let us not forget, also, that Jesus and his twelve friends were wanderers, and that Jesus's one attested moment of anger was directed at the merchants in the temple, city-dwellers to a man. Trollope's country characters are all more simple, good, and naturally virtuous than the cynical manipulators whose habitat is the greedy city, shown at their worst in his only bitter novel, *The Way We Live Now*, and personified by the arch-villain Melmotte.

For an instance of natural education, we can do no better than return to the Wild Boy of Aveyron (though there have been a few others snatched from the dark, notably Kaspar Hauser in 1828, who was so sweet of disposition that he picked his fleas off with great care to avoid crushing them, and set them free. He also vomited when offered meat and passed out after a glass of beer).[19] When the boy first came out of the forest, and for weeks afterwards, it was evident that he had no guile or cunning, no notion of advantage to self or victory over others. He was without doubt a perfect innocent, incapable of wishing harm to anyone. The scientist who studied his behaviour was astonished at his lack of nastiness, or even naughtiness, and to describe him best used the word *doux*, a complex amalgam of all the nicenesses of human character – gentle, soft, sweet, mild, good-natured, of harmless disposition. When he had first been spied, he instinctively ran away from humans, yet there were no reports that he had attacked children or raided farms. It was estimated that he had lived in the forest for up to six years, but he had not terrorised the neighbourhood. On the contrary, he had seemed fairly satisfied with his lot and had kept to himself without complaint. He had appeared reasonably well fed, subsisting on roots and plants, and perhaps small animals, but he had not known any shelter. Despite which, Roger Shattuck holds that 'from many material and moral points of view, he must be seen as better off and better behaved than, say, a child living in the lower depths of a big European city of that era. A really destitute and neglected slum child ... is no better nourished than the Wild Boy, may well carry disease, and is probably corrupted by vice, crime and squalor.'[20]

Even after years of life in civilisation, albeit as a curiosity to be studied, the Wild Boy never entirely lost his innocence, remained unconcerned with power or status, uninterested in self-advancement or sexual competition. His ego was forever unsullied by Freud's Id. In a moving passage, Shattuck describes the subtle drawbacks as well as the joys of such primal innocence. The boy was like a deaf mute, for he was utterly unaware of himself:

> A million tiny events in our bodies and nerves and minds keep telling us that we are alive and how we are doing. We can be deaf to them, particularly if our survival depends upon our not listening. That was the Wild Boy's initial condition, which continued for some time after he left the woods. He had existed without being alive – alive to the fact and the miracle of his own life . . . He couldn't hear himself; he couldn't hear himself living. And for three months Madame Guérin and Itard watched a thirteen-year-old boy come to life in front of their eyes.[21]

But coming to life meant learning fear and reproach and deceit, to the point where Itard felt guilt at the intrusion of science into the boy's untutored moral world, and he lamented the 'barren and inhuman curiosity of those men who first uprooted him from an innocent and happy life'.[22]

The innocent natural state necessarily involves ignorance of those subtle skeins of human intercourse which have to be learnt, practised and refined throughout life. The nomads would have had no time for psychology.

It is, incidentally, an intuition of this original unspoilt goodness that engendered one of the most disastrous social and political philosophies of recent times. Marxism has been called the triumph of optimism over experience. The sequence of its catechism seems to be this: since man's original nature is peaceable and good, it must have been corrupted by something, and that something can only be the artifices and inventions of human society. These in turn are represented by the ownership of property, non-existent in the natural nomadic state, which must

85

mean that some own while others are owned – hence the exploiters and the exploited. If only one were able to cancel the so-called progress of capital and revert to the happy condition of primeval innocence, moral goodness would once again be at the centre of the human condition.

Thus far, Marxist theory is a direct descendant of Rousseau's *Contrat Social*, which almost seems like a dress rehearsal for it. But Marxism carried in its breast the fatal element of compulsion, and if there is one matter upon which all moral philosophers are more or less in agreement, it is that goodness cannot be made compulsory, with an attendant baggage of fear and deterrence to promote it. Goodness manufactured on these terms leads inevitably to the Orwellian nightmare of values switching to reflect their opposite, where everything that is the most contrived, bloodless, passive and unnatural in human behaviour is held to be the Good. (Indeed, even Rousseau's plans contained a degree of coercion.)

R.D. Laing's warning that obedience must not be mistaken for goodness may perhaps here be anticipated. If his analysis of the Divided Self were to be applied to the social conditions of the late Union of Soviet Socialist Republics, we might have found, on one level, that the entire population was schizophrenic, presenting a false self to the world and concealing a real identity which was deemed dangerous and subversive. So, if Marxist socialism is the Romantic Fallacy put into practice, and its effect is collective madness, the flaw must reside not in the premiss that man is naturally good, but in its application – that he will turn to evil unless he is carefully watched and constantly prevented from digression. Which brings us back to another thread, that a certain amount of natural, beneficent aggression is important if men and women are to mature and become capable of real altruism. Marxist theory smothers this, and thereby renders goodness impossible.

It is difficult to think of any saints who flourished in the Soviet era. There were courageous intellectuals like Pasternak and Solzhenytsin, visionaries such as Gorbachev, but no shining stars of sacrifice. Annoyingly for the communist theologians, Mother Teresa, King Baudouin of the Belgians, St Francis of Assisi, Bob Geldof all emerged from capitalist societies, and, pertinently to our present subject, nearly all of them felt the urge to move, to travel, to bestir themselves into far-off places in order to bestow goodness (the exception being King Baudouin, obviously constrained by his regal status from going very far.)

Which returns us to our nomadic origins. If the original humans were not belligerent fighters bent upon murder, but pacific wanderers at ease with themselves and the earth which supported them, what could their lives have been like? It is at least possible that it resembled in most respects the lives of those remote tribes of hunter-gatherers who survive into modern times. It is reasonable to suppose they have more effective weapons than those that would have been available to the earliest men, yet studies show they do not rely upon the slaughter of big game for their nourishment. Most of their calories are found in plant food which is gathered and prepared by the women. Only in the Arctic, where little plant food is available, does big-game hunting become the dominant food-source, and human beings did not reach the Arctic until extremely recently, within the last few thousand years. The American zoologist Jared Diamond suggests that big-game hunting contributed only modestly to the food intake of early nomadic men until *after* they had evolved modern anatomy and behaviour. This would mean that the enlarged brain and social organisation of *homo sapiens* was not the result of our having become hunters but preceded that development. 'For most of our history we were not mighty hunters but skilled chimps, using stone tools to acquire and prepare plant food and small animals.' Whence, then, did the myth of our fierce past arise and why did it deceive anthropologists for so long? Because, says Diamond, men have ever boasted. He calls it the 'locker-room mentality' and proposes that it is so ingrained in our psyche that scientists who found large animal bones on the same site as the remains of human ancestors were tricked into thinking the animals were prey rather than predators.[23]

When one considers early man to be the prey object, ever on the move and alert to danger, defensive of his brood, a great deal of human behaviour becomes more explicable. Bruce Chatwin, inspired by Dr John Bowlby's seminal work on *Attachment and Loss*, pressed his imagination to apply Bowlby's insights retrospectively, and came to some intriguing conclusions. Noting that a mother can always distinguish between her baby's cries of alarm and those of mere hunger or cold; that the child is variously frightened of strangers, the dark, and rapidly approaching objects; and that it is preoccupied with monsters, Chatwin thought the explanation lay in the memory of the species. If there was always the threat of predators in the primeval home of man, and especially at night, when the big cats hunt and men have no ability to see in the dark, then no wonder the baby cries when left alone in his cot, as indeed I remember doing myself for hours at a stretch, terrified of abandonment. 'The child is yelling', says Chatwin, transposing the cot to the African thornscrub, 'because, unless the mother comes back in a couple of minutes, a hyena will have got it.'

Chatwin goes further, with an insight of revelatory power: 'Visitors to a baby ward in hospital are often surprised by the silence. Yet if the mother really *has* abandoned her child, its only chance of survival is to shut its mouth.'[24]

Let us follow Chatwin to the end. He points out that animals are superior to mankind in many obvious ways. The spider is a better weaver and mender, the bat has better radar, the swallow is a better architect. Although he does not say so, I think he implies that the recognition of these superiorities is an echo of that respect and humility which early man must have felt *vis-à-vis* his predator, and is therefore a precursor of value distinctions. I have never felt this more keenly than when watching a bullfight. The animal is so self-evidently stronger, sleeker, more confident than his opponent, who must resort to subterfuge in order to subdue it. The bull is weakened before it appears by having its eyeballs sprayed with an irritant and its testicles similarly tampered with. The colourful *banderillos* sever the animal's shoulder muscles so that it cannot hold up its head and is losing great quantities of blood. By the time the matador makes his glorious entrance, the bull is confused, disoriented, disabled, and would die anyway if left alone. But he has to be despatched by a 'noble' thrust between the shoulderblades down into the heart, blood gushing through its mouth as from a bucket. Seldom can Jared Diamond's 'locker-room mentality' have been more dramatically illustrated. The men *have* to make themselves look resplendent in gold costumes and theatrical gestures precisely because they *know* the bull is their superior in every natural way and they would not stand a chance of survival in those circumstances without ritualised cheating. You would not find a Spaniard to agree, but the boastful bullfight is ultimately an expression of humility.

Humility is essential for the nomad faced with a potential predator, and the Spaniard's remote ancestors would not have been so foolish as to pretend otherwise. The moral universe of the nomad encompassed respect for the earth and all it supported, towards animals, plants, rocks, as well as towards their fellow men, colleagues within their group and strangers without it. Positive values enhancing co-operation evolved naturally, and all those moral precepts which today exhort us towards co-operation and respect have their roots first in animal conduct, and, by extension, in the conduct of early nomadic root-eating man, an animal among animals.

Nomos, we have seen, was Greek for 'pasture', and the nomad a man of the earth. The elders among the nomads presided over the allocation and fair distribution of pasture, hence *nomos* came eventually to mean that which is allotted by custom – in other words law, which is the social application of morality. The Jewish prophets were themselves nomads, and the Saviour they foretold would be a herdsman. Remember the Wild Boy's finest pleasure? To stare out of the window at the landscape – the earth his mother, while drinking a glass of water – his mother's milk. Trapped in a house, he yearned to wander and touch the ground, the trees that had been the décor to his untroubled life.

Chatwin writes:

> Psychiatrists, politicians, tyrants are forever assuring us that the wandering life is an aberrant form of behaviour; a neurosis; a form of unfulfilled sexual longing; a sickness which, in the interests of civilization, must be suppressed. Nazi propagandists claimed that Gypsies and Jews – peoples with wandering in their genes – could find no place in a stable Reich. Yet, in the East, they still preserve the once universal concept: that wandering re-establishes the original harmony which once existed between man and the universe.[25]

From this harmony springs the natural disposition to do good, to be as humans were, to add to the order of the world. The just man is, as Socrates said, the one whose soul is harmoniously ordered, who has an integrated personality, whereas the unjust man's personality is disintegrated. Harmony betokens inevitably right, beneficent behaviour, and disharmony breeds disruption and chaos. If goodness is part of our nomadic genetic inheritance, it follows that something must have broken that harmony and caused the disintegration which leads to bad behaviour. We are talking, in fact, of what are now called 'personality disorders'.

4

OUT OF ORDER

It may appear ambitious to make the huge leap from a contemplation of early humans as pacific nomads to a discussion of those latter-day neuroses gathered under the generic umbrella of 'personality disorders', but in fact the link is clear and direct. We spoke in the last chapter of moral goodness deriving from harmony with the universe, and bad behaviour resulting from an interference with this harmony, or its disintegration. Psychiatrists who talk about personality disorders presuppose, by the very words they choose, that there is a natural 'order' from which the personality has been deflected, and they further take for granted that this 'order' is antecedent to the 'disorder' which has brought the patient to them. Each sufferer from personality disorder has been removed by his illness from that desirable state of harmony and integration which is his birthright. The psychiatrist's job is as far as possible to restore him to that state, to bring him (literally) back to earth, to rediscover the nomad or the animal in him.

People with personality disorders habitually create chaos around them, behave badly, cause unhappiness, commit crime. They cannot do good or make any positive contribution to general well-being until their disorder has been remedied, the possibility of moral beauty, what Cicero called 'the splendour of abstract moral worth',[1] being denied them. A close examination of the careers of those saints who, with modern knowledge, we can almost certainly say were sufferers from personality disorder, will reveal that they did no good at all. Joan of Arc was arguably a harmful neurotic leaving a pile of destruction in her wake, while Theresa of Lisieux merely twittered away her nonsense, self-absorbed and alien, without doing any real mischief except to herself.

The number of disorders which may afflict us in the modern world is very great, filling hundreds of pages in the *Diagnostic and Statistical Manual* used as the only work of reference in American courts of law. Some are so bizarre as to be scarcely credible, while others fall into several broad categories which we may more easily recognise, from manic depression to schizoid disorder, paranoid schizophrenia, and psychopathy. These conditions have in common a long period of gestation and a very low degree of detection, which makes it extremely difficult to spot sufferers in time. They may in every obvious respect lead perfectly normal lives, but such is their affliction that they are as far removed from human nature as it is possible to imagine.

The most common disorder is depression, and though it may seem unkind to depict depressives as inhuman, I mean only that they are divorced from that harmony which should be the lot of the fully integrated human being. Severe depression may declare itself in a marked listlessness, unwillingness to indulge in any activity, loss of appetite, disturbance of sleep, lack of sexual desire or responsiveness. Unfortunately, these symptoms are often mistaken for laziness, lack of character, or just a disposition to be bored, and nobody may know that secretly the depressive is convinced of his or her own worthlessness, and that they may blame themselves for all the ills and unpleasantnesses which have befallen their family and friends for years past. In the face of all evidence to the contrary, they are convinced that they are fundamentally unlovable, and will therefore conceal their feelings lest these should elicit a response to confirm this belief. Most of all, terrified that any display of aggression will reveal them for the loathsome creatures they think they are, they stifle all natural self-assertion which, as we saw in Chapter Two, is essential to the fully integrated personality. Thus, they slowly kill themselves by attrition, and many do finally commit suicide.

An unhappy description of this state of mind is afforded by D.J. West in a study published in 1965. Depressives may become 'so convinced of the utter hopelessness of their misery that death becomes a happy escape', he writes. 'Sometimes before committing suicide, they first kill their children or other members of the family. Under the delusion of a future without hope and the inevitability of catastrophe overtaking their nearest and dearest as well as themselves, they decide to kill in order to spare their loved ones suffering.'[2]

I knew a lady who was depressive, although, typically, one did not realise it at the time. Mercifully, she did no harm to her children, but her suicide was one of the biggest shocks of my life. To describe her now is not only to show love and respect for her memory, but to illustrate how this disorder can make a person who is good behave in a way which is bad.

Nicolette Harrison led a charmed and favoured life, marred only by some errors of judgement which were forgiven. Beautiful, elegant, a trifle grand, with long blonde hair cascading on to broad shoulders, she was one of the statuesque figures of London life in the 1960s, an asset in any gathering, with what then appeared to be a delightful touch of girlish shyness, but what must with hindsight be regarded as something more serious. She was barely seventeen when she married the 9th Marquess of Londonderry and became mistress of an ancestral palace, Wynyard Hall in County Durham, as well as the magnificent Londonderry House in Park Lane; this latter was sold not long after the wedding and destroyed to make way for a nondescript hotel where nobody wanted to stay.

As Marchioness, Nico was ravishing. She gave birth to two daughters, Sophia and Cosima, who are now respectively Lady Sophia Pilkington and Lady John Somerset, but after some infidelities she and Lord Londonderry were divorced. Nico's second husband was Clive Powell, better known as the jazz musician Georgie Fame, with whom she went to live in a small farmhouse on the borders of Somerset and Wiltshire. Mrs Powell had two sons, Tristan and James, who also grew into fine young men of whom she was justly proud.

Nico had more than one reason to be content. Not only was she securely and happily married, and doted on her two boys, but she also resumed an uncomplicated and cherished friendship with her first husband, who became a neighbour. She was a much appreciated hostess and cook. We thought she would slide neatly into middle age as a much-loved matriarch, especially when her daughter Sophia made her a grandmother for the first time. Then, one summer's day in 1993, having first given her car keys and identity papers to passers-by on the Clifton suspension bridge at Bristol, and evidently full of calm purpose, Nico hurled herself off the bridge into the oblivion she thought she deserved.

The last phrase above is, of course, speculative. Nobody knows what she was thinking as she jumped. But it is inconceivable that she would have done so had she been able to predict the pain and grief she would cause to her husband, children, and all who knew her. Nico must surely have come to the conclusion that all these people would be happier if she were out of the way, and it is precisely this kind of mirror-image of the truth, as strong and persuasive in every respect as the truth itself, which besets the depressive. Many were those who chastised themselves for not having noticed any unhappiness in her, but they were wrong in this for she was not unhappy. Depression is something different. It may creep up in the very shadow of happiness and poison it fatally.

Looking back, I now see the purport of her incredible and unexpected shyness. She spoke in such a whisper that one had to bend to hear her, and nearly always get her to repeat her words. Even then, Nico would not, could not raise her voice. She was afraid of giving offence, not because she might say something rude (which was hardly likely) but because she might say anything at all. She must have seen herself as so insignificant, so negligible, that she scarcely dared show that she was present. I also recall how nearly every sentence she uttered was a question, pushing the attention away from herself immediately. She was far too diffident to make a statement.

These are simple matters, which could not have been interpreted as dangerous without the interpreter looking a fool. But they were indicative of that disorder of the personality which can fracture one's grasp on reality. Depression distorts behaviour, diverting it from the natural path to the unnatural, unwholesome one built upon disharmony. It caused a good woman such as Nico to plan an act which caused pain to those who loved her.

Another form of depression, known as Münchausen's syndrome, appears at first glance to be quite unlike Nico Powell's secret, buried trouble, both because the sufferer seeks attention rather than avoiding it, and because he does no obvious harm to anyone. Baron Münchausen was a fantasist in the eighteenth century, an incorrigible but soberly convincing liar. Those unhappy people who bear his name today are typified by the hospital addict, who will go to great lengths to gain admission to hospital for totally spurious reasons, and do so repeatedly. Such people make up long case histories with a list of plausible ailments, simulate pain and discomfort, and are prepared to submit themselves to surgical archaeology which most of us would do anything to avoid. They are frequently also unco-operative, demanding that consultants should run back and forth in their service, undertake yet more investigative operations, and react to the negative results in a very hostile manner. After all this work, they often discharge themselves in a huff, but if their feigned symptoms are exposed, they become very angry.

There is the world of difference between this severe personality disorder and the behaviour of the mere confidence trickster, such as the man who in 1987 was admitted to twenty-three hospitals in a row on suspicion that he had a kidney stone. He carried a small stone with him and concealed it under his back each time he lay on the X-ray table. The man conceded in court that free hospital accommodation was preferable to cheap bed and breakfast when you have no money at all.

The genuine Münchausen is severely disturbed and incapable of that integration which is necessary to the benign person. A number of explanations of this bizarre conduct have been offered, and are usefully summarised by the distinguished forensic psychiatrist Dr Herschel Prins as follows (though I interpret in abbreviated form):

- a feeling of power, that one has managed to fool the doctors
- excitement derived from taking repeated risks with anaesthesia
- the receipt of affection from nurses
- being given drugs legally
- the provision of security and protection, albeit provisional[3]

To this comprehensive list I would add the one motive which I suspect dominates and encompasses them all, namely the feeling of being special, and moreover *knowing* that the feeling is undeserved. These people are ultimately and paradoxically worthless in their own eyes. Because they could never, they think, be valued for themselves, in their own right, on their own unadorned terms, they manufacture a more interesting specimen who is worthy of attention, and enjoy the pretence while it lasts. But they feel that their real self, of which they are well aware, is boring and unnoticeable. Their Münchausen deception is a variant on Nico's tentative whisper.

The case of the Dutch woman who went seventy-five times to hospital with the story that she had taken an overdose of tranquillisers, and subsequently had her stomach pumped, illustrates the point. There were no pills in her stomach, just a lot of rather good recently digested food. She had often gone straight to the hospital from a restaurant. She was not saying 'Give me the attention I deserve,' but rather, 'I am useless and serve no purpose. I merit no attention. I don't even deserve to eat.' She is asking the hospital to confirm her low self-esteem by negating the food which would have nourished her.

Even more disturbing is the willingness of mothers occasionally to submit their children to unnecessary surgical procedures, a phenomenon known as Münchausen's syndrome by proxy. It was first introduced by R. Meadow in *The Lancet* in 1977, under the heading 'The Hinterland of Child-abuse', and became known to the public at large with the arrest and trial of Beverly Allitt in 1993. Miss Allitt, a nurse, was accused of the murder and attempted murder of several babies in her care. Her lawyers put forward the Münchausen defence, that she made the children ill in order to be in a position to become their saviour, but the jury would have none of it and found her guilty of murder. Nonetheless, Miss Allitt is a prime exemplar of that distortion of human nature which, in wanting to do good, sows wickedness instead.

Necrophilia is, surprisingly perhaps, yet another form of depression, with a fair claim to be considered beneficial in intent. Here one must be careful in defining terms, for the popular concept of necrophilia is a narrow one, based upon too few instances of murder followed by sexual congress with the corpse. The most famous of these was John Christie, the diffident ex-policeman at 10 Rillington Place in Notting Hill Gate, in whose garden and behind whose wallpaper were found six female corpses in 1953. But necrophilia is far more various and complex than this, covering florid aberrations such as vampirism, necrophagy or cannibalism, as well as the simpler and weaker desire to be in the presence of death (a disorder common among people who seek jobs in morgues, and others frequently found by police sleeping in cemeteries).

Incidentally, necrophilia *per se* is not an offence in

law, because it is not deemed to exist. Jeffrey Dahmer's clear trouble in Milwaukee was the most dangerous form of necrophilia, in which he collected parts of people he had killed to be used as props in his private pornographic fantasies. But no mention could be made of this in court, because necrophilia is not catalogued in the heavy *Diagnostic and Statistical Manual* except in one definition as 'paraphilia not otherwise diagnosed'.

Dahmer is, however, a digression in the present context. That form of necrophilia which is a manifestation of clinical depression is best seen in Romeo's wild leap into Juliet's tomb to clasp the dead body to his breast, or King Herod's refusal to be parted from his dead wife, whom (if mythology be credited) he kept by his side for an unconscionable period of time. This is quite clearly a type of bereavement, a disinclination to be consoled, a desire to perpetuate a state of happiness which threatens to slip away because, alone, the mourner would be reduced to his own insubstantial personality and would not amount to much. Necrophilia, understood thus, is a kind of comfort.

A case quoted by Herschel Prins is perhaps helpful in this regard. It concerns Michael Telling, who murdered his second wife Monika in 1984 and was found guilty of manslaughter by reason of diminished responsibility. The fact of the killing itself is not disputed, nor is it particularly unusual as far as domestic homicides go. Monika had been taunting Michael about her sexual encounters outside the marriage, and under this provocation he shot her dead. It is what happened afterwards that makes the event peculiar. For a week or more, Michael moved Monika's corpse around the house, frequently talking to it, and even kissing it as it lay on the bed. Then he placed the body in a half-built sauna, where he presumably went on visiting it, and left it there for five months. Eventually, he decided to take it to Devon. Unable to dig the hard ground for burial there, he dumped the body in some bracken, first taking Monika's head off so that he could keep it by him. Police found it in the boot of his car.[4]

Prins is chiefly interested in the case for the light it throws upon legal definitions of insanity, but I think it is also an illuminating instance of unconquerable bereavement. Michael loved his wife and could not live without her. So he went on living with her. While the murder itself was an act of jealous rage, its aftermath was a signal of depression.

Like most depressives, Michael Telling dissembled. By holding on to his wife's body he was true to himself, no matter how disordered that self was, but in secret. To the insights of R.D. Laing we owe the notion, already referred to in the last chapter, of the divided self. Briefly put, Laing suggested that the personality disintegrates when it is forced to split into two halves, one a false self presented to the world and vetted in advance for its acceptability and likelihood to earn approval, the other an authentic experience not revealed to others and subjected to strict control. (Dr MacKeith, appearing for the defence in the Nilsen trial of 1983, posited a false self syndrome to explain his apparent normality.) It is when that authentic self is smothered in order to hide it from view, because its rejection would be too painful to bear, that the personality fragments. Nico Powell kept her true self concealed because she thought nobody would like what they saw.

Laing gives an example in the personality of 'Julie', who is excessively good, excessively compliant, no trouble to anyone. As a child she had been goodness itself, and Laing suggests that it would have been healthier for all concerned had she felt free to stand up for herself. 'It is a fallacy of momentous proportions to regard obedience as good and rebellion as bad,' he wrote, 'to insist on yielding and not assertion.' Even doctors collude in the fallacy, by defining her false self as sane and her real, buried self as mad. 'The real disease lies in the splitting of these values, so that the false self seems docile and dead and the true self wildly animated.'[5]

Laing is nowadays out of fashion. He has been chided as offering excuses for the indulgence of wild fantasy and for suggesting that the well adjusted have no monopoly on sanity. His reply is that he meant to point out only that the hidden self is as valid and as truly experienced as the false self, and that integration of the two is the key to renewal and cure. As we are presently engaged upon a quest as to the sources of bad behaviour in people innately disposed to do good, his insights remain apposite and in direct descent from Socrates' warning about harmony and integration. For if the false and true self are not properly integrated, equally accepted and openly embraced, then a deep and perhaps irremediable schizoid condition may result.

The schizoid person is severely disjointed, having divorced his apparent personality from his concealed one so successfully that the latter is able to realise subterranean ambitions which the former might well denigrate. Whereas the depressive is unwilling to reveal himself because he is convinced he is unworthy, the schizoid will avoid all real contact with other people because he thinks everyone is unworthy. He is incapable of trust, and feels threatened by friendship as well as by hostility. He therefore maintains his human relations on a superficial and seemingly efficient level, but all the time is seething with discontent and self-willed isolation. He needs affectionate attention and sympathy to restore his balance and re-establish his essential humanity, but will repel them as soon as they are tendered and retreat into aloof indifference. The trouble is, he is certain that he will be diminished by friendship, that he will lose something of himself and his control over his own fate, and this terrifies him. He is obliged to manufacture a feeling of superiority over others which is so successful that he comes to believe it himself (because it *works*), and the slightest criticism is a terrible worry in so far as it undermines this construction and threatens to reveal the vulnerability upon which it is based. Schizoids are therefore ruthless with critics and merciless towards perceived enemies, as well as being infuriatingly ungrateful.

Nearly all these personality disorders which subvert the natural state of equilibrium are invisible except to the accustomed eye, and so it is no surprise that, just as the depressive may appear happy, the schizoid often excites unsuspecting admiration. This is because he is often a high achiever and a famous person. The number of schizoid personalities whom we know as historical figures is, for this reason, above average, for disproportionate ambition is part of their disorder.

Napoleon and Hitler were manifestly schizoid and notoriously suspicious, and Hitler especially was never really known by anyone. Beethoven was sullen and morose, convinced of his superiority and alienated from every human with whom he came into contact. Field-Marshal Lord Montgomery was stupidly touchy and absurdly vainglorious. President Nixon of the United States of America was irredeemably mistrustful, and ultimately ruined by his obsessive hatred of dissent; he saw in every pair of eyes an enemy who could unmask him and provoke the world's mockery. Margaret Thatcher, British Prime Minister from 1979 to 1990, could not tolerate criticism of any sort, was famously ungrateful, and wont to see herself as some kind of mythic heroine. General de Gaulle, isolated soldier during the period of France's disgrace and then President after her resurgence, was perhaps the most startling example of a schizoid character in an historical role. I do not think it is seriously doubted that Charles de Gaulle actually believed he was the personification of France, the embodiment of *la gloire*, the reincarnation of Joan of Arc, and yet nobody has suggested he was mad. He must have been close to it at times.

When a schizoid personality achieves a position of supreme political power he is capable of great mischief, for the country whose fate he controls is but a pawn in his real endeavour, which is the publication of his strained and stretched personality and its desperate need to overcome all obstacles rather than risk exposure as vulnerable and dislocated. One has only to remember the perceived 'character' of France in de Gaulle's time, of Britain under Thatcher, or the United States during Nixon's office, to recognise the great harm that may be done by these damaged people. They thought to earn respect for their countries by the vigorous display of ambition and, in the long term, earned only the pity reserved for a boastful child.

It is not only in politics that schizoid people may rise high. In literature, too, there are manifold examples. Marie Corelli was the best-selling novelist at the end of the nineteenth century, a woman whose books went into over eighty editions, whose opinions were sought and valued, whose house in Stratford-upon-Avon attracted more visitors than Shakespeare's birthplace. But her whole being was a confection (she was really Minnie Mackay, illegitimate daughter of the Scottish poet Charles Mackay who wrote *On the Madness of Crowds*), she thought she was the greatest name in literature for centuries, she made enemies of everyone she met, misinterpreting gifts and suspecting slights, and died a derisory figure. Almost her contemporary was Frederick William Rolfe, who wrote under the pseudonym Baron Corvo (*Hadrian the Seventh, The Desire and Pursuit of the Whole*), a man of staggering ingratitude. The number of those who tried to help him and who received in return the most ignoble contempt matches more or less exactly the number of people whom he knew.

By the very nature of their disorder, schizoid personalities may become famous, but there are many who do not, and who wreak havoc in an ordinary home by their utter inability to trust. They may be called 'delinquents', or be thought simply to be in the throes of adolescent rebellion, but when a schizoid condition underlies their emotional remoteness and suspicion, they are ungraspable and no longer susceptible to encouragement or exhortation. They have slipped away. Their ambition to be superior is as strong as it is in the famous, but because it is thwarted by the ordinariness of their lives, they can become destructive, even dangerous. Such a one was my foster son of two years, Gary, who interpreted all advice as insult and every gift as demeaning. But I fancy his disorder was more profound even than the schizoid.

One step further takes us to the paranoid schizophrenic, whose mistrust is so deep that he is convinced the world is in conspiracy against him. Projecting onto others feelings and intentions they do not have, and which originate only in his imagination, he sees his ordained importance as under perpetual attack from malign persecutors all around, and will lash out with hideous effect to protect himself from the hidden enemy. Paranoid schizophrenics usually end up in mental hospitals or prison rather than the White House, though it may well be that President Nixon was close to this level when he was most besieged. Stalin, more certainly, was well advanced into delusional paranoia, with devastating results for his political colleagues as well as his foes. His is a chilling instance of paranoid schizophrenia allied to unbridled power.

Another was Peter Sutcliffe, commonly known as the Yorkshire Ripper, who murdered and mutilated several women in the North of England during the 1970s. Psychiatrists at his trial attested to his paranoid schizophrenia, based upon his delusional belief that he was undertaking the work of God in clearing the streets of prostitutes (though not all his victims were such), sometimes in direct response to divine instructions. There did not appear to be evidence, however, that he felt threatened or persecuted by them, which made the diagnosis odd. The jury presumably thought so too, for they sent him to prison; it was some years after his conviction that doctors recognised his disturbance and transferred him to Broadmoor Psychiatric Hospital, where he still resides. The ferocity with which Sutcliffe eviscerated and disfigured the wretched women who crossed his path ought to have indicated to the jury that some pathological hatred was at work, but they were otherwise impressed by his ability to stay in employment, run a house, have a wife (who suspected nothing), and plan his attacks methodically. This disparity between the apparent sanity of the procedure leading towards a completely insane act is one which is often confusing, and will need to be examined when we come to determine what is legal 'sanity'.

For the purpose of the present discussion, as to how disorders of the personality may stray people from that natural harmony which is their species' inheritance, it is enough to note that the paranoid condition is one of the most distressing and disruptive one may encounter. Nor does it have to be as grotesque as Stalin's or Sutcliffe's. There is a level of paranoid schizophrenia which is episodic, may erupt for a few months and disappear, and which may be recognised by more than half the readers of this book. It is that temporary derangement which occurs when sexual jealousy is aroused, a force so potent that it cannot be dispersed even when the cause of the jealousy is proven to be delusional. If ever one wanted to demonstrate the distance one may travel from harmony, the route of the jealous lover is probably the most dramatic.

Poets have grappled with this theme so exhaustively that we have reason to suppose it the most common personality disorder of all, despite its being not recognised as such by any court of law save the French, whose famous *crime passionnel* defence tends to be dismissed in Anglo-Saxon jurisprudence. Yet anyone who has experienced it, or watched its effects upon others, can scarcely doubt that it involves a distortion of the personality so severe as to upset normal equilibrium and cause behaviour which is often entirely out of character. Shakespeare dealt with it in *Othello*, wherein a man of noble spirit and decent instincts becomes a suspicious, vindictive wretch who finally murders his wife Desdemona, though she is entirely innocent of any treachery and his love for her has not weakened in any way. To my mind, even more pathetic is the cruel change in personality which befalls

Leontes in *The Winter's Tale*. At the beginning of the play he is secure and happy, at peace with the world and a properly organised individual, whose calm and trusting love for his wife makes him bestow benignity all around. When jealousy intervenes, entirely without reasonable cause, he rapidly disintegrates into a pitifully scattered man who unsettles friends and admirers, brings terrible pain to his bewildered wife and, in Richard Pasco's searing performance at Stratford in 1977, ruined himself by degrees before our eyes.

Racine's *Phèdre*, too, displayed the destruction of a woman at the mercy of an incestuous passion which intellectually she loathed but emotionally could not resist. And the entire plot of Trollope's *He Knew He Was Right* revolves around Louis Trevelyan's irrational and destructive obsession with his wife's supposed flirtations, pursued

> with the hope of the insane man, who loves to feed his grievance, even though the grief should be his death. They who do not understand that a man may be brought to hope that which of all things is the most grievous to him, have not observed with sufficient closeness the perversity of the human mind. Trevelyan would have given all that he had to save his wife; would, even now, have cut his tongue out before he would have expressed to anyone . . . a suspicion that she should in truth have been guilty; was continually telling himself that further life would be impossible to him if he, and she, and that child of theirs, should be thus disgraced – and yet he expected it, believed it, and, after a fashion, he almost hoped it.[6]

Clinical psychiatrists from Mairet (1908) and Jaspers (1910) onwards have long recognised the syndrome as morbidly delusional, and several case studies have related the most bizarre extremes to which the jealous man may resort in order to substantiate his suspicions, including the surreptitious examination of the spouse's underwear for signs of seminal staining.[7] I have myself observed a similar situation evolve in my own family, with results that would be risible were they not so tragic.

My parents married in 1938 and were blessed (if I dare say so) with two sons, myself in 1939 and my brother Colin in 1945. Their lives continued placidly enough for the next thirty years, unbesmirched by scandal or suspicion, first in a prefab in Camberwell, near the Old Kent Road, and from 1957 in a council house on the edge of Barry, South Wales. My mother's health had always been bad, and she rarely went out or met anyone. In addition to which, her congenital deafness precluded social gathering, for she avoided talk lest she might give offence by guessing wrongly what somebody might be saying to her. I mention this only to make it clear that she was the very antithesis of a flirt, even in the mildest sense.

My father decided one day that his wife was conducting an affair with the milkman, who delivered daily but whom she saw only when he collected payment once a month. She was by now over sixty, hunch-backed, grey, solitary in her silent world, and hardly a woman to excite desire. She was also extremely loyal by nature, unwilling to do or say anything which might cause distress. But the idea that my father had generated all by himself could not be shifted, and for almost a year his jealousy made every day miserable to her. When he woke up, he would watch carefully to see if she was asleep. From his work in Cardiff, he would telephone her every ten minutes throughout the day, asking her where she was, in which room, next to which piece of furniture, what she was doing. He demanded that she should not sit in any chair which might be observed through the window, that she should not look out of the window at any time, later that she should draw the curtains all day long. He would do the shopping for her; she was not to budge. When he came home, he would question her closely to see if she might trip herself up by giving an account of the day at variance with what she had said on the telephone, and follow her from room to room, even if she went to the kitchen to make a cup of tea. He steamed open the electricity bill lest it might contain a *billet doux*. I saw this on my visits home and remonstrated with him, as did my brother, but to no avail. It need hardly be said that my mother's days were uniformly dull and predictable. That they should also become a torment for no reason at all was ghastly to behold. Had she been younger or more resilient (or indeed wealthier) I should not have been surprised if she had walked out. As it was, the experience told dreadfully upon her health, until eventually my father 'came to his senses' (as it is aptly put), gradually resuming his equilibrium and allowing peace once more to enter the claustrophobic household.

I have no doubt now that he was in the grip of a severe personality disorder which could have been clinically diagnosed. Should anyone wonder why Colin and I did not propose the intervention of a psychiatrist, I have only to refer readers who may remember it to a television series called *Till Death Us Do Part*, and promise that Warren Mitchell and (to a lesser extent) Dandy Nichols portrayed characters who were virtual copies of my parents; they will then immediately understand the kind of reception which would have greeted such a proposal.

Explanations given for this disorder vary. Some suggest that the man so afflicted has a guilty past which makes him fear his wife will avenge herself by behaving in like fashion (and there is some evidence my father may have been a philanderer in the early years of his marriage). Others say that actual or feared impotence which comes to some men in late middle-age is the source of a disastrous transference of failure onto the unwitting spouse. Whatever the cause, its effect is transparently a change in character, reflected in behaviour which does immense harm, though the perpetrator may be a person who wants only to do good. My father was certainly not a wicked or unkind man, and once the madness had passed he reverted to the gruff but solicitous husband with whom my mother had always felt at ease.

Beyond paranoia is the most dangerous disorder of all, that exemplified by the so-called psychopath. I say 'so-called' because the term has been emasculated in recent years by over-use and has come to refer to anyone whose behaviour is not only brutal and disgusting in the extreme, but incomprehensible. It has even descended to a mere term of abuse applied to persons whose conduct excites strong reprimand by reason of its savagery. But it has a proper history and its meaning used at one time to be more specific. Moreover, the definition of psychopathic behaviour has a great deal to do with our understanding of moral value, for the psychopath challenges such value fundamentally.

As long ago as 1835, J.C. Pritchard advanced the concept of 'moral insanity', which he described as a madness 'consisting of a morbid perversion of the natural feelings, affections, inclinations, temper, habits, moral dispositions and natural impulses, without any remarkable disorder or defect of the interest or knowing and reasoning faculties'.[8] Note how Pritchard assumes 'natural feelings' which have been 'perverted' by this disorder, in other words a moral compass that has been knocked awry. He is suggesting that the human starts from a position of primal innocence and disposition to do good, which position is undermined and traduced by moral distemper. In many ways, it is a pity the moral dimension in this definition has been gradually wiped away by legislators who have tended to think it offered too easy an excuse.

It was not forgotten by Henderson, who first coined the term 'psychopath', at the same time pointing out that it was an illness and not simply a punishable delight in crime.[9] Successive parliaments have disagreed, and the Mental Health Act of 1983 sticks to the definition 'persistent disorder or disability of mind', having removed all reference to morality. This is tantamount to instructing greengrocers not to sell tomatoes in future, as they are no longer to be defined as either fruit or vegetable. The whole point of psychopathic behaviour is that it is to do with the stifling of the moral sense. A man is a psychopath because he is a moral being who does apparently immoral things, not because he is a malfunctioning brain.

The psychopath, like the depressive, the schizoid and the paranoid schizophrenic, is notoriously hard to detect, and there is a sense in which nobody is psychopathic until he has committed a psychopathic act. His life is utterly normal, rational, organised and even satisfactory, in every respect save that of emotional recognition of the consequences of his acts. Where emotional understanding normally resides, there is an unnerving hole. He is completely ruthless in his determination to have what he wants, no matter what harm may ensue to others in so doing, because he does not understand how other people can be hurt. They are not people to him so much as props in his personal stage set, there to serve his momentary advantage and be discarded with indifference, as one might swat a fly. Because his emotional connections have been snipped off, gratification for him is extreme and unbounded by frontiers of acceptable behaviour, and so his acts are characterised by an unreflective self-interest and brutality. Murder, disembowelment, dismemberment hold no terrors for him, and since his moral understanding is nil *in so far as his own acts of murder are concerned*, he will feel no remorse whatever. (His moral understanding with regard to matters which do not issue from his psychopathic disorder may be perfectly attuned, and he may collect funds for an orphanage, protest against social deprivation, or be the most popular Father Christmas in his community, as three convicted multiple murderers have so been.[10])

The person with psychopathic disorder, being emotionally arid, is at his most dangerous when he feels threatened by demonstration of emotion, which he can only interpret as something alien and incomprehensible. Thus, the saddest aspect of this condition is that its victims are often those who attempt to help the one afflicted. This was the case with a young British murderer in the 1950s, Patrick Byrne, who had killed old ladies in their homes but had not yet been apprehended; his local priest, whom he had known since adolescence, intuited that the young man was deeply troubled and sought to show him some affection in the hope of gaining his confidence. The priest was butchered in his bathtub, and Byrne seemed bewildered by what he had done, mystified and perplexed. He has now been in mental institutions for twenty years.[11]

The psychopath is frequently (but not always) socially isolated, timid, withdrawn, secretive, and liable to sudden explosions of wrath. This is true of the addictive repetitive murderer, whose attacks are episodic, and of the mass-murderer, who kills several people all on the same occasion and usually then kills himself. There have been several such cases in the United States (Austin, Texas, in 1966, San Diego, California, in 1983), and one notable instance in England. Michael Ryan walked out of the house he shared with his mother in Hungerford on 20 August, 1987, and shot sixteen people at random. He had no previous history of violence. He simply ran amok (or amuk – the word is Malayan), suddenly undergoing a complete change of character, or so it appeared – the murderous impulses must have lain dormant and unsuspected for years. It is typical of amok behaviour that it seems possessed and is often followed by a comatose state. Eye-witnesses of Ryan's demeanour that day confirm his apparent transformation. A friend of twenty years said that he did not recognise him, that he seemed 'brain-dead' with 'a terrible vacant look in his eyes and a funny sort of grin on his face'.[12]

It is important to remember that all these instances suggest a previous uncontaminated self which has been changed and diverted from the ordinary path, taken down a poisonous route away from true nature. The boys who slaughtered James Bulger and left his little body on a railway line may possibly have been the youngest specimens we have of incipient psychopathic disorder, which is by no means incompatible with their having been bereft of a true intellectual understanding of what they had done. Psychopathic explosion does not usually occur, after some years of unsuspected preparation, until early manhood. If Robert Thompson and Jon Venables were indifferent to the pain they caused, then circumstances appear to have advanced the expression of their disorder by some years. I think this may be the case with Thompson, but Venables, who asked the police to tell James's mother he was sorry, appeared to have his moral vision intact. It is difficult in this distressing case to foster any tolerance for the perpetrators of a fearful act, yet, if the effort is made, it becomes possible to see that even a psychopath, for whom no sympathy is felt, was once but a harmless promising child, and that severe aberrant behaviour is precisely that – a wandering away from the norm. Robert Thompson's smashing of James Bulger may represent a very rare example of the diversion from that path of ordinary morality caught at its inception, in which case there is still time to save him.

Save him from what, exactly? For some, the answer is obvious. Noting the episodic occurrence of personality disorder, its eruption in spasms afterwards subsiding into normality and peace, and the titanic psychic struggle which often precedes it, priests and sages have little hesitation in identifying a classic instance of diabolic possession. The very language used assists them, for *dis*order and *im*balance are negatives without an agent; the psychiatrists and doctors do not tell us what caused the diversion from order and balance. The priests do, and they have a name for it: the agent of disorder is the Devil. It is the Devil who possessed Venables and Thompson for two and a half hours that February day of 1993, and it is from the Devil that they must be protected in the future.

5

TICS AND DEMONS

It is easy to be deceived into thinking that modern psychological methods have rendered obsolete all ancient religious concepts regarding diabolic possession. We are assumed to have matured in understanding and liberated ourselves from the clutter of superstition. Thus we are apt to scoff when we read of exorcists operating in the twentieth century, and to sigh at remarks such as that attributed to Reverend Trevor Dearing, vicar of St Paul's, Hainault, who has declared on record that 'I believe it is possible for the human mind to be invaded and taken over by evil forces in the same way as the body can be taken over by germs.'[1] The statement is not, however, as outrageous as it might appear, nor is it automatically incompatible with a more sophisticated approach. The eminent moral philosopher J.L. Mackie said much the same thing when he wrote that 'irresistible impulses are ones which arise outside the central personality and are seen by it as alien, but which are strong enough to get their way not through the parliamentary procedure of deliberation but in defiance of it'.[2]

Penetrate the slightly dense language, and one may see that the philosopher allows for an agency outside an individual's personality which *has a will of its own* and can impose that will on the impotent individual *who may try to resist but cannot*. What else can that mean but that there is a malign force at work which may poison a man and deflect him, against his will, from doing the good which he would normally intend? What separates the exorcist from the philosopher is a choice of words, and while the latter identifies only a neat abstraction, the former knows the enemy with whom he has to deal by name. Both admit the occurrence of possession and imply a connection between mental disorder and the supernatural.

For the ordinary citizen there has never been any doubt. Even those who profess to be free of superstition may unconsciously invoke or chastise the Devil with such unguarded remarks as 'I don't know what came over me', or 'got into me', or indeed 'possessed me', when trying to explain a temporary lapse in good behaviour or descent into anger and vindictiveness which are quite out of character. Even more revealing is the expression 'to take it out on somebody', which presupposes an 'it' which has invaded the mind and must somehow be got rid of. How? By allowing it to vent its fury upon someone else, thereby cleansing oneself and transferring the influence elsewhere. Psychiatrists will agree that allowing 'it' to fester inside will eventually destroy one's mental equilibrium. All these common speech habits are evidence of a long-standing acquaintance with the Devil and his tricks, whether he is reduced to an 'it' or is more bluntly identified.

There have been many other names for this source or 'irresistible impulse', from Lucifer to Beelzebub to Satan and Old Nick. The paradox is that, though we might seek to weaken its influence or even paralyse it by refusing to name it, as is commonly the case today, our recognition and fear of it remain intact. As Baudelaire wrote, 'everybody feels the devil is there but nobody believes in him – how wonderfully subtle he is!'[3] Or later, 'la plus belle des ruses du diable est de nous persuader qu'il n'existe pas'.[4] Modern scepticism is the Devil's ally; the more certain we are that such an old-fashioned and absurd superstition has no place in an enlightened world, the more efficiently are diabolic influences able to penetrate our slack defences. Though we rarely say so, we all know this in our bones, and the notion of a malignant devil threatening to knock us awry, push us out of order into disorder, is practically

113

impossible to root out. 'It's the Devil who holds the strings which make us jump.'[5]

One might have thought that such ideas could only survive in times of deep ignorance, and that medical knowledge would have swept them aside. What seems to have happened is that medicine has not so much swept these ideas aside as swept them under, banishing them to a subterranean, furtive life in a concealed limbo. When acquaintance with the Devil was taken for granted, in the Middle Ages, the recognition of his presence led to barbaric cruelties which we would now consider matters for criminal investigation. It was a Christian's duty to cast out the Devil wherever he saw him, and since he might be manifested in an epileptic fit, in dissident opinion, in sexual ardour or aberration, even in the enthusiasm of one's religious faith, the number of murders committed in the name of Devil-hatred has stained the history of humankind from the Crusades to the Spanish Inquisition and beyond. Senator McCarthy in the United States carried his mediaeval certainty into the 1950s, and would not have hesitated to torture and execute his devils ('communist sympathisers') by the thousand had the law so permitted him.

There are obviously some ailments, such as epilepsy, which are now cleared of diabolic content, and some of Jesus's miracles may well have been performed on people who appeared to be possessed but were in fact having a fit (if there is a difference; those of us who have suffered one do not mock the comparison). Also, some manifestations of diabolic possession in nuns, involving masturbation, thrusting the pelvis in a lewd manner, uttering obscenities and displaying the genitals, would today be recognised as the explosive release of quite natural sexual energies, long frustrated by an abnormal mode of life. The Quakers were always rather advanced and tolerant in their views on how to deal with the Devil. Rather than slaughter the unfortunate person whose body and mind were harbouring him, they thought a period of peace and quiet with nothing but the Bible to read would nurse the afflicted back to spiritual health and drive out the diabolic presence. Consequently they shut people away, quite decently, to reform, and their places of incarceration were called reformatories. Jeffrey Dahmer was sentenced to serve over nine centuries of prison term in the Columbia Correctional Institution, where his diabolic propensities would be *corrected*. There are many in Wisconsin who rejoiced that he was instead eliminated by a fellow prisoner's attack in 1994.

If one is to believe those examples of true diabolic possession for which there is documented evidence (and some psychiatrists do believe them, distinguishing such events from false possession, which is self-delusion), then one may well understand why. Symptoms may include levitation, speaking in an unknown language (*glossolalia*), speaking in an existing language of which the afflicted person is entirely ignorant (*xenolalia*), exuding an unbearable stench of putrefaction, spontaneous bleeding with no physical cause before or scar afterwards, a sudden access of superhuman strength, roaring like an animal, and, most incredible of all, the ability to swivel the head round a full 180 degrees. William Peter Blatty's novel *The Exorcist*, published in 1974 and since made into an internationally notorious film, was based on an actual case recorded in Washington state which involved a fourteen-year-old boy who cursed loudly in dead languages and displayed huge scratches on his body despite having been firmly strapped to his bed.

In their recent book Brian McConnell and William Tatum list several other examples which are even more distinctive and bizarre. Theobold and Josef Bruner, brothers aged ten and eight respectively, in 1865 in Alsace displayed terrible signs of disorder. 'At times their bodies became bloated as if about to burst,' recalled a contemporary. 'When this would happen, the boy would vomit, whereby yellow foam, feathers and seaweed would come out of his mouth . . . these feathers filled the air with such a stench that they had to be

115

burned.' In 1906, Germana Cele, a sixteen-year-old South African, was given to floating five feet above the ground, either vertically or horizontally, her clothing as rigid and unnatural as her body. The combined strength of witnesses could not pull her down. She slithered over the earth like a serpent, howled in such decibels as to drive away people protecting their eardrums, and vomited and defecated in astonishing volume after having consumed barely a spoonful of milk in twenty-four hours.

A similar event occurred in Iowa, USA, in 1928, involving the exorcism of a young woman over a period of twenty-three consecutive days. Apart from the usual howlings, levitations, prodigious vomitings and smells, the woman's head sometimes swelled to the size of an inverted water pitcher, and her lips to the size of hands. She was possessed by four different devils, who contrived to speak, very loudly, without her ever moving her lips or opening her eyes; the voices issued from somewhere deep inside her. Though there are many witnesses to these events, the account of them makes some demands upon credulity when we read that the Devil interfered with the pastor's car to make him late for the first bout of exorcism, and that he could refer to the vehicle as 'that dandy car' and to the pastor himself as 'you dumbbell'.[6]

The more recent case of Annaliese Michel in Germany is especially upsetting for the implications of religious mania which it suggests. Annaliese was a peculiarly devout Roman Catholic. As an adolescent, she lived only for God and the saints, resembling in her simple exclusivity the more happy example of St Theresa of Lisieux. She was diagnosed an epileptic, which her parents refused to accept. In 1975, Annaliese underwent a series of seventy-two exorcisms, with appalling consequences. Not only did she writhe and foam in the expected manner, but she uttered disgusting obscenities in a high tenor or deep male bass, describing sexual adventures of peculiar inventiveness. She would speak in Latin, which she had never learned, or an archaic

German known only to linguistic historians, all recorded on tape. In April 1976, she began to refuse food, and died a few months later, aged twenty-three but with a body which weighed little over four stone and could have been carried in a shopping bag. Her head, at the end, was no more than a fleshless skull covered with darkened skin.

To the lawyers it was clear that Annaliese had been starved to death by her parents, who insisted in stating that the Devil had possessed her. To the doctors it was equally clear that she had suffered from a paranoiac hallucinatory psychosis in which the demons were self-generated – an expression of spiritual malaise. As for the bass voice, it was a 'psychohysterical transposed voice' adopted for the purpose, but there seemed to be no medical explanation for Annaliese's familiarity with languages she had never heard spoken. The doctors were probably right, in so far as medical knowledge can interpret the supernatural, but Annaliese herself, in moments of clarity and peace, begged to be released from the devils that tormented her. Perhaps she was right, too.[7]

If these extreme instances are thankfully rare, there is no rarity at all in the idea that every person is potentially stalked by an *alter ego* of malicious intent, a personal devil who may claim ascendancy at any moment and against whose influence one must be constantly vigilant. We have already looked at literary examples (Frankenstein, Jekyll and Hyde, Steppenwolf), and suggested that the most illuminating is Wringhim in James Hogg's *Confessions of a Justified Sinner*, stalked by a stranger who causes him to act malevolently whether he wants to or not, and who turns out to be an alternative, unsuspected expression of himself. This is Jung's shadow, and it is essential to Jung's concept that the shadow is not an episodic companion but part of the wholeness that makes the individual; the man with no shadow does not exist, and both the substance and its reflection are real and constant. Only, the shadow may not always be noticed.

'I am split mentally and horribly afraid of it,' says Versilov in Dostoievsky's *A Raw Youth*. 'It is as if you have your own double standing next to you.'

When we turn to the remarks made by convicted multiple murderers in recent years, we find corroboration which is astonishingly uniform. 'One thing I know for sure,' said Jeffrey Dahmer after his arrest, 'it was a definite compulsion because I couldn't quit. I tried, but ... I couldn't quit.' When he came to wonder what it was that caused him to change character so disastrously on seventeen separate occasions, he said, 'The Bible calls him Satan. I suppose it's possible because it sure seems like some of the thoughts aren't my own. They just come blasting into my head.' He felt at those moments that his actions were being *guided* towards malignancy. 'These thoughts are very powerful, very destructive, and they do not leave. They're not the kind of thoughts you can just shake your head and they're gone. They do not leave.'[8]

On the other hand, they are episodic, not continuous. Under the influence of the 'stranger' the personality disintegrates totally, but it is generally re-integrated quite quickly, enabling the murderer to resume normal innocuous living. Dahmer had a job, looked after his grandmother, donated to charity. Dennis Nilsen stood in picket lines, and organised an office Christmas party which his colleagues so enjoyed they all signed a card of gratitude to him. They could not know that the cooking pot he used at the party would later serve to boil human heads.

When Ted Bundy was convicted of a series of brutal murders of young women, he told the court, 'I cannot accept the sentence, because it is not a sentence to me ... it is a sentence to someone else who is not standing here today.'[9] There could hardly be a more graphic description of possession than this, for Bundy was not suggesting that the police should have arrested somebody else, only that the distorted personality responsible for the crimes felt as alien to him, in his integrated state, as it did to the rest of those present. He had a name for the murderer who possessed him – 'the Hunchback' – and when he felt the Hunchback was about to take control, that the urgings were about to begin, he would make great efforts to stay off the streets where he might see a young woman who could innocently trigger the explosion. He knew that 'what was inside him was not a figment of his imagination, it was real'.[10] It is for this reason that Bundy always discussed the murders, whether with journalists or lawyers, in the third person. Sceptics interpreted this as a ruse, a mark of cowardice in the face of his guilt. But for Bundy it was perfectly natural that the killer should be designated by the third person. He was not a stupid man; a personable and persuasive young lawyer, he conducted his own defence in a professional manner. For him to have used the pronoun 'I' when making reference to the murders would have been more than legally embarrassing – it would have been philosophically inaccurate. Bundy would have been, in a certain sense, telling a lie.

William Heirens likewise had a name for his devil. He called it George, and felt it was really George who was responsible when he went berserk in the course of a burglary and murdered Frances Brown. Hence the message scrawled in lipstick on the wall: 'For God's sake catch me, I can't stop myself.' These words are almost echoed by Bobby Joe Long, the Texas murderer – 'I wanted to be stopped because I couldn't stop myself.' Long claimed to be horrified at what was done by his hands. 'It was like there was a dream of me doing what I really wanted to do even though I knew I shouldn't be doing it . . . I couldn't believe what I'd done the next morning. I was sick. I threw up.' His mother recalled the moment when she recognised a devilish transformation sweep into him, and said that 'at the time she was so frozen with fear at the change in her son's personality that she thought he had been possessed'.[11]

Across the world in Russia identical sentiments are expressed in similar language. Andrei Chikatilo, executed for a series of apparently motiveless murders over a period of seven years, was anguished that his 'real' self was not paid attention by the courts. 'I gave myself to my work, my studies, my children, my grandchildren,' he said, 'but when I found myself in a different setting I became a different person, uncontrollable, as if some evil force controlled me against my will and I could not resist.'

David Berkowitz, the so-called Son of Sam who terrorised New York in the 1970s, saw himself as the conduit through which the Devil ('Sam') worked – 'Sam used me as a sort of tool.' In his taunting letter to Captain Joseph Borelli, who had desperately consulted forty-five psychiatrists in an attempt to build a picture of the totally unpredictable man he was hunting, Berkowitz wrote, 'I feel like an outsider. I am on a different wavelength then [*sic*] everybody else – programmed too [*sic*] kill.' Once he was caught, he averred that this alienation had been with him for as long as he could remember. 'There is no doubt in my mind that a demon has been living in me and in my mind since I was born,' he said. 'When I was a child I had to sleep with the light on, or I had to sleep with my parents because the demon gave me severe nightmares. [The second syllable of 'nightmare', incidentally, derives from a word meaning 'spirit', 'demon' or 'elf', as does the second syllable of the equivalent French *cauchemar*.] I feel this is not me. It is someone inside me. I'm certain of that . . . This belief of an alien presence is not an escape of responsibility because I am looking forward to a jail cell as opposed to having an apartment filled with demons . . . this is what happens to people who are possessed. They want their souls back. I want my soul back. I want what was taken from me. I have a right to be human.'[12]

Time and again one comes across accounts of the most brutal and vicious murderers described in the gentlest of terms by those who never had occasion to observe them in their possessed state. Edward Paisnel was known as Uncle Ted by dozens of children on the island of Jersey, and was a popular Santa Claus. In 1971 it was revealed that he had also been responsible for a series of previously unsolved killings. Ed Gein in Wisconsin, whose use of the skin and nipples of his victims was particularly abhorrent, had been known as a reliable babysitter. One of the men who just escaped finding himself with Dennis Nilsen during one of his murderous moods called him a 'saint', and another, who survived only because the devilish power evaporated before the murder could be completed, added that Nilsen had been a considerate companion during the preceding two hours. 'The most cruel and destructive behaviour', wrote Dr Hyatt Williams, 'can be perpetrated by a person at one time, while almost immediately before or after such conduct he can be kind and compassionate.'[13]

Perhaps the most vivid evidence as to the essential invisibility of diabolic presence, when it is dormant in an otherwise benign individual, is offered by Sonia Sutcliffe, wife of the so-called Yorkshire Ripper, Peter Sutcliffe, who was found guilty on thirteen charges of murder in 1981 and sentenced to serve at least thirty years. For several years the industrial north of England had been virtually paralysed with fear as the horribly mutilated bodies of young women were found in ditches and behind bushes. Mrs Sutcliffe was just as apprehensive as everyone else, for the Yorkshire Ripper's terrible career was the subject of daily conversation. But she felt safe, because she had a very decent and devoted husband to protect her.

For years after the trial, Sonia Sutcliffe refused to reveal what it 'felt like' to have been the Ripper's wife, despite fortunes offered her by the cheap press. When she broke her silence in the *Mail on Sunday* in 1987 with an article by Barbara Jones, it was said that the interview had been gained by deception practised over a long period and that the journalist had cunningly betrayed a friendship. It is, probably for that reason, authentic.

> Take the night my mother came with us to view what was to be our new house. I remember it well – Saturday, 25 June 1977. We couldn't have been happier. I was just about to qualify as a teacher and we'd been saving for

three years for our own house. And there it was, the perfect home in Garden Lane, Heaton, the best part of Bradford. We loved the Victorian features and the neat little garden. It appealed to the artistic senses of both of us. Later that night I went off to the hospital where I worked as a nursing auxiliary. Peter dropped me there and told me he was going for a drink with friends. Three years later, I was to hear that in the early hours of the next morning my husband had bludgeoned 16-year-old Jayne MacDonald to death with a hammer and stabbed her repeatedly, leaving broken glass in her chest . . . [it had been] probably the happiest evening we had ever had . . . How could any wife imagine that her husband was busy hacking off a dead woman's head?[14]

One answer is that it was not her husband who was hacking off a dead woman's head, but a temporary inhabitant of her husband's body and soul, a diabolic parasite. Such a view is commensurate with the notion of true, undeviant, harmonious and integrated personality being diverted by an actual agent who must be fought and conquered. St Augustine believed that evil was a separate power, though he uncharacteristically shrank from naming it. 'It is not we ourselves that sin,' he wrote, 'but some other nature (what, I know not) sins in us.'[15] St Theresa of Avila was not nearly so hesitant. A highly intelligent woman with an acute sensitivity, both spiritual and physical, she thought a great deal about the Devil and regarded him as her personal enemy, bent on stealing souls from God. Theresa blamed him sometimes for the strange seizures with which she was periodically afflicted. 'These ecstasies come upon me with great violence and in such a way as to be outwardly visible,' she wrote, 'I having no power to resist them, even when I am with others, for they come in such a way as to admit of no disguising them unless it be by letting people suppose that as I am subject to disease of the heart, they are fainting fits. I take great pains to resist them when they are coming on – sometimes I cannot do it.'[16]

The use of the word 'ecstasy' is interesting, being literally a 'coming out of' oneself, since it is the Devil's purpose to cause his victims to abandon their social, dependable character and release their shadow, and neither Dahmer nor Bundy, Nilsen nor Long would have quarrelled with this description of their own submission to the tormentor. But I have deliberately chosen a quotation from St Theresa which is ambiguous, for she is here referring to those ecstasies which she thought were inspired by God, and which she describes in much the same language as those other distortions she ascribed to the Devil's work. This raises the whole matter of whether a religious sensibility may be more conducive to doing good than doing evil, or vice versa, or indeed whether the one may be mistaken for the other when the resulting conduct is thought to be divinely directed.

The crucial point is that these ecstasies are involuntary, that those who experience them attribute their source to something alien and wilful with which they must constantly join battle in order to maintain their own integrity. Otherwise the personality risks being swamped and cancelled out. While it is semantically and ontologically impossible to say what diabolic possession 'looks like', there are some conditions which so resemble what we think it *ought* to look like that they make the observer feel very uncomfortable. Korsakov's syndrome, which involves the obliteration of all memory older than a couple of seconds, and Tourette's syndrome, which condemns the sufferer to a manic sequence of tics and twitches, both illustrate the swamping of a personality. In Korsakov's, it is swallowed into a perpetually renewing void, always disappearing, escaping, ungraspable, unable to endure, therefore to exist; in Tourette's, the personality suffers the opposite fate of being crowded out by mimics and interpreters, elbowed aside by frauds, smothered by a multitude of mischievous demons who use it as their marionette. Unlike murderers and saints, whose possession is sporadic, the victim of Korsakov's or Tourette's is possessed *all the time* and can only achieve peace through sleep. It would be much more frightening to be with a Touretter for an hour than to spend an equivalent time chatting to a Dennis Nilsen.

Since the Korsakov sufferer is a profound amnesiac, he can never know who he is or what he has been. Two seconds after saying something, he will have forgotten it, so he can have no continuing identity, no past, no structure, no connections with anything outside his perpetually inventive mind. He may often appear to be a chronic liar because his fabulous stories are soon revealed to be empty of reality. But they are not lies, because the man who is relating them does not know what a lie is; nor are they the truth, because he has no measure to test the veracity of anything. They are indifferent, and he is indifferent to their indifference. He is condemned to mythomania because he has no way of knowing whether what he is saying has any relevance. He has no past, and therefore no personality, but must make it all up all the time, re-inventing himself in an unending sequence of presents. His soul has been stolen, but by what, or by whom?

At first, the Korsakov sufferer will be an entertaining companion, for he seems to have been everywhere and known everyone, and can recall his 'experiences' in what Oliver Sacks has aptly called 'narrational frenzy'. When you spot that the 'experiences' are confabulations, you might feel you are being made a fool of and be consequently resentful; then it dawns on you that the man has been several different people in the last half hour, and that none of them is genuine, that he doesn't really know who he is, and you begin to feel nervously apprehensive. For he is a body and a voice, he is talk and no more, talk for its own sake, talk which is desperate and fruitless. Such a man (or woman) may well seem to be possessed, for whoever he was, he is no more, nor will he ever be. 'He' has been obliterated and supplanted by this chronic yarn-spinner.

The freedom to invent is only an illusion of freedom, for the Korsakov patient is not inventing because he *wants* to, but because he *has* to. 'Whatever else free-will may be, it is not randomness,' writes Mary Midgley. 'Somebody who may act at any time in a way which has no roots in his previous life is not free, but disordered. To be unpredictable, not only to other people but to oneself, is to have lost all control over one's destiny. That is a condition as far from freedom as rolling helplessly downhill.'[17] Korsakov's is as much a compulsion as was Dahmer's necrophilia, even though it does not lead to doing harm. Whether the Korsakovian does harm to himself one cannot say, as it is difficult to assess how deep his self-knowledge may reach.

Dr Sacks, describing an actual patient called William, referred to his great gift of perpetually bridging the abyss of amnesia as his damnation, and the word is carefully chosen. 'If only he could be *quiet*, one feels, for an instant; if only he could stop the ceaseless chatter and jabber; if only he could relinquish the deceiving surface of illusions – then (ah then!) reality might seep in; something genuine, something deep, something true, something felt, could enter his soul.' If not, then William is like a person 'pithed, scooped out, de-souled, by disease'.[18] One could hardly depict diabolic intent more succinctly.

Tourette's syndrome, named after Gilles de la Tourette who first studied the disease in 1885, is characterised by an excess of nervous energy, and instead of trying to fill a baleful void, it overloads an already brimming tank. We have all at some time or another seen people in the street who hold loud conversations with an interlocutor who is not there, accompanied by gesticulations, jerks, tics, jumps, glances over the shoulder, dodges, defensive gestures, frowns, a vertiginous kaleidoscope of pantomimic oddities. I do not mean the simple rehearsal of arguments which a person afraid of his own aggression may not wish to expose to the possibility of rebuttal, and which denotes delayed frustration, but the physical acting out of a whole drama of apparently imaginary devising. Except that the

Touretter has not devised his or her manic display; they are imprisoned by it, and cannot stop it happening.

If we see such a person, we tend first to wonder whether the performance is intended for us, and as soon as we realise that it is not, to stare or avoid an embarrassing encounter by crossing the road. The Touretter may shout obscenities, keep touching things, or flail about as if evading a blow. The explosions occur every few seconds, during which the man is clearly not in command of himself and his whole body seems to be controlled by a malicious puppeteer. To restrain him would be the deepest cruelty, and yet ordinary life, constructed with quotidian volitions and blessed with a wilful peace, seems to be denied him.

Fortunately, this is not always the case. The Touretter is often astonishingly musical and can find repose from slavery to his tics in singing and dancing. He can also be tremendously quick, darting in and out of revolving doors with a dexterity which a normal person could not risk. Indeed, many a Touretter simply cannot resist the attraction of a revolving door to give his jerks employment and, dare one say? – amusement. He also excels at games like table-tennis, because his speed defies the predictable and his improvisatory flair attempts the impossible stroke in a split second. He can be competitive, playful, funny, but he more or less has to be, because his condition dictates he should be so. His levity is a burden.

He may also be astonishingly competent. In another book Dr Sacks introduces us to a victim condemned to invent and juggle with strange words or lie on the floor and throw his legs in the air, who is also a successful, distinguished surgeon. His compulsive twitches entirely disappear when he is operating.[19]

There are some Touretters, however, who are so seriously at the mercy of their tics and impulses that these completely stifle the genuine identity of the sufferer and fragment or, to revert to the root of our subject, disintegrate the personality. Dr Sacks describes one such person, a woman in her sixties, whom he observed by chance in New York, and only lengthy quotation can do justice to the vividness of his experience. He eventually realised the woman was imitating, caricaturing all the passers-by in a performance of such gusto and panache as to reduce everyone to admiring laughter.

I have seen countless mimes and mimics, clowns and antics, but nothing touched the horrible wonder I now beheld: this virtually instantaneous, automatic and convulsive mirroring of every face and figure. But it was not just an imitation, extraordinary as this would have been in itself. The woman not only took on, and took in, the features of countless people, she took them *off*. Every mirroring was also a parody, a mocking, an exaggeration of salient gestures and expressions, but an exaggeration in itself no less convulsive than intentional − a consequence of the violent acceleration and distortion of all her motions. Thus a slow smile, monstrously accelerated, would become a violent, milliseconds-long grimace; an ample gesture, accelerated, would become a farcical convulsive movement.

In the course of a short city-block this frantic old woman frenetically caricatured the features of forty or fifty passers-by, in a quick-fire sequence of kaleidoscopic imitations, each lasting a second or two, sometimes less, and the whole dizzying sequence scarcely more than two minutes.

And there were ludicrous imitations of the second and third order; for the people in the street, startled, outraged, bewildered by her imitations, took on these expressions in reaction to her; and those expressions in turn, were re-reflected, re-directed, re-distorted, by the Touretter, causing a still greater degree of outrage and shock . . . This woman who, becoming everybody, lost her own self, became nobody. This woman with a thousand faces, masks, *personae* − how must it be for *her* in this whirlwind of identities? The answer came soon, and not a second too late; for the build-up of pressures, both hers and others', was fast approaching the point of explosion. Suddenly, desperately, the old woman turned aside, into an alleyway which led off the main street. And there, with all the appearance of a woman violently sick, she expelled, tremendously accelerated and abbreviated, all the gestures, the postures, the expressions, the demeanours, the entire behavioural repertoires, of the past forty or fifty people she had passed. She delivered one vast, pantomimic regurgitation in which the engorged identities of the last fifty people who had possessed her were spewed out. And if the taking-in had lasted two minutes, the throwing-out was a single exhalation – fifty people in ten seconds, a fifth of a second or less for the time-foreshortened repertoire of each person.[20]

If the Korsakovian is mercifully unaware of his affliction, because he cannot remember it any more efficiently than he can remember anything else, the florid, total Touretter knows that he cannot own himself, that he is destined to be captured and smitten by these absurd impulses, that he is a perpetual prey to them. He can never know the simple harmony and order that the rest of us take for granted, for his soul is distracted. Whatever anyone else may say, it must certainly appear to him that he is possessed by demons.

It is only we, modern sophisticated man, children of the Enlightenment, who are surprised at such an interpretation. Primitive peoples closer to the pagan sources of religious belief and superstition take it as a matter of course that a man must be vigilant against demonic possession. Amongst some North American Indian tribes there persists a fear of one's personality being under siege by, and ultimately occupied by, the devil whom they call the Windigo. Those who fall prey to him suffer what psychiatrists have called the Windigo psychosis, a depressive lethargy leading to compulsive cannibalism. The man possessed feels the Windigo must be fed and sated, and though cannibalism is the strongest taboo of his tribe, he cannot resist the demands of the Windigo. His consequent inward struggle causes a dramatic disintegration and classic nervous disorder. What has this to do with Tourette's or Korsakov's syndrome? That all three may admit of a rational, medical or psychological explanation, but all three *with equal justice* can be attributed to possession at one and the same time. Medical science and superstition do not have to be incompatible, and for our purposes it is important to take note that all three behavioural aberrations are involuntary and have been caused by *something*. One may personify that 'something' without altering its validity as an abstraction or a medical definition. It has always been so.

From time immemorial it has been held as given that the spirit world is abundant with demons of all sorts and sizes, from sprites to fairies to goblins and elves, all of which have responsibility for moods, envies, jealousies, rages, generosities and so on. A 'demon' was not originally malevolent, but a guardian and helper from the spirit world – Socrates talked of his *daimon* with affection and trust. There gradually evolved the notion of some spirits being held accountable for good behaviour, and others blamed exclusively for bad behaviour, thus eschewing autonomous will and self-control on the part of the individual. Morality was the province of the 'demons'.

Bad demons would eventually prove poisonous unless they were periodically purged. They could be transferred to plants, to animals, to saints, or to the dying god himself, and they could be expelled *en masse* at annual festivals held precisely for the purpose. A man's sins (i.e. the manifestations in his conduct of evil spirits) could be transferred to a calf just as his warts might be transferred to a tree. In some parts of India a holy man would happily take into himself those adverse powers in return for payment. The Incas would rid themselves of evil spirits once a year by having four noblemen with spears run down the four roads leading out of the city to the four corners of the world, while all the townsfolk came to their doors and shook their clothes, quite as if they were shaking off dust, with joyful cries of 'Let the evils be gone'. In parts of Africa it has been reported that the Devil must be deceived into thinking nobody is paying him any attention, by an enforced period of four weeks' absolute silence, during which no sound is permitted and even the grief of the bereaved must be held in check. When the time is up, there breaks forth a great din and clatter as everyone bangs things to frighten the Devil out of their houses, going so far as to empty all their furniture on to the street so that he should have nowhere to hide.[21]

The Holi festival in Rajasthan and the Saturnalia in Europe, when people are encouraged to let off steam by behaving with licence and to make propitious gifts to placate the spirits, were meant in part to be a safety mechanism to keep the devils at bay. Walpurgis Nacht was assigned to the expulsion of witches. We still celebrate the feast of Saturnalia today, although we now call it Christmas.

The very fabric of drama, not only at its most sophisticated in Aeschylus or Racine, but in its primitive form in jungle chants or narrative dance, has to do with the expulsion of demons which would otherwise lodge dangerously in the breast. The spectator is meant to purge his emotions of those spirits which may cause him to behave badly, by watching an enactment of their terrible potential effect on stage (*catharsis*). When I watch Nuria Espert playing Lorca, or Edwige Feuillère playing Racine, or indeed Elizabeth Taylor in the films of Albee's *Who's Afraid of Virginia Woolf?* and Tennessee Williams's *Suddenly Last Summer*, I am being purged of demons. A recent example was David Mamet's play *Oleanna*, in which the two protagonists on stage so aroused us that arguments about the play continued afterwards in the street outside. The purging of demons was as visible as Dr Sacks's little old Touretter lady in New York spewing out all her accumulated compulsive mimickings. You could practically see the demons sprawling over the pavement, and one suspected that the people who released them thus after Mamet's play conducted themselves better at home as a result.

It frequently occurs in pagan cults that the ultimate deliverer from evil, who would take upon himself all the expelled demons of the populace, is the dying god himself. The great J.G. Frazer suggests that the savage mind confused the material and the immaterial, and imagined that, just as it was possible to shift a physical burden from one pair of shoulders to another, so ought it to be easy to offload one's pains and sorrows (read sins and demons) to the divinity, who would bear them away forever, leaving the people once more in peace and harmony. If so, then it is a misconception which persists in our own major religion, wherein the dying god is deemed to assume the sins of the world. By His sacrifice on the cross, Jesus carries off our demons and leaves us cleansed and refreshed. What is more, He does so regularly, once a year.

The early Christian Church took the doctrine further and proposed that the demons themselves could be purged and rendered pure and harmless once more. It caused much confusion and led to serious squabbles lasting for generations. One of the four heresies of Origen held that all men, devil-infested or not, should be saved at the last, that the devils themselves were open to salvation. Behind the idea lay an optimistic assessment of man's redeemability and the belief that his tormentor, Satan, though he was condemned to tempt, longed most to be rejected so that he, too, could re-attain that place with the divinity which he had lost. Marie Corelli developed this idea in her most successful novel, *The Sorrows of Satan*, in which the protagonist, Geoffrey Tempest, is educated in the ways of wrong-doing by a shady, insubstantial character with no discernible past called Rimanez. We soon learn that Rimanez is in fact the Devil, though Tempest is infuriatingly obtuse in refusing to see this. The situation echoes James Hogg's Mr Wringhim and

131

his shadowy demonic self in *Confessions of a Justified Sinner*, but Corelli's originality is to make Rimanez a tragic figure. 'Every lost soul would of necessity remind me of my own fall, my own despair,' he says, 'and set another bar between myself and heaven. Remember, the very Devil was an angel once.'

The novel reminds one that Christianity was originally a biophilic religion full of hope, and on the level of moral philosophy it taught not only that the disposition to do good was paramount over the periodic capacity to do ill, but that the former would always conquer the latter, given time. It was an essential theme of Jesus's own moral teaching. Whether he would be pleased by the way in which the Church which bears his name (and whose very foundation, one imagines, he would have considered blasphemous) has, over the centuries, given greater weight to the Devil's work, is another matter. The remorseless and discouraging sequence of inquisitions, wars, papal bulls, denunciations, heresies, punishments and hatreds nourished in his name would have horrified him. 'If he had foreseen such a thing, it is actually hard to suppose that the Jesus of the New Testament would have found it tempting [to establish a Church], since it would have seemed to him so obviously like the work of the Devil.'[22]

The above is to a large extent an historical digression, except in so far as it reminds us of our central point, namely that abnormal, eccentric actions, those which divert from innate goodness to produce harmful results, must be devil-inspired and devil-induced. It follows that vicars of the Christian Church, productive of more harmful results and human misery than virtually any other organisation over the last two thousand years, must have been possessed by demons. The fact that they often suspected as much themselves is testified by the extraordinary lengths to which they went, and still go, to rid their adherents of these pernicious influences. The Catholic Church is in perpetual fear of the Devil, contriving to keep him at bay by daily concentration and repetitive confession. Above all, there is available the final resource of exorcism.

Exorcism was originally a much milder operation than it has become, and was intended as a preparation for entry into the Church rather than a last-ditch attack when everything has gone wrong. It was essentially a cleansing operation, for the assumption was that new converts (and everybody was a convert at the beginning) needed to purge themselves of the misguided influences of paganism before they could be pure enough for the entry of the Holy Spirit. Baptism today is a legacy of this primitive cleansing.

However, when the demons return despite such careful preparation, then something more vigorous is required to drive them out again, and recourse is made to the ritual of frightening the demon (and everyone else, it might be said) in ways very similar to those adopted by the African tribesmen previously mentioned, who send the Devil packing by driving him crazy with noise. (The Jews of the Old Testament had their exorcists, and Jesus was one of them, but their rituals appear to have been somewhat gentler in tone.) It becomes a shouting match, with the possessed victim screaming obscenities or defiance in excruciating decibels, and the priest/exorcist raising his voice to an uncharacteristic bellow in an effort to drown out the Devil's protests. It can certainly be a dramatic encounter, and often a terrifying one.

Exorcists are reluctant to operate inside a church, lest the departing demon defile the holiness of the surroundings, and so the ceremony, which may have to be repeated several times over a period, takes place privately, often in the house of the victim. It may, on the other hand, take place virtually anywhere, although stories of exorcism by television and telephone, emanating naturally from the United States of America, serve only to make the entire process appear risible.

It is important that a full ritual of exorcism should be permitted only as a last resort, when doctors and psychiatrists have had a chance to examine the patient and

133

determine whether or not there are other explanations for his behaviour. To their great credit, most churchmen are in favour of such precautions and co-operate with the doctors. It is generally agreed that the vast majority of so-called possessions, perhaps as many as 99 per cent, can be attributed to psychological causes; a distemper of personality which has been allowed to develop without hindrance and must seem to the sufferer, whose unhappiness has not been sufficiently noticed, to come from devilish sources. A few sessions of therapy, with psychiatrist or priest, may be enough to help such a person. But in 1 per cent of cases for which exorcism is requested, psychiatrists and priests alike are forced to admit that there is no viable explanation for an obviously profound and complete reversal of personality, other than severe diabolic possession.

They have to be sure, for the process which then takes place is exceedingly dangerous and, if unsuccessful, can lead to the most appalling consequences. One such occasion occurred in the north of England in 1974, and was the germ of a tragedy so grotesque that, when it ended in a court of justice, some of the evidence was too upsetting to be presented. Defending counsel at the trial was Harry Ognall QC, now Mr Justice Ognall. The story is Greek in its dimensions and its implacability.

At the time of these events, Michael Taylor was thirty-one years old, hard-working, ordinary, pleasant and companionable. He adored his wife, Christine, and their five sons ranging in age from twelve years down to six. They were known to everyone in the village of Havercroft, eleven miles from Wakefield, as a manifestly happy family. It is important to record that neither Michael nor Christine had ever consulted psychiatrists, nor had ever been suspected of suffering from personality disorders or mental defects or even difficulties in intimate family life. There was no need to. There was nothing whatever to worry about. Their personalities were perfectly well 'ordered'.

The only trouble was that Michael was out of work and

rather low as a result. He and Christine were not deeply religious people, although they did have some crosses in the house and a Bible or two. Then a sect called the Christian Fellowship came to their area and they found themselves hosting a meeting in their home. It promised to be a social affair, quite a change for a little place in which nothing much happened, and if there were to be readings from the Bible and some hymn-singing, what harm could it do? Neighbours thought it all went rather nicely. There was even a form of holy communion, using sliced bread and Ribena, performed by a music student strumming a guitar. Her name was Marie Robinson.

The following day there took place another prayer meeting, at which Miss Robinson began to exorcise the evil spirit which she said dwelt within a neighbour, Mrs Smith, until Mrs Smith burst into tears and asked her to stop. She went home. Michael Taylor, meanwhile, was so worked up by the emotional tension of the occasion that he started jabbering in a language nobody could understand. This was a perfect example of *glossolalia*, or 'speaking in tongues', and another neighbour present, Mrs Wardman, said that it was a gift of the Holy Spirit, and rather beautiful.

Other meetings of the group occurred within the next few days. At one, Marie Robinson herself was shaking and chanting in an apparent state of possession. At another, Michael kissed Marie, and their bodies bounced off one another as if being repelled by an irresistible force. Michael now told all and sundry that he had seen the Devil, that the world was coming to an end, that he had been seduced by diabolism. He took to kneeling in front of neighbours in the street and of emptying his house of every scrap of religious significance. A member of the Christian Fellowship, alarmed at Michael's deterioration, suggested a drive in the country. It was agreed, but then suddenly there emitted from Michael's throat a scream so piercing and hideous that it terrified the children. At that point, it was decided Michael Taylor should be taken to see Father Vincent at a nearby vicarage.

Michael behaved violently at the vicarage. He punched Father Vincent and threw the cat out of the window. Food presented to him was chucked on the floor. Mrs Vincent declared that she was sure this was an authentic case of diabolic possession and that only genuine exorcism could hope to deal with it. She summoned a Methodist minister and a lay preacher and their wives, and the six of them spent all night, for six uninterrupted hours, submitting Michael Taylor to the question. They laid him on his back in the vestry and took turns standing over him casting out devils one by one. They said afterwards, exhausted, that they had managed to cast out forty. It could be maintained that they had put them there in the first place, for each devil had to be named before it would admit to being present within Michael, and so his confessions to bestiality, incest and the like were all echoes of the exorcists' suggestions. There are times when one wonders who in this terrible tale was the most sick.

Every time Michael puffed out his cheeks and gasped for breath, the exorcists jubilantly cheered the departure of another demon. By this time he was in a state of hysteria and was hyperventilating. Christine Taylor, who was present throughout, thought her husband had been pledged to the Devil by Marie Robinson, and that he had the seed of murder in him.

The various ministers did not disabuse her. They were convinced they had driven out every evil spirit but two: those of violence and murder. The Methodist minister's wife said she knew that, if Michael went home, he would kill his wife. Father Vincent also believed this was about to happen. Yet they let him go. The same group member who had taken the Taylors for a drive the previous afternoon and heard the beginning of this ghastly saga in that piercing scream, drove the young couple to their home early on the Sunday morning after a bruising night. Fortunately, he had the foresight to leave the five Taylor children with their grandparents.

At this point the reader should be warned. There

are more notorious murderers than this obscure and gentle young man, but none whose crime was quite so supernatural and inhuman. At 10.00 a.m. Michael tore his wife's face apart with his bare hands. He pulled her eyes out of their sockets and tore her tongue from its roots. He ripped and scratched and scraped until he had taken her face apart and left but the bones of the skull remaining. He then killed a pet dog and strangled it like a chicken before walking out of the house, naked except for his socks and covered in blood. He was kneeling on the ground when a policeman approached him, asking why he was so saturated in blood. 'It is the blood of Satan,' he replied.

At the police station Michael was asked if he had killed his wife. 'No, not her,' he said, 'I love her. I destroyed the evil within her. It had to be done. I'm relaxed . . . Chrissie was good. The evil had been put into her by them. I had to kill it . . . I felt compelled to destroy everything living within the house . . . It used my wife, my love. Oh Hell, I loved that woman. I destroyed the evil within her. It had to be done. No, no, not Chrissie, Chrissie, Chrissie, she was good. I loved her. I loved her so.'

It was subsequently suggested that Michael had felt lustful intent towards Marie Robinson and was distracted by the guilt which this engendered. The doctors also pointed out that he had been in an hypnotic and dissociated state when he had attacked his wife, that he had in fact been brainwashed. It was for others to wonder how and why such a massive transformation of character should occur, who or what had been the agent of dissociation.

In his closing address to the jury at Taylor's trial, Harry Ognall had this to say:

> Michael Taylor was a decent, hard-working, public-spirited and well-liked young man. He was described by a friend as a cheerful, friendly and in no way a violent man. He was a devoted father and loving husband for whom marriage was one long courtship.

He then encountered the Christian Fellowship and this particular branch of that fellowship was a group of tormented souls who simply fed neuroses to a neurotic and in a few short days he was returned to a homicidal maniac. In that condition he was the subject of what we submit were grotesque and wicked malpractices posing in the guise of religion. And, in the light of all the evidence, supervised by members of two branches of the Christian Church, he was made to confess sins of which he was wholly innocent and indeed did not understand and was subjected to indignities which defy comprehension. At the end he was allowed to go home with the spirit in his heart and no reason in his head, and within minutes he had killed the darling of his life with unspeakable brutality.[23]

Taylor was adjudged not guilty of murder, but guilty on the lesser charge of manslaughter because he had not known what he was doing or had not realised that what he was doing was wrong. In other words, he was not responsible for his act of outrage. Who, then, was? Marie Robinson didn't do it, albeit her reaction to Taylor and his to her contributed to his state of mind. The vicars of Christ didn't do it, though their words and deeds may well have amounted to inducement and incitement. The lust was not there before, the brain had not been washed before, the capacity for wrong-doing had been entirely absent before. Was this a question of morals, or of sudden and unexpected disorder of the moral sense? Is there perhaps a way in which, when balance is obliterated and harmony crushed by a spirit of malevolence coming from outside the personality, matters of moral decision become irrelevant? To behave wickedly, as well as to do good, requires autonomy, or the words are meaningless. Intent has to be part of the equation, otherwise moral judgements have no target.

As Graham Greene said of his amoral character Pinkie in *Brighton Rock*, he was, in the end, evil. 'What did it matter in that case whether he was right or wrong?'

6

TO DO OR NOT TO DO

It certainly would not matter if anyone were right or wrong if his acts were not his own. Greene implies that Pinkie is not Pinkie but the spirit of malevolence working through him. Michael Taylor was not himself the day he savaged his wife's face; on the evidence, I think it is incontestable that he was something other. We have considered, from the beginning, whether or not people can or should be held responsible for their conduct, whether they can, in short, be saints. They cannot, if hostility and cruelty are so ingrained within human nature that to be anything other than wicked is to be less than human. They cannot, if their genetic architecture has determined that they should not, or, conversely, that they are bound to behave altruistically by virtue of their DNA and not of their free volition. Nor can they be good if God has ordained they should be born with the black stain of sin in their hearts.

We can turn from these pessimistic assessments of man's nature and look for refreshment to the optimistic ones, but even they, paradoxically, have led us to further grim conclusions. If man is inherently good, decent, pacific, as many from Rousseau to Bruce Chatwin have maintained, then his appalling behaviour must be attributed to influences which have caused him to stray from his nature and prevented him from being good. These might include personality disorders, mental illnesses, or straight invasion by diabolic forces, as we saw in the last chapter. In each instance, the afflicted person is robbed of his *will*, is denuded of autonomous volition to such an extent that he does not even know that what he is doing is interpretable, that it can be described as good or bad. It is simply what he does at that moment.

This matter of the will is of crucial importance, and it is interesting that it emerges now through the negative evidence of its absence. We best understand the crime of Michael Taylor by envisaging his will as being kidnapped. We best imagine the hell of Tourette's syndrome by cherishing those moments, at the piano or on the dance floor, when the Touretter's own will reasserts itself and he can master his tics instead of being manipulated by them. Even the Korsakovian has his moments of will-assertion – hundreds of them, every few seconds, when he (desperately, one thinks, but probably not so to him) invents a new identity for himself. His is one endless, adventurous, but fruitless assertion of will, leading nowhere and meaning nothing. But it begins to become clear that, within all these manifestations of aberration from the norm of human harmony and peace, is inherent the notion that it is individual will that has been stifled, and that if only the will could be resurrected, then the human in all his natural goodness would follow.

Almost every serious study of the addictive repetitive murderer has made the observation that he is a man whose will has somehow been obliterated at the moment of his crimes, thus agreeing with the self-assessment of many of them quoted in the preceding chapter. One of many moving passages in Lionel Dahmer's memoir of his son, relating to a period before he had any idea that Jeffrey was a murderer, specifically pinpoints the moment of realisation. 'I saw a young man in whom something essential was missing,' he wrote. 'I saw a young man who fundamentally lacked that element of will which allows a human being to take hold of and direct his own life.'[1]

A salient ingredient of the human description, then, one which differentiates us from the other animals, is the possibility of choice. When a goose tears up grass rather than enter into a potentially damaging conflict with another goose, we cannot say he has chosen to do right, to take the path of peace, for he is responding automatically to genetically bred instructions. No thought or decisions are involved. If genetic reproduction may be said to have a purpose, it is to maximise the potential continuance of the species. Yet in the human species we are aware already that there is an ethical dimension which has to be considered parallel with the deterministic one, and it is the glory of the species that the ethical dimension can be seen occasionally to override the genetic. This is why the notion of free will is so precious, and we shall find as we go along that those people who deserve our admiration for saintly behaviour are generally those who have been free to exercise their will and have done so with thought and concentration.

We shall also see, alas, that free will, unencumbered by illness or disorder, is not enough by itself to guarantee conduct in accordance with pacific human nature; it is also possible to exercise the will freely for malevolent ends.

Just as the addictive murderer is imprisoned by his disorder and the Touretter by his tics, my late father by his period of irrational jealousy and the Ulster politician Ian Paisley by his rage, so might the audience at a mass political or musical rally temporarily submerge their individual freedom of will in the mass, and surrender their wills collectively to the painless joy of obedience. Such was observable at the Nazi meetings of the 1930s, the meetings of Mosley's Blackshirts in London during the same period, the solid cemented behaviour of football crowds and Beatles enthusiasts, and the collective suicides of religious fanatics.

Then there is the battery of mechanisms thrown up by the unconscious in order specifically to thwart the exercise of free will by the conscious, identified by Freud as 'defence mechanisms' (displacement, regression, denial, and so on). Add to these the environmental conditions which may render the expression of will either impossible or pointless, such as abject poverty, starvation, brutalisation, oppression, and one must readily acknowledge that there are powerful obstacles to be overcome before the will to do good may breathe freely. In Zola's *Germinal* (1885) there is not a single character who may be said to be ill, or diabolically possessed, or seriously disturbed. Nor is there a single one among the miners who has the freedom to exercise his will. They are all imprisoned by blind, implacable circumstance. Their choices have been removed, and with those choices, their humanity.

In parenthesis, total freedom of choice is not available in every circumstance. On a trivial level, the milkman is unlikely to exercise his free will by dumping all his bottles in the Thames because he does not feel like delivering them, nor is the train driver likely to send his engine backwards at sixty miles per hour because he wants to know what it feels like. Certain common assumptions have to be made, that safety and continued employment have a greater attraction than untrammelled exercise of free will. Of course, such observation does not invalidate the theory; the milkman and the train driver retain their freedom but choose, in the interests of common sense, not to give it expression. But theoretical philosophers often fail to take note of such ordinary exceptions to their abstractions as manifested in regular life.

On the other hand, it is equally impossible for the free man – undiseased, unpossessed, unaddicted – *not* to exercise free will and, by extension, *not* to make choices which have moral implications at every turn. This has the unexpected effect of making freedom a kind of burden, in so far as the free man is bound to demonstrate it; he is imprisoned by his inexhaustible liberty. With her usual taste for paradox, Iris Murdoch has one of her characters express it thus: 'I've always imagined that I could just give up morals, but it's not so easy. I'm not as free as I think.'[2] Hence, the exercise of free will requires more than merely being human, it requires making an *effort* to be human, to make one's humanity manifest and vibrant.

It is not passive. It demands vigilant resistance to all those influences which we have seen work continuously to upset the natural in human nature.

This is hard work. It suggests that the mere absence of evil-doing, a kind of bland, shapeless innocence, is not human at all, but lifeless. Montaigne makes the distinction between a casual and fortuitous harmlessness (which he claims describes himself) and real virtue, 'for the word virtue, I think, presupposes difficulty and struggle'. Real goodness can only arise when the will is constantly pressed into conflict with its enemies, stretched and strained, eager for battle (*avida est periculi virtus*) and proud of victory: 'la vertu refuse la facilité pour compagne ... elle demande un chemin âpre et épineux.'[3] We have already seen in an earlier chapter that Jeffrey Dahmer struggled for nine years with the force that was devouring his will, and therewith his humanity, only to fail in the end and succumb to murderousness. But Montaigne would have approved of the effort, and not been embarrassed to call it virtuous.

One of the awful ironies of religious thought is that it has tended, at least within the Christian tradition, to denigrate effort, free will and humanity in favour of obedience, helplessness and immaturity. Historically, the Church has been terrified of free will and its concomitant implication that men can be good by their own devising, a notion it has often regarded as heretical. Montaigne's sensible attitude had been anticipated a thousand years earlier by Pelagius, who likewise affirmed that, when men acted virtuously, it was as a result of their own moral effort. For this outrageous remark he was hounded by the priests, themselves goaded especially by St Augustine, and declared a heretic.

Pelagius lived from about 360 to 420 and was British. His real name was Morgan, which might suggest he came from the Welsh hills, but there is also a tradition he was of Irish birth. A ponderous man with a gentle disposition, he went to Rome at the beginning of the fifth century, was shocked by the licence he there discovered and by the excuse offered for it ('men will be men', more or less), and set about informing his contemporaries about the potential in human nature. He insisted that the will had to be absolutely free, in order to be able to choose between doing good or evil, and that no fault could possibly be attached to a deed if the will was constrained in any way. Theorists called this 'the liberty of indifference' or 'the power of contrary choice', but in plain terms it meant that men were born characterless and unformed. They did not have an indelible predisposition to do wrong, nor were they bound always to do right. The individual will was, at every moment and in each separate situation, in equipoise, free to go one way or the other. Thus the individual will was creative and energetic, a point of view remarkably close to another which would emerge fifteen centuries later and be called 'existentialism'.

All this was anathema to St Augustine, obviously because it placed God in a subordinate role, and it would prove equally indigestible to the Jansenists of the seventeenth century with their hopeless doctrine that goodness was a blessing bestowed at random. Martin Luther, too, preferred to believe that it did not matter what you did, good or bad, life-warming or life-chilling, harmful or beneficent, because you could not earn God's approval; therefore good conduct was useless, and free will an encumbrance.

These are horrible concepts by which to guide one's life and utterly foreign to the view of human nature towards which we are moving, namely that each man is master of his character, providing always he not be susceptible to those circumstances which may poison it despite his will. And that saintliness is not only possible, but natural, given the free expression of will to release it. Lastly, that goodness, though natural, requires effort to prevent it being swamped. Ultimately, as Don Quixote says, 'Cado uno es artifice de sa ventura.'

A perfect example of goodness through effort is afforded by the life of Thomas More, the man whom

Dr Johnson considered 'the person of greatest virtue these islands ever produced'. One can best appreciate what he meant (and Johnson was himself, for different reasons, a man of exemplary goodness) by looking at More's career, what it promised and how he coped with its destruction.

Thomas More, the son of a barrister, rose to a position of eminence in the land by reason of his sharp intelligence and winning charm. He was a brilliant and prodigious scholar, an intimate friend of the great humanist Erasmus, with a legal brain much admired by his contemporaries. He also wrote one of the classics of English literature, *Utopia*, and a *Life of Richard III*. His family life was extraordinarily vivacious and happy, with wife, children, sons-in-law and grandchildren all gathered together. Elected to parliament in 1504, More's abilities marked him out for a glorious future, so much so that Erasmus feared his head would be turned by worldly ambition. He was especially in favour with the King, Henry VIII, whom he had first met when Henry was nine years old, and whom he was now encouraged to regard as a dear friend. The King would often invite More to dine alone with him and Queen Catherine, or drop in unexpectedly at More's house in Chelsea to spend an evening with him. They were seen walking in the garden, arm-in-arm, and competed in heaping praise one upon the other. Thomas said the King was courteous and affable, while Henry enjoyed More's amusing wit and clever talk. In 1521 More was knighted.

Two years later he was Speaker of the House of Commons, and two years after that Chancellor of the Duchy of Lancaster. Already a bencher of Lincoln's Inn and a privy councillor, More's popularity amongst his peers was renowned, and nobody was surprised when the King made him the first layman Lord Chancellor in 1529, taking the oath of office from the Duke of Norfolk, who delivered the King's instruction that he should administer justice impartially. Erasmus wrote, 'I do indeed congratulate England, for a better or holier judge could not have been appointed.' In view of his subsequent reputation, and with our subject very much in mind, it is a trifle shocking to discover that Sir Thomas More was a stern Chancellor, responsible for the execution of six heretics (his predecessor Wolsey had executed none). It has been said in his defence that he would have considered heretics in much the same light as racists might be viewed today, but that is to beg the point; racists, however objectionable, are not murdered by the state. Suffice it remind us that More was not perfect. True saints rarely are.

The rest of the story is well known. Henry VIII wanted to divorce the Queen so that he might marry Anne Boleyn, and required parliament to pass several radical legislative measures of enablement. More was uneasy, and said so. He would assent to the idea that parliament could amend legislation to permit the succession to the throne to descend according to the King's wishes, but not that the King could usurp the supreme authority of the Pope. It may appear now to be a point not worth arguing about, but to More it was the most important matter of conscience he had ever faced. Anne Boleyn was furious and probably influenced the King against him, but Henry was not in any case a patient man. More resigned the Lord Chancellorship in 1532, was imprisoned in the Tower of London in 1534, and remained there until his execution the following year.

More's sanctity rests upon the last two years of his life, and on his manner of leaving it. His behaviour is held to demonstrate that every man is able to reach his own moral decisions, and is responsible for the dictates of his conscience. Therein lies his autonomy and his humanity. Having made his decision, which was neither pragmatic nor political, it must be said, More was in harmony with himself, whole and integrated, in command of his will and undamaged by adverse influence. His prison cell was terrible, damp, cold, and infested with rats. When he politely and calmly refused to reconsider his decision, he was deprived of books and writing material, and was reduced to writing to his wife with a piece of coal on a scrap of paper. Then he closed the shutters on his cell window and spent the rest of his days in the dark.

Despite all this, More was cheerful, completely at ease and kind to his gaolers. He retained his wit and was never embittered, though he might possibly be chastised for stubbornness and causing his wife and loving family much unhappiness. On the day before his execution the King rescinded the sentence of hanging and allowed him to be beheaded as a nobleman. More's death on 6 July, 1535 is an occasion which has passed into the collective memory. When he came to the steps leading up to the scaffold, he said to the man on duty, 'I pray thee see me safely up, and as for my coming down let me shift for myself.' Every person present averred that More's conduct on the scaffold was without parallel. It represented at once the triumph and the peace of free will.

A modern equivalent might be the incredible stoicism of Brian Keenan, held chained to a wall in cruel darkness for years beneath the streets of Beirut, yet discovering within himself, through the purposeful exercise of free will in conditions where freedom was banished and the will of others always prevailed, the core of his humanity. Deprivation, torture, despair all besieged him and threatened to engulf him, but his will to resist disintegration, to resume the harmony which is natural to our species, was so powerful when accompanied by intense concentration and effort, that no hostile influence could ultimately subdue it. The most moving page in his account of this ordeal is that on which Brian Keenan suddenly recognises the acute bewildered anguish of his young guard, Said, and weeps for him. 'At times his voice broke and he cried out in desperation for Allah. I felt my own tears. I was transformed with a deep and helpless love for him. I had become what he was calling out for.'[4]

Sir Thomas More was canonised in 1935. Brian Keenan never will be. But I do not think there is a chink of difference in the difficulties they faced, nor in the nobility of their struggle to affirm their humanity. They both demonstrated how, when all freedom of choice appears to have been removed, the freedom to find and reassert one's own goodness even in the blackest of all holes can and will always remain. They were both existentialists in their way, for they both refused to have designations pinned upon them – 'traitor' in the one case and 'hostage' in the other – but devised their own description.

The characters of Corneille's plays (*Le Cid, Horace, Cinna*) are likewise heroes of choice and will. Faced with a conflict between conscience and expediency, or between an expression of self and submission to adverse influences, they choose the former of the equation and thereby keep intact their humanity (unlike Racine's *Phèdre*, for example, who allows herself to be buffeted and finally destroyed by the Dionysian devils who would distort her). *Cinna* shows that forgiveness is not an act of weakness, but rather an act of self-realisation, of mastery over disorder and fragmentation of the personality. To the extent that Corneille's heroes choose themselves, they are as existentialist in their philosophical position as any of Sartre's fictional and actual idols.

Since it may appear odd to yoke together a fifth-century theologian, a sixteenth-century martyr, a twentieth-century hostage and some seventeenth-century dramatic characters, all under the label of existentialist, it is as well, perhaps, that we should examine the salient points of that philosophical construct and see how they fit in with the present discussion. That a sane and integrated man, in harmony with his nature, is free at all moments to choose how he will behave, is the crux of Pelagius's philosophy. So, too, is it at the heart of Sartre's vision of the active man.

Sartre, of course, goes much further than Pelagius or Corneille, for he does not posit a free choice between ready made alternatives of good and evil, but the far more demanding task of choosing to *create* the notion of good from scratch. Moreover, not only is each man free, but he cannot choose *not* to be free – his freedom is ineluctable and terrible. This is the sense of his famous phrase 'je suis condamné à être libre',[5] and the lonely cry of Orestes, 'I am a man, Jupiter, and each man must invent his own path.'[6] Sartrean freedom is harsh but noble, exigent but emancipating. As Maurice Cranston wrote, Sartre is a 'stern moralist [who] believes that virtue is possible, but difficult'.[7] Just like Thomas More, in fact.

The existentialist ethic starts from the premiss that men, unlike things, have no immutable, imprisoning essence to glue them for ever in a description. They cannot be pigeon-holed by adjectives purporting to fix and nail their personalities, so denying them the choice of self-creation. In anguish and solitude, they must make a resolute effort of lucidity and consciousness to *exist* rather than just 'be', as a table 'is'. Sartre tells us that when he was a child, he felt he was being objectified by the gaze of adults and the assessment of the world, reducing him to passivity. 'Breathing, digesting, defecating in apathy, I went on living because I had been born.'[8] Once he was able to escape this trap, this mire of non-meaning, he realised he was able to define himself as he went along. Man is responsible for himself and for everything he does, without the possibility of refuge in the insulting viscosity of 'essences'; he is not 'essentially' anything – he is what he does.

Man must constantly make choices between various possible courses of behaviour. In his total and terrifying liberty, he can only give justification to himself by the choices he makes; he will define himself by those choices. Against the famous initial truth of Descartes – *cogito, ergo sum* (I think, therefore I am) – one might propose a parallel existential truth, which would be *eligo, ergo sum* (I choose, therefore I am). Immorality in the Sartrean sense would therefore be a refusal to exercise this choice, not so much to do wrong wilfully, but supinely to accept that there is an absolute idea of Right and Wrong (or Good and Evil) by which one's actions must be measured. The four characters of Sartre's play *Huis Clos* (1945) have lost this power of choice. They are dead, and therefore doomed never to change. Nothing they do can alter the way each sees the other, and nothing they can say will have any effect. Human beings, once their freedom of choice has been removed, cannot be good or bad – the words would be as irrelevant as they are to the flapping of a moth. As Iris Murdoch has put it, 'Good is an empty space into which human choice may move.'[9] Without human choice, the space will remain unoccupied.

Baudelaire, ever conscious of the power of evil and determined to embrace it, is a coward as far as Sartre is concerned because he is willingly subservient to a notion extraneous to and independent of himself.[10] By continuing to regard his immoral acts as immoral and recognising that his acts are wrong, he gives silent approbation to the notion of an *a priori* conception of what is right. Immorality is not a valid choice for a free man to make, because implicit within it are the seeds of remorse which suppose a pre-established and non-autonomous morality. Sartre says that Baudelaire commits evil in order to repent it immediately afterwards. This is not his idea of existentialist man. Similarly, the character Goetz in another of Sartre's plays, *Le Diable et le Bon Dieu*, is devoted to committing evil in the first act, then dramatically swaps to a parallel commitment to doing good. By the end of the play he realises that he has all the time been trying to clothe himself with an essence composed of recognisable attributes, first the qualities of the evil man, then the qualities of the saint. In both cases, he has been denying his humanity by avoiding his responsibility to create through choice.

Such a profoundly anthropocentric view of ethics and morality is a direct descendant of that intellectual crisis unleashed by Darwin's extraordinary insights. For the first time in centuries, man's moral dilemmas were left floating, waving without anchor, helplessly irrelevant. Darwinism offered no answers and promised no cures. The feeling of contingency engendered by the discovery of evolution was deeply unsettling. Here was man, devoid of importance, bereft of moral guidance, abandoned in a world of accident, chance, fortuity and terror, reduced to a clump of genes – a marvellous clump, to be sure, but a clump nevertheless. For many, it was a vision of despair. The existentialists, however, converted what appeared to be a moral void into an opportunity for greatness. Because it was no longer possible to say that God created Man, at last men would be able to create themselves and proudly reap the consequences of their independence. If goodness was revealed, there was no-one to thank; if evil, no-one to blame. We are alone in the world, without excuses. We cannot fall back on any concept of human nature to explain why we are what we are. We *are* only what we *do*. And by our acts, we create and invent values.

Examples of authentic existentialist heroes may be plucked from many centuries and different callings. Sartre himself chose the pederastic convict and writer Jean Genet as his demonstrator of the existentialist ethic, and devoted a huge book to his life and career, significantly calling Genet a 'saint' in the title.[11] Others, also significantly regarded by history or public opinion as saints, may include Bob Geldof, Joan of Arc, and Oskar Schindler. They all, separately, escaped petrifying definitions to release goodness in creative action.

Bob Geldof, an iconoclastic, painfully scruffy, oath-splattering pop singer from Dublin, made his name as lead singer with a notably loud group called the Boomtown Rats in the 1970s. Once the image was fixed, it appeared immutable; even his fame and his wealth could not loosen its bonds. Geldof did not seem to be troubled by this at all. His hair grew longer and more tangled, his taste in swear words more exotic. One journalist called him 'a devoted exponent of verbal profanity',[12] and he seemed perfectly content to retain this reputation. In fact, he gave every impression of not caring a fig. The fact that he was supremely articulate, had been a keen debater both at school and within the family where he grew up in Dublin, was eloquent, passionate and well informed, were not newsworthy traits, so 'loudmouth' it was and loudmouth it remained.

Until, that is, the tragedy of Ethiopia in 1985 released and transformed him. A combination of unending drought and political cynicism had reduced an entire population to pitiful destitution and literal starvation. It is not, alas, an uncommon occurrence, and the privileged, overfed Western nations may usually be permitted to ignore it. Not this time. First, a BBC news report showed pictures of human beings so visibly bereft of hope or dignity, brittle bones sticking through paper-thin skin and eyes big and dull with despair, that viewers were shaken out of their apathy. (Some telephoned to complain that such unpleasant scenes spoiled their evening.) Second, Bob Geldof was jerked into activity as if by an electric shock. Appalled by what he saw, Geldof dropped everything to do *something* for the people of Ethiopia. He lobbied politicians and ministers and shocked them with his refusal to accept evasions or polite expressions of concern. He even bearded Margaret Thatcher, then Prime Minister and so famously obtuse and stubborn that most of her cabinet were afraid of her, and asked her point-blank what she intended to do. Well, she said, it is not as simple as you think, she said, the money has to come from somewhere and government has responsibilities towards the taxpayer, and so on. Geldof interrupted her and told her that it was simple and that he would show her. It is the only occasion on which Mrs Thatcher was seen to be dumbfounded.

Geldof then organised the biggest fund-raising effort yet seen in Britain. Galvanising the whole of the popular music world to lend him support, and bullying many others (banks, suppliers, transporters) into doing his bidding, he inspired the whole nation and put Thatcher and her government to shame. Individuals could contribute to Band Aid, as it was called, by letter, over the counter, or by television. Everyone from children to old age pensioners contributed in a flood of compassion and fellow-feeling, and when a special massive concert was arranged at Wembley Stadium, in the presence of the Prince and Princess of Wales, all eyes were on Geldof, the singer-become-saviour. With the concert, record sales and personal contributions, a total of £50 million was raised, almost entirely due to Geldof's relentless effort. Not only was he principal organiser and inspiration, but, mindful of the waste which sometimes ensues, with much of the money falling down the hole of administration and precious little of it ever reaching the needy, he went personally to Ethiopia more than once to supervise the transport and delivery of food, making sure that supplies got through even if it meant he might have to drive the lorries himself. It is no exaggeration to say that he brought the attention of the world to Ethiopia and made politicians of other countries stir themselves out of their habitual self-regard.

Bob Geldof was knighted by the Queen for his Band Aid initiative. Being an Irish citizen he cannot be addressed as Sir Robert, but in print he is Bob Geldof KBE. To the young he immediately became Saint Bob, although it was cheap newspapers who contrived the expression and he was obviously irritated by it. 'I only did what needed to be done,' he has said, 'what any decent person with a conscience would have done.'[13] Not so. Being decent and having a conscience are not enough; they are characteristics which can be decorative, somnolent, or moribund. The psychic energy required to galvanise them into activity is quite separate from simply 'minding about' something, which is all that is expected, generally, of decency and conscience. What Geldof did was creative; he re-invented himself. He was, for a moment, the quintessential existentialist hero. 'I can be exactly who I want,' he once said. He found freedom in submission to a cause, and in the recognition that famine, being an issue of morality, was too big a problem for politicians. Unlike most people, Bob Geldof found it impossible to be indifferent or pusillanimous. In his commitment lay his humanity and in his radiant will-power there shone an expression of the latent goodness of mankind.

It would be silly to pretend that Geldof changed his personality or became someone else. To this day he remains the same foul-mouthed rogue. In this he resembles Joan of Arc, who was also 'rough-tongued' (as it is elegantly put by Vita Sackville-West), impatient of and rude to politicians, bold, resolute and dismissive of excuses. Even after she had led the French army into battle and victory and had stood trial for heresy, she remained the same ordinary little peasant girl she had always been. Her huge demonstration of will was a creative act which transcended her femaleness and social condition and existed in addition to these, not instead of them. She was the existentialist heroine of the fifteenth century.

Jeanneton, to give her her real name, was born in 1412, the daughter of Jacques Darc, a peasant farmer of Domrémy in the Vosges. Her mother was pious and good, and gave her the only religious instruction she ever received. Joan was illiterate, unable to read or write at all, and had never been on horseback. Yet when voices told her, at the age of about sixteen, that she had to save France from the alliance between the Burgundians and the English, and crown the King, she did not hesitate. She demanded an audience, and after three days was granted one. She somehow managed to convince old experienced men that she could lead troops into battle to relieve Orléans, did so, and won. She was at the Dauphin's side when he was crowned at Rheims. If it were not such a well-attested story, it would be difficult to believe.

This adolescent and untried girl, unexposed to the cynical manoeuvrings and shifting standards of the political world, was immediately abandoned by those she had benefited, sold to the English, denounced by the University of Paris, tried on charges of blasphemy, condemned and burned. There was nothing of the hysteric about her, no excessive religious zeal, no exaggeration of temperament. 'Neither ecstasy nor despondency affected her unduly. She was neither disproportionately lifted up nor disproportionately cast down.'[14] A pretty stable and balanced girl, in fact, who would much have preferred to remain in her fields. But she could not.

The pioneering Victorian psychologist F.W.H. Myers compared Joan's voices with Socrates' inner counsel, his 'daemon' or guardian spirit, and identified them both as the release of subconscious thought into active and conscious life, which effectively also describes Bob Geldof's sudden eruption of action. The implication is that many of us are capable of this kind of regeneration, but prefer to cushion thought in habit or resignation ('I wouldn't be any good at it', 'There's nothing I can do about it'). Joan of Arc was above all *active*, she defined herself by her acts, by what she did, and was not especially attractive or lovable for her personality. This is why she is one of the least sentimental of saints. 'She is a hard, not a soft, saint. There is nothing of the poetic quality in her, as in Saint Francis. She is too heroic and bracing to appeal to the average mind . . . heroism may command the tributes of the populace, but sentimentality wins its heart. Jeanne never makes any appeal to sentimentality at all.'[15]

St Anthony of Padua offers a stark contrast. He died in 1231, but, as I said in Chapter One, his funeral is still going on. From the day after his death until today there has been an endless stream of people touching his tomb, paying respect to the love and trust he inspired. Joan died exactly two centuries later, in 1431, but no line of grateful mourners stretches up to her statue at Domrémy (her remains had been thrown into the river Seine), and she had to wait five hundred years for canonisation, whereas Anthony was sainted within the year. Joan of Arc's genius was practical, as befits an existentialist heroine, and her qualities all the harsher for being effective. In a similar way, Winston Churchill inspired Britain in 1940, not by his charm, in which he was singularly deficient for all but his close family, but by his single-mindedness. This is precisely the quality which Geldof brought to his Band Aid initiative, and he was admired, rather than loved, for it. Vita Sackville-West has written of Joan that 'it was her single-mindedness which enabled her to inspire disheartened men and to bend reluctant princes to her will.'[16]

There is, unfortunately, an obverse aspect to these positive examples. What if the existential decision to refuse deterministic self-description should lead to destructive behaviour? Cannot the individual freely choose to re-invent himself as a dominant, entirely egocentric force? Is there such a thing as too much free will? These are difficult and uncomfortable questions, to which there are no easy answers. In logical terms, there can be no sustainable objection to the exercise of free will and independence in order to make oneself a torturer. There are, of course, other objections, and the synthesis towards which this book is struggling will take account of them. But on the level of the existentialist ethic, freedom can lead to dominance, and for every Bob Geldof there will be a Marquis de Sade. As for Joan of Arc, her transformation from country girl to conqueror may be regarded as a disaster as well as a triumph. She made herself dominant and fearless, indifferent to the suffering she might cause, and a potential killer armed with lethal *sang-froid*.

There are many philosophers who have argued that this progression towards dominance is inevitable. It is Adler's will-to-power, or Abraham Maslow's 'hierarchy of needs' rising by stages towards the 'peak experience'. Most people never reach their ultimate existentialist peak, but those who do may turn upon the rest with fangs bared. Colin Wilson has written a great deal about the 'dominant 5%' of the human race, those who have drive and initiative, those who achieve and endure, those who satisfy their needs often at the expense of the other 95%. He tells how the Chinese in the Korean war found they could economise on the number of guards they needed to post by simply identifying the dominant 5% of their American prisoners and separating them from the rest. The remaining 95%, docile and compliant when

156

deprived of their leaders, no longer needed to be guarded at all.[17]

The dominant 5% will include all the people who affect life in some way, either by running affairs or adorning them, be they tycoons or politicians, actors or judges, composers or painters. Margaret Thatcher belongs to the club, as do Liszt, Penelope Keith and Mary Whitehouse. But though the club is small, it has a wide membership, and amongst those sharing space with Mesdames Thatcher, Keith and Whitehouse you will find Hitler, Sweeney Todd and Charles Manson. All habitual murderers belong to the dominant 5%, and some of them know it. Dostoievsky understood this better than most, and though his *Crime and Punishment* thankfully eschews percentages, the character of Raskolnikov who is at the centre of the novel realises full well that his act of double murder has changed him, elevated him in a way, lifted him among the 5% who are different and impervious to essentialist laws. Raskolnikov has created himself by his act, has become an existentialist hero and master of his will.

Let us pause for a moment to remind ourselves of an earlier chapter. Dominance is not a peculiarity of the human species. It exists in nature to promote co-operation and survival. Tribes of baboons have their dominant 5% of members, to whom the rest defer, and it has been observed that these invariably lead in the defence against predators as well as impose the coherent social structure which enables the tribe to function as a co-operative unit. They do so by the establishment of a strict hierarchy of rank which determines the place of each individual within the community. The much-quoted 'pecking order' amongst birds is a similar recognition that each individual (save the very first and the very last) must dominate some and be dominated by others. In human societies we see a parallel organisation among aristocracies, whether of wealth, land, or inheritance, and in England the hierarchies of rank are actually listed, so that the monarch is number one in order of precedence, followed by her consort and male members of her family, the Archbishop of Canterbury, the Lord High Chancellor, the Archbishop of York and the Prime Minister. Dukes of England take precedence over dukes of Scotland, Great Britain, Ireland and the United Kingdom, and are themselves numbered 1 to 24 (number 1 is the Duke of Norfolk, and number 23 the richest of the lot, the Duke of Westminster). All dukes come before marquesses, who come before earls, who come before viscounts, and so on. The Lord Chief Justice, oddly enough, is way down on the list, below the eldest sons of barons. While some of these (those eldest sons, for example) may no longer be properly regarded as among the dominant 5% of the people, they benefit from an inherited principle that they *should* be.

The practice of dominance still obviously applies in military establishments, where the matter of rank is of supreme importance and is never challenged without the direst consequences. In my schooldays it still applied amongst boys, some of whom emerged as more dominant than the rest and were appointed monitors, and of these some became prefects, and one alone of the latter was elevated to school captain. In my day, the school captain still had the power of discipline over other boys, to the extent that a teacher would send a miscreant to him for punishment with the slipper or the cane. That may have passed into history, but there can be no doubt that boys continue to organise themselves into a hierarchy of dominance relative to one another whether or not the authorities will recognise it.

Dominance is also allied to sexual arousal and receptiveness. Anthony Storr has pointed out that, after competition between two snakes for a female, the loser will crawl away and be sexually inactive for weeks, while the winner will copulate immediately.[18] I cannot resist pinching Dr Storr's example of a human equivalent in Sarah, Duchess of Marlborough, who noted in her diary, 'My lord returned from the war today and pleasured me twice in his top-boots.' The so-called 'flasher' is also, though he may not realise it, seeking to dominate observers by drawing attention to his manhood, and the masochist reinforces dominance by willingly submitting to it.

The purpose of this digression is to remind ourselves that dominant behaviour, by a forceful exercise of will, is a natural phenomenon, not necessarily to be discouraged or lamented. It has given us heroes and saints. But when it is used for entirely destructive ends, it becomes worrying, and such is the case with many of the most disturbing murders, not all of which can be ascribed to those personality disorders or mental defects we considered earlier. There are some in which the motive can only be a florid expression of the will-to-power.

Such is the case with rapists as well as murderers, and there are many rapists who do not intend murder (who may not even think about it) but whose degradation and humiliation of the victim sometimes leads to murder as the lust for power increases and feeds upon itself. That the satisfaction of will and power rather than sex is the purpose of the attack is often demonstrated by the excessive amount of force employed, far more than would be necessary to induce compliance in sexual intercourse; also by the occasional use of objects to penetrate the victim and cause fear, as well as reducing the sexual act to ridicule and contempt; finally, by the accompaniment of angry noises, insults, verbal abuse and a disproportionate display of disgust.

The closer one examines the evidence of rape, the more obvious it becomes that the rapist is an inadequate individual who is deeply insecure about how to exercise power and worried that it might not work. Victims who have survived sometimes testify that the rapist wanted her to hold his penis and insert it into herself, as if he did not have the confidence or courage to do it unaided. ('Get hold of me, hold it, put it in . . . put it inside you . . . put it back . . . you do it, you'll have to put it in.'[19]) One may discern that this strategy also serves subconsciously to exculpate the rapist if and when guilt should overwhelm him (i.e. I didn't do it, she did it herself, she wanted it). When it comes to the full sexual murderer, however, no such tentative inhibitions operate at all, and the resulting attack can be so horrific as to defy belief.

Lust murder is statistically rare, but when it occurs it naturally attracts frantic publicity. Not even the worst newspapers can bring themselves to report some of the details, and I shall forbear to fill the gap; those with the appetite for it may find full reports elsewhere. The Moors Murders of thirty years ago are still vivid in the minds of everyone then alive and literate. Ian Brady and Myra Hindley tortured and slowly killed a number of children in the sitting-room, even going so far as to record their victims' screams and pitiful pleas for release before they died. These were played in court at the trial, but some other specifics were withheld. It was fitting that Emlyn Williams, who knew what these were, entitled his book on the case *Beyond Belief*. There is some reason to suppose that the Brady/Hindley affair was an example of *folie à deux*, wherein one partner initiates the offence while the other is swept along by the display of power and its insidious control of normal reaction. Lord Longford is probably right to pursue his advocacy in favour of Myra Hindley, who he insists has long since been a fundamentally different woman, a stranger to the puppet she was, despite the fact that it was she who procured the children for her lover Brady to kill. Brady, on the other hand, has never repented or taken the measure of what he did, and properly belongs in another chapter. He is now in Ashworth Hospital, Liverpool, and grows progressively more insane.

Another well-known example is that of Charles Manson in California. If Brady and Hindley were *folie à deux*, then Manson and his 'family' were an illustration of the even rarer *folie à plusieurs*. Manson exercised such power and influence over his three girlfriends and disciples, Patricia Krenwinkel, Leslie van Houten and Susan Atkins, that they were happy to slaughter and eviscerate filmstar Sharon Tate, heavily pregnant, and remain utterly indifferent to her cries for mercy. Yet these three young women were more or less the same age as their victim and had, a year or two before, been reasonably normal girls. More murders were committed by them at the instigation of Manson before they were caught. This is clearly a case of power, although unusually exercised by proxy, for Manson was not himself present at the killings. His power was not over the victims but over his slaves – the murderers – and they absorbed his extraordinary will, allowing it to operate through them. It could be argued that Manson, too, belongs to another chapter, for he seems on the face of it to be the perfect embodiment of the Devil. Yet he showed no more signs of possession than did the three girls. His was a perversion of the will to power, and theirs a culpable acquiescence in it.

Time and again one finds that the need to have control over the victim (and by extension, over the attacker's own life, identity, self-description and ultimate fate) takes precedence over the desire to kill. In the cases of both Nilsen and Dahmer, killing was only part of the exercise of power, a power grown exigent by its systematic denial on a lower level over a period of years. Nilsen kept the bodies of his victims for months, proud of his ability to resurrect them from beneath the floorboards whenever he chose, and force them to be his companions whether they liked it or not. When they were alive he found himself repeatedly in the Sartrean dilemma of being 'fixed' by their gaze, the person they described; he 'belonged' to them in so far as their description was finite and constricting ('boring, long-winded, self-opinionated, stubborn, egocentric'), and by killing them he escaped them. It would be facile to point out that he cancelled their power and asserted his own – that much is obvious – but it is worth saying that this was his aim and his need, to the fulfilment of which death was incidental.

Jeffrey Dahmer had lost power over his own body at the age of four, when he was subjected to a double hernia operation. The rest of his life was spent in a void of uselessness, accepting the world's view that he was powerless to have any influence over his own life or anyone else's. His voice assumed the unnerving blandness of a flat monotone, he never smiled, he did nothing. His father despaired of his future, but he meanwhile discovered he could have some control over dead things, the corpses of animals whom he would dissect, deconstruct, and put together again. By the time of his arrest, he had performed the same operation upon seventeen young men, whom he had first murdered. However unpleasant it may be to think about, and however distressing for the families of those who died, the deaths of those boys restored to Dahmer his evanescent sense of power and seriously improved his own self-image.

Three final cases may serve to show what may happen when the will is hungry and unfettered. The most upsetting is that of Roy Norris and Lawrence Bittaker, who kidnapped and murdered teenage girls in the summer of 1979 in southern California. Their crimes were remarkable for the degree of unspeakable torture they inflicted upon their victims and the consistency with which they photographed each girl at various moments of subjugation and unexampled terror. They had a special van with a sliding door to facilitate the kidnap, and most of the assaults were conducted in this van. All the girls were raped several times as a matter of course. One was stabbed in the ear with an icepick and then strangled with a coathanger. Another had her nipples torn off with pliers while she screamed in agony. 'The rape wasn't really the important part,' said Norris, 'it was the dominance.'[20]

This is even more clear in the notorious abduction of Colleen Stan, again in California, on 19 May, 1977. She was hitch-hiking and was offered a ride by a young married couple, he bespectacled and timid, she with a baby on her lap. They seemed safe enough. It was not long before Colleen found herself in the cellar of a house, where she was subjected to a series of terrible and bizarre humiliations. She was suspended

162

naked from beams and whipped, before the couple had sexual intercourse beneath her feet. Then a wooden box was placed over her head, and she was locked in a larger box where she defecated and urinated and became filthy. The man held her under water until she nearly drowned, taking photographs the while, and his wife clipped off Colleen's tangled hair. She remained in this state for six months, until she was given minor jobs to do, like shelling walnuts. She was then made to sign a document giving herself over body and soul to her captor, as his slave, part of the contract being that she should keep her orifices ready for him at any time, never wear panties and in his presence keep her knees apart. If he shouted 'Attention' she had to strip naked and stand on tiptoe with her hands raised above her head. Afterwards, she went back into her box.

After three years of this incredible treatment, Colleen was so brainwashed by her captor, whose name, by the way, was Cameron Hooker, that she was allowed to go jogging, to go to a dance, to telephone her parents, without ever feeling the wish (or perhaps the ability) to escape. She always returned to do her duties as slave and went back into her box. Once Hooker gave her permission to stay with her family for the weekend, but after she had spent one night there he telephoned to say he was coming to fetch her. She was disappointed but not disobedient.

Cameron Hooker, his wife Janice and Colleen the slave began reading the Bible together and going to church. Meanwhile he would routinely strangle her to the point that she passed out. Eventually, she got a job in a motel, always going 'home' to her box afterwards. It was Janice, probably jealous by now, who spilled the beans to the local vicar, who in turn informed the police. Colleen's imprisonment had lasted seven years.[21]

As an illustration of the aphrodisiacal properties of power, the Cameron Hooker case can scarcely be bettered, but it is the compliance of Colleen Stan in her own degradation which must cause the most disquiet. Can one person's will really be so strong as to cancel that of

163

another, to radically undermine the other's personality? If so, then it may not be so easy to condemn the activities of ordinary German citizens who found themselves herding fellow humans into gas ovens. The whole subject of mass acquiescence in evil conduct is too big for a parenthesis, and we shall return to it in a later chapter.

As we have seen, sex and power often interweave, and one may easily be mistaken for the other. Many rapes use sex only as a means to a different end, as Nilsen killed in order to have corpses about the house. One case of almost pure power control, with virtually no aphrodisiacal content, came before Liverpool Crown Court in 1988, when June and Hilda Thompson were tried for the murder of their father Tommy. They were not the sadists, but rather the victims of over forty years' abuse by their father, who had systematically erased any personality they might have evolved in the service of his overweening will. The sisters' lives were regimented to a maniacal degree. They had to draw the curtains at 7:35 precisely every evening, or they would be beaten; a minute premature or tardy deserved punishment. Cups and saucers had to be placed exactly three inches from the edge of the table, food had to be stored according to equally mathematical instructions, and the washing-up had to be performed noiselessly, without a single plate or knife touching any other plate or knife. When Tommy felt like bashing his wife, the daughters would stand silently either side of her as he punched her in the face or kicked her in the shins, so as to prevent her falling (one of her eyes was permanently dislodged as a result of repetitive beating). June and Hilda were routinely raped by their father from puberty until well into their forties, but there was never any sexual excitement involved on his part; the rape would take place between television programmes, as a result of a slight nod of his head, interpreted after long practice as a signal for one of the girls to go upstairs and prepare herself. The girls eventually shot him dead as he lay one day on the couch. Passing sentence of two years' suspended imprisonment, the judge acknowledged that their lives had been one uninterrupted torment and that they had been punished long before the crime.[22]

Tommy Thompson refined the art of control by effort of will to a degree which, fortunately, is extremely rare, though some readers will have noticed marriages in which the husband contrives to create a domestic dictatorship with less gruesome results. Free will, when it becomes the sole expression of personality, can be a dangerous and mournful thing. For Thompson, his choice was the only value he knew how to recognise, his exercise of power the only event in the daily life of a family which knew no solace or pleasure.

June and Hilda now live quietly and peaceably in their tiny house. They still do the washing up noiselessly and still place the cups in the allotted position on the table. Their dead father controls them to this day.

7

LOOKING OUT

Thus far, it is evident that the development of a conscience and the capacity to do good depend upon the healthy exercise of will-power. Conversely, the denial of conscience and the disposition to do ill result from an unhealthy, or perverted, exercise of the same will. I hope it is gradually becoming clear that, in the former case, it is proper to talk of 'free will', while in the latter it would be more accurate to speak of 'trapped' or 'stunted' will. Its power remains strong, but its direction has been distorted or turned awry by circumstances.

We are not talking here of the various deterministic theories which seek to ascribe behaviour to an ineluctable 'human nature', to genetic programming, or to the preoccupations of our pre-hominoid ancestors, all of which have been considered earlier. Mental disease has also been removed from the debate. Once the exercise of individual will through choice is accepted (and conduct which is morally describable is *always* a matter of choosing from alternatives), the question as to why that choice sometimes falls upon doing harm must belong to the circumstances in which the individual has been placed in the world. This is what the nineteenth-century French historian and moralist Hippolyte Taine called *le milieu* and *le moment* (to add to *la race*, by which he meant the whole baggage of genetic determinants), and what we tend rather too neatly to call 'nurture' (as opposed to 'nature'). *Le milieu et le moment* represent all those social, historical and familial conditions which help shape the person and either release or thwart his will.

It is obvious that harsh physical conditions must to

some extent atrophy the development of conscience. The man who lives through one Arctic winter after another is likely to have the survival of his family and the provision of their food higher on his agenda than the niceties of decent interfamilial conduct, and these will anyway be dictated by the need to maintain his health and happiness, as provider, before the others. Similarly, it is useless to ask a starving Saharan nomad or an Indian untouchable to think about the advisability of doing good in this world. Extremes apart, and given relatively ordinary geographical and social conditions in Western civilisations, we still find that the will can be rendered un-free by aberrations of upbringing, and for an examination of these we must return to a theme adumbrated in Chapter Two on the naturalness of aggression – namely the emotional environment of the growing child.

'The chief enemy of excellence in morality,' writes Iris Murdoch, 'is personal fantasy: the tissue of self-aggrandizing and consoling wishes and dreams which prevents one from seeing what is there outside one.'[1] In simpler (and shallower) terms, selfishness is the enemy of morally good conduct, which is so obvious as to seem tautologous, but this trite remark holds a deeper and more complex truth, namely that the ability *not* to be selfish, that is the capacity for empathy, has to be *learnt*, and through it must come one's freedom and the will to do what is good. The newly born infant is completely dependent upon its mother and greedily looks to her to provide succour and survival. Total self-absorption is both natural and necessary at this stage. But when the need to be fed has been satisfied, a second, equally imperative need arises, the need for approval and love. This, too, the parent has to provide, and in such measure that the infant learns to trust that love, to rely upon it, and to feel secure with it. The child is still egocentric at this stage, although he has made one step towards altruism, in so far as he has learnt that mother is not just a mammary gland or fast-food shop, but a person

167

too, one whose approval is to be sought and cherished. It is the first step in recognising that there *is* somebody else, that others exist in the world.

The next step is to realise that these others also have their needs, also want to be approved and loved, and that in the reciprocity of giving and receiving love and approval lies the satisfaction of everyone. This is the very source of empathy, without which no morally good behaviour would be possible, for it is only by being able to place oneself in somebody else's position that we can conceive of what might be good or bad for that other person. Empathy is the imagination of the soul, the projection outside oneself by feeling (obviously in imagination only) what the other person is feeling. It is not only the source of all goodness, but the premiss for all art, the *sine qua non* of Greek theatre, Shakespeare, Arthur Miller. Without the imaginative leap necessary to adopt somebody else's position, all drama would be mere parcels of words. So empathy is the very root of both conscience and intellectual understanding.

Just as empathy is lacking in the newly born infant, so is it in the fully grown psychopath; in the one it has not had time to grow, in the other it has failed to grow. In this sense alone, the psychopath is but an embryonic person, one without a conscience. It is as though there were no space, apart from the mathematics of years, between his infancy and his adulthood. Anti-social personalities share this characteristic of being utterly unable to identify with other people, to imagine what it might be like to be them, and therefore unable to notice or care if they suffer. Virtually all studies of anti-social criminals reach the conclusion that they have not learnt the reciprocity of love because they never had the opportunity to discover that approval may be bestowed as well as earned. Having been denied approval, they never sought to give it. They do not know what it is. Empathy is unintelligible to them, and so appeal to their conscience is shouting into the wind.

This is why child abuse, of which we hear far more

these days than its actual incidence should merit, is so fatal. The worst abuse is that which denies the child the possibility of developing its own internal regulator of what is right and wrong and ultimately condemns him to being *unable* to do good. That is a worse deprivation than silly sexual play, for it deprives the victim of his humanity.

Even in adulthood, the damage may be revisited. Brian Keenan spent long years as a hostage chained to a wall in a dark, silent cellar in Beirut. 'Humanization is a reciprocal thing,' he wrote. 'We cannot know ourselves or declare ourselves human unless we share in the humanity of another.'[2] Isolation threatened to reduce Keenan artificially to the helpless, dependent condition of an infant, and it was only his fierce stability of personality which prevented him losing grip on his conscience and on his ability to think goodness.

When a child receives the required amount of love and approval from his mother, he banks it. It provides him with the confidence that he is in fact lovable, and gives him an inner reserve of self-esteem which he can call upon when faced with disappointment or rejection later in life. As I have said, he is then free to mature into an emotional understanding that others need love as well as he, and develop the altruism which equips him to give it. In other words, once he knows that other people are good to him, and he knows how and why they are good, he is able to be good towards them. By looking at examples of children in whom this development has been interrupted or stifled we may better see the conditions in which altruism can flourish. Alas, there are all too many of these bruised individuals.

(This is why the fashionable right-wing theory that self-interest is the first duty and altruism defeatist is so terribly wrong. The whole edifice of political and social selfishness was recently demolished by David Selbourne in *The Principle of Duty*, and before him frequently by Bertrand Russell. As far back as Cicero we find condemnation of the notion that as long as I look after myself I am doing the right thing. 'There are some also who, either from zeal in attending to their own business or through some sort of aversion to their fellow men, claim that they are occupied solely with their own affairs, without seeming to themselves to be doing anyone any injury. But while they steer clear of one kind of injustice, they fall into the other; they are traitors to social life, for they contribute to it none of their interest, none of their effort, none of their means.' And again, it ought to be the chief end of all men 'to make the interest of each individual and of the whole body politic identical. For, if the individual appropriates to selfish ends what should be devoted to the common good, all human fellowship will be destroyed.'[3] One wonders how much development has been denied to those Tory ideologues who cannot see this.)

Dr Lionel Dahmer has been candid about his evasiveness and aloofness towards his son Jeff as he was growing up. Jeff was never 'abused' in the sense in which the word is generally used today. His parents were comfortably well off, they lived in a decent home, he was not battered or beaten or sexually tampered with. But his father, himself inhibited by shyness and exaggerated reserve, was distant and barely tactile, while his mother was self-absorbed, filling herself with pills and medicines. The parents quarrelled repeatedly, leaving Jeff to form the inner conclusion that he did not matter. From this, it was an easy route to the notion that nobody mattered, and that emotions had no part in his life.

Dr Dahmer paints an uncomfortable scene of an encounter with Jeff after his arraignment on sixteen charges of murder. He says he saw the mark of his son's madness, like a scar across his face, when he said he was sorry:

> It was impossible to tell whom he felt sorry for, or what he felt sorry about. He could not even imitate regret, much less truly feel it. Remorse was beyond him, and he could probably sense it only as an emotion

felt by people in another galaxy. He was beyond the call of a role, incapable of acting a part. His 'Sorry' was a mummified remain, an artifact retained from that distant time when he'd still been able to sense, if only to imitate, a normal range of feeling. Suddenly, I thought of Jeff's childhood, and his general remoteness no longer looked like shyness, but like disconnection, the opening of an unbridgeable abyss. His eyes no longer struck me as merely expressionless, but as utterly void, beyond the call of the most basic forms of sympathy and understanding, beyond even the capacity to ape such emotions. As he stood before me at that instant, my son, perhaps for the first time in his adult life, presented himself to me as he really was, destitute of feeling, his emotions shaved down to a bare minimum, a young man who was deeply, deeply ill, and for whom, in all likelihood, there was no way out.[4]

It is part of my thesis that the impulse to do good is a free expression of the will, and the action of doing harm is a distortion of that will (in a sense, therefore, not really 'wilful'). Dr Dahmer found himself confronted with a son whose will had been wrenched from him, leaving him as an empty shell. Cognitively, his grasp of right and wrong was intact, but there was no emotional reflection of this knowledge and therefore no proper way of applying it to people. He had never learnt the empathetic response and was bereft of imagination. He could not escape the claustrophobia of his egocentricity; as his father intuited, the route had been blocked. Jeff was trapped in the infant's condition.

The idea that a child's freedom of will can be removed by abuse or emotional neglect finds frequent corroboration in the accounts of the childhoods of many violent offenders. There is usually a feeling of having been subjected to overwhelming energy from outside, which robbed them in some way of their autonomous power, depleted them, emptied them. This in turn made it impossible for them to relate with other people except in terms of the power of one over the other – never in terms of reciprocal delight. We have already seen in Chapter 2 that Dahmer's history carries an actual physical event which allows one to specify precisely when this kidnapping of the will occurred. At the age of four he was taken to hospital with severe abdominal pains. A double hernia operation ensued, involving the invasion of his body by strangers' hands. In the light of his parents' peculiar distance, this was virtually the first intimate contact he had had with anyone, and it resulted in his violation (in his eyes), the snatching away of part of him into the power of others. It was never explained to him what had happened. From that day, he was unable to think of people as sentient beings, but only as purloiners of power. It is significant that, when as an adult he did spend time with someone, he liked best to place his ear to the person's stomach in order to listen to the burblings of the machine inside, and that with all his killings, the first incision he made to the corpse was in the abdomen, so that he could plunge his hands into the intestines. His victims had become his objects.

It is commonplace, too, that the lack of empathetic responses in small children leads them into speculative cruelty towards animals. Usually, it is cats and dogs that are the most vilely treated, specifically because they have an emotional symbiotic relationship with man and can form affectionate ties. Cruelty thereby violates this bond, negates and besmirches it, in a way that cruelty towards an ant could not. It is a sure sign that the child's development is at risk and that the internal regulator of his behaviour is not functioning as it should. Oddly enough, though Jeffrey Dahmer was not cruel to animals, he was indifferent to their souls, as it were. When he cuddled a rabbit or a puppy, it was to feel how they were put together, where the bones were, and how they worked. As to the life which animated them, he knew nothing. Later he would collect the corpses of animals killed on the road and take them apart; to him, they were machines.

In very rare cases, the absence of empathy may result in the child withdrawing into the featureless, mechanical world of mathematics, taking refuge in numbers and avoiding effective contact with people altogether. Not only can they not imagine the lives of others, they do not even see other people. They are cocooned, protected and, in every moral sense, dead. Fortunately, they are also entirely harmless. A famous case in the 1960s brought to international attention twenty-six-year-old twins, John and Michael, whose 'eidetic memory' enabled them to say with accuracy on what day of the week a certain date far in the future would fall (or had fallen in the far distant past). They were scrupulously detailed in their attention to facts as well as figures, which they related, when invited, in a monotonous, 'necrophilic' voice, but were totally obtuse in their responses to anything human, emotional, interesting or vivid. In truth, they did not respond to such matters at all, for these subjects did not exist for them.

Oliver Sacks has described an encounter with Michael and John, who had been in institutions from the age of seven, because they had been thought retarded, autistic, or mad. They answered his questions in a childlike and clockwork manner. 'Give them a date,' he wrote,

> and their eyes roll for a moment, and then fixate, and in a flat, monotonous voice they tell you of the weather, the bare political events they would have heard of, and the events of their own lives – this last often including the painful or poignant anguish of childhood, the contempt, the jeers, the mortifications they endured, but all delivered in an even and unvarying tone, without the least hint of any personal inflection or emotion. Here, clearly, one is dealing with memories that seem of a 'documentary' kind, in which there is no personal reference, no personal relation, no living centre whatever.[5]

It is interesting that Dahmer had the same blank, dead, unvarying voice, and Nilsen had a small degree of the same accuracy about numbers, as if he were in thrall to them. He could recall the exact date of every significant event of his life, or even the insignificant ones, such as the day he started work at a particular job fifteen years previously. It is as though both these men went down the same road as Michael and John, but did not go so far. Had they done so, and sought 'safety in numbers', they may well not have had to treat people as if they were numbers, too, and a lot of young men would not have died. All these people have something in common; they are slivers from the same trunk.

When one examines the history of convicted murderers, the long, nasty process of squeezing out the juice of their humanity in early childhood makes very unpleasant reading. It cannot be known for sure how many people Henry Lee Lucas murdered (at one point he confessed to hundreds), but it is known that he had miserable beginnings. His mother, a prostitute, beat him without mercy at every opportunity, with any weapon which came to hand. She would not let him cry. She dressed him in a girl's frock and made his blond hair into curls on his first day at school. The teacher, seeing that he was seriously undernourished, saved some of her sandwiches for him and gave him a pair of shoes. He smelled very bad, was filthy and verminous, and was shunned by every other child. Lucas recalled that his earliest memory was of his mother, having finished with one of her customers, shooting him in the leg and spattering her son's body with the stranger's blood.[6]

A fourteen-year-old murderer identified only as 'Tom' was kept in a garden shed and fed scraps from the family table; he had brothers and sisters who were treated normally. Tom's only friend, the only object of his faltering empathetic sense, was his cat. One day his uncle strangled the cat before his eyes. Tom prepared a neat grave for his pet. The uncle trampled it down and smashed the wooden cross. It was then that Tom killed his family with a shotgun. They were effectively the instruments of their own deaths; though they had not succeeded in removing Tom's capacity to feel altogether (his killing of them was a *crime passionel*, the result of feeling), they had conquered his capacity to care.[7]

Charles Manson, the organiser of pitiless murders committed by his 'Family' in 1969, was also the son of a prostitute. He had no known father, and grew up on street corners and in bars, while his mother hustled. No affection was ever shown towards him; on the contrary, whenever his grandfather tried to show any warmth towards his grandmother, he was rebuked as a sinner, so that the young Charles had demonstrated to him the dangers of empathy. He spent all his youth in remand homes and prisons, was raped and tormented by other prisoners and warders, was taught, in fact, that people treat one another as objects to be used for personal gratification and promptly discarded. There was never any chance that he would develop the necessary emotional skills to want to be kind and altruistic.

The most graphic example, however, comes from fiction. Mary Shelley's *Frankenstein*, first published in 1818, is known to virtually every literate person in the English-speaking world, at least by name. There have been many film adaptations of the story, nearly all of them deeply misleading, not to say fraudulent, with the result that most people assume the story is about a wicked doctor who creates a monster in a laboratory, which monster then runs amok and frightens everyone rigid. It is often also assumed that the name of the monster is Frankenstein. In fact, Viktor Frankenstein is the doctor, and the human being he manufactures is called the Creature. Mrs Shelley's powerful parable has a strong moral point which is often missed; she purports to show that the Creature is inherently good and potentially beneficent, but that his moral parameters are broken down by the people around him and he is forced to become wicked when he is rejected by society. The professor of psychology David Canter lists the consequences of this treatment:

One is that he is never able to develop productive, warm relationships with other people, thereby becoming increasingly callous. The second is that the only illustrations he is given of how to behave are those of other people reacting viciously to him. One other most important consequence, central to Frankenstein's tragedy, is the monster's desire to have a female of his kind with whom he can form a mutually supportive relationship . . . Viktor refuses this request, realizing that there are some fatal flaws in the make-up of the fiend that would only be magnified if he had a sexual partner with whom to produce offspring. Mary Shelley's novel leaves us with the question of whether the evil nature of the monster was really created by a lack of emotional shape and support, as would be expected of any child abandoned by its family at birth, made worse by the vicious way he is treated.[8]

In contrast, the Abbey of Rievaulx in the twelfth century, under the direction of the saintly and patient Aelred, was a model of what blessings may ensue from a truly empathetic society. All Aelred's monks were encouraged to care and feel for one another to such a degree that one writer referred to the abbey at this time as being infused with 'a radiance of affection',[9] and everyone felt loved and appreciated. It was a veritable school of psychological well-being and it demonstrated, better than anywhere else, how the development of a moral sense and disposition to behave well derives from close emotional bonding. Aelred of Rievaulx did not merely tolerate friendships between his monks, he encouraged them, for he was convinced that all life was a progression, and the development of emotional maturity was an essential prerequisite to good deeds. People flocked to the monastery, and on feast days they would be like bees in unbudgeable clusters. Aelred never turned anyone away, and he soon banished the old custom of silence which had enjoined the novice to address no-one but the abbot, the prior, or the novice-master.

According to his own account in *Speculum Caritatis*, Rievaulx Abbey bustled with chatter as groups of monks assembled in amity and unity of mind.

Many monasteries today cite Aelred as an example of far-sightedness in his tolerance of affectionate social bonds. Schools of both psychology and moral philosophy would do well also to look to him as the celebrator of empathy in the formation of character and kindly disposition.

The knowledge that one is lovable, then, gives one the freedom to develop one's potential for benevolence and grow into a moral being; without it, there is little chance of either. Even so, such knowledge of lovableness is insufficient by itself, for there follow other exigent needs to be fulfilled before a properly integrated, beneficent personality can emerge. One of these is the need to achieve, to do something well or be someone impressive, be it only within the tight family circle, so that the seeds of self-esteem might be sown. As with affection and empathy, the inter-relation of these forces is almost circular. You must esteem yourself before you have the emotional wherewithal to esteem others, and without the regard of others, you are unlikely to think much of yourself. But it is possible to disentangle the carts and horses in order to observe that, yet again, the onus of fruitful progress towards moral equilibrium must lie with the parents. Part of their function is to ensure that the developing child has some reason to be proud of himself. He must feel the glow of admiration upon him.

It is perfectly possible for a child to feel secure in so far as he is loved, but disappointed that he appears not to be valued, as if the love bestowed were undeserved. When there occurs this mismatch between potential and achievement, the resulting frustration can be just as damaging as a failure of empathetic development, as a resentment may fester for years and revenge explode in the most unexpected situations. The typically under-valued child will feel that he is constantly put upon by his

177

father, his teachers, his schoolfellows, but that he should not be angry about it because he does, after all, have some kind of love, which should be enough. Incipient guilt may accompany this unravelling of desires and satisfactions, and the child, fearful of showing ingratitude, may well get his own back on total strangers.

Lionel Dahmer, who mercifully did not, like his son, take symbolic vengeance upon an unappreciative world, nevertheless was manifestly an under-achiever, and he passed this characteristic genetically on to his son. His account of his own early years is so typical of thwarted self-esteem that it deserves lengthy quotation:

> When I look back on my childhood, I see its continuing theme as a reaction against my own pervasive sense of powerlessness, that dreadful feeling that I could not do anything right, could not control anything, could not take charge. More than anything during my childhood, I was plagued by the certainty that I was both physically weak and intellectually inferior. As a young boy, I was almost the stereotype of the weak skinny kid, the last to be picked for any sports team. I was the elementary-school kid who was bullied, the kid who was easily frightened, the kid who had glasses and was called 'four eyes'. In high school, I was the kid the girls hardly noticed, except as an object of curiosity, the kid who never even had a date until he was eighteen, the kid who finally decided that a 'great body' was what the girls wanted, and who then methodically went about the task of creating one, working out three times a day until the 'skinny kid' had been replaced by someone else . . . I was an average student, slow to learn, particularly in math. From the first grade onward, my parents tried to help me become a better student by drilling me. My father spent countless hours tutoring me. My mother spent almost as much time making flip cards in addition and subtraction, multiplication and division, and by constantly quizzing. The idea that I developed was

178

that I had to 'overstudy' everything, and that if I did not, I would fail ... Though my mother never intended it, and was only trying to help me, a feeling of personal incompetence overwhelmed me during those early years. It was made more obvious by her extraordinary ability to assert herself, to take charge of things ... Compared to such a force, I naturally saw myself as weak and inept. As a result, of course, I began to develop a feeling of nearly complete powerlessness and dependency. Even more telling, however, was my mother's tendency to finish things for me before I had a chance to complete them myself. I would start some task, working slowly through it, as I always did, and suddenly my mother would appear, and in a few quick strokes, either of mind or hand, she would finish it for me. Even though done in a helpful, loving manner, it was a gesture that powerfully reinforced my sense of myself as slow and inept and which caused me to doubt my ability to do things, to carry through, to complete even the simplest tasks. I think that in order to act against my own corrosive and infuriating sense of weakness and inferiority, I began to gravitate towards violence.[10]

He means *thoughts* of violence, and refers to making bombs with his chemistry set and hypnotising a little girl, in itself an act of power- and control-assertion. With Lionel, the compensation for his inadequacies went no further and he plunged into the scientific life, studying well into adulthood, constantly keeping at it lest he lose the knack and the admiration of people close to him. But his depiction of the prevailing atmosphere of a childhood sunk in failure, *despite* the admitted love he received from his parents, could not be more accurate.

Among psychologists it was Adler who first spotted that the need for achievement was an essential building-brick in the evolution of a harmonious personality (and, by extension, of a moral being). In a phrase that has since become a cliché, he established that the unfettered continuance of an 'inferiority complex' was a potentially dangerous phenomenon. Whereas Marx had thought the need for health and security was all that mattered, and Freud had insisted upon emotional security, happiness and sex, Adler added the element of self-esteem and social regard. After him Jung would point to the need for self-fulfilment as the final ingredient in the brew. For none of these insights is exclusive of the others, although it was not until Abaraham Maslow's work was published in 1962 that their fusion was realised.

Maslow said there was a 'hierarchy of needs', all omnipresent and simultaneous in the individual, but requiring satisfaction in a certain order. First, there were the basic physiological needs to sustain life, such as food, protein, water and exercise, which presumably were shared by every living creature. A human child who was always undernourished would never progress beyond this animal stage of stomach-need and would therefore be denied the opportunity to grow into a fully human person. He would forever remain indifferent to questions of moral choice and perception; they would not arise, would have no relevance. (Although, as we have seen in Chapter Three, even at this level some kind of embryonic ethical sense may be observed among animals who will share food when they are themselves hungry.)

When the need for bodily sustenance is satisfied, there emerges the second rung of the hierarchy, the need for order and security, which includes shelter, routine, and protection from fear. These Maslow calls 'safety' needs, which, once satisfied, are followed by 'social' needs, or the craving to belong. On this level will come the love from and for parents and siblings and the search for friendship, to be supplemented in adolescence by tense and exclusive love for one person. When these needs are satisfied, as we have just seen, then empathy for others and identification with them will emerge, permitting the development of a rich moral sense.

Maslow places the need for self-esteem, status, acknowledgement and success on the fourth level, to be reached only when hunger, safety and emotion have been well catered for. This is the Adlerian level, just as perilous as the Freudian level which preceded it. The number of personality crises arising from an inability to satisfy this level of need is alarming, as both testimony from psychiatrists and crime statistics indicate. The final level is 'self-actualization', or the realisation of one's full potential in personality and ambition. It was this fifth stage in the hierarchy which gave rise to Maslow's fame in the culture of the 1960s as encourager of the drop-out or apologist for the 'do-your-own-thing' generation. He was said to support the notion that to be one's true self was the height of bliss and his celebration of the 'peak experience' was used as an excuse for shallow exultism.

Maslow was misunderstood, and he later detracted somewhat from the beautiful synthesis of his scheme by pointing out that the fifth stage did not necessarily follow on from the previous four, but was arbitrarily distributed. In other words, it was possible to be an integrated and effective person when the first four needs were addressed, without the necessity to soar like Beethoven on to the fifth. It was, however, important to insist on the *simultaneous* nature of these needs; they were always present, and did not disappear once they had been satisfied. The need for love may be fulfilled at one point in a person's life, enabling him to progress on to the next need, that for status. But if love floundered, a retrogressive crisis would be created, and the hole made by that need would have quickly to be plugged before concentration on esteem could be resumed. An example might be the character played by Penelope Keith in Alan Ayckbourn's trilogy *The Norman Conquests*, who is compulsively removing invisible specks of dust and folding napkins because a crisis has resurrected that childhood second level of need, that for order, security and routine. This must be resolved before she can turn her attention back to love-needs.

181

When all four levels of need are harmoniously fulfilled, a person may be said to be whole. All too often, however, the progression breaks down at the fourth level, and some very curious types of behaviour may then occur. The man who sees himself a failure *as a human being* will behave, for the most part, in an inadequate, listless, colourless, ineffective manner, as if to confirm his low worth, unable to think or do anything useful for anyone; he is almost zombie-like and ethically flat. This condition is once again perfectly caught in Lionel Dahmer's description of his son Jeff after his arrest:

> My mind recalled only a young man who was passive and more or less nondescript, a failure at almost everything he'd ever tried, a mixer in a chocolate factory, a job that placed him barely above a menial labourer. Now he was not only famous, but the catalyst for a thousand different reactions. All his life, he had been so very small, it seemed to me. There were times he'd been so small that I'd scarcely seen him at all. Now he was gigantic, the public personality around whom enormous forces swirled. How could this be the same Jeff who spoke in mumbled sentences, who'd sold blood for liquor, who'd muttered his characteristic 'Sorry!' at every offence, then slunk away, embarrassed and ashamed? How could so small and insignificant a man be blown up to such dimensions at such a blinding speed? How could so grey and unaccented and generally pathetic a figure generate such passion? Never had the vast gulf that had separated what Jeff was and what he had done seemed so wide.[11]

The same could be said for many a serial killer. Ted Bundy had likewise seen himself as a loser, though he had presented a far more plausible mask to the world than had the featureless Jeffrey Dahmer. His murders may be interpreted as erupting from a long-disguised failure to attain Maslow's crucial level of self-esteem, as may the terrible crimes of David Berkowitz, 'Son of Sam', in New York.

Fortunately, most men compensate for their failure in far less gruesome fashion. A typical response might be to slide into what Colin Wilson has called the 'Roman Emperor syndrome', whereby inadequate men manufacture a situation in which they can pretend to have massive power. There are men who as soon as they enter the married state assume dictatorial influence over their wives and children, treating them as their subjects; their every whim must be honoured, their every instruction, however absurd, immediately obeyed. (The cruelty of Thompson to his wife and daughters, mentioned on page 164, is akin to this behaviour, though we know too little of Mr Thompson's early life to ascribe it specifically to his inability to reach Maslow's fourth level of need.) If the miserable wife plucks up courage to leave her spouse, he generally crumbles and can become suicidal. Other manifestations of the Roman Emperor syndrome are the office brute, the megalomaniac entrepreneur (Robert Maxwell), the politician wracked by insatiable ambition.

The point is that none of these people, whether or not they resort to murder in order to shore up their pitiful personalities, could ever be capable of an act of goodness. The ethical dimension of life is denied them, for that must come with maturity and integration of soul. One may look for saints among sinners, but not among losers.

8

AVOWED INTENT

And so it is to sinners that we must turn. Having established that it is possible to do good when the inheritance is pure, the brain unpolluted by disease, and the will unfettered by circumstance, the question must arise whether, given all these perfect conditions, good behaviour is inevitable. And if it is, should it be measured by intent or by result? A blockage of the will must surely cancel intent, for the agent of the intending would not be efficient; but can a free will do harm by accident, where no intention is involved? Conversely, can one intend to do harm and achieve no such consequence, thus being good by default? Is saintliness in the mind or in the effect?

David carried the Ark of the Covenant on a cart which jolted as it passed over rough terrain. In order to protect the Ark, Uzzah stretched up his hand to steady it. For this impious act he was immediately struck dead. His intention had been good, but that did not prevent his being punished.[1]

Conversely, St Thomas Aquinas thought that one could not commit an evil act with intent. Evil came through second causes (like a good artist with bad tools) and was therefore accidental.

We come back to the matter of responsibility, the *leit-motif* of this enquiry, and how this affects our ethical distinctions and, ultimately, our legal definitions. It is assumed in most systems of jurisprudence that the intent to do wrong must be present for a defendant to be found guilty of doing wrong. Where the intent is absent, by virtue of an inability to distinguish right from wrong, it is usually deemed that, despite the effect, no crime has been committed. But before looking at the legal perceptions of right and wrong, it is important we should be clear about the ethical presumptions underlying them. We should not confuse our understanding of what is an intentional action with how laws decree that such intentional action should be treated.

The mediaeval philosopher Peter Abelard said that a sinful act not intended to be sinful was in essence innocent, because the soul could not be corrupted by what the body did. He held that sinfulness *must* therefore involve intent.[2] Lifted out of religious language, this means that you have to want to do something bad in order for badness to be an inherent quality of your act; the will must be intact and active. Eight hundred years later, we still enshrine this principle in our law, for the crimes of theft, burglary, fraud and murder, for instance, all require what lawyers call a 'specific intent' to be proven for the offence to be designated 'criminal'. In many cases it has been held that no such specific intent can be present if the offender was so drunk at the time of the offence that he literally did not know what he was doing (although both Nilsen and Dahmer, whose crimes were committed in a state of intoxication, failed to convince the courts that this impaired their responsibility, and Dahmer did not even try). Similarly, mental disease or defect must preclude wilful intent.

The most famous modern example of a defence of no wilful intent is that proffered by Adolf Eichmann in Israel. He did not claim drunkenness or mental illness, but simply lack of any wish to do harm to anyone. Eichmann had been responsible for the organisation of first the deportation of Jews, later their transportation to death camps, under Hitler. A boring, cliché-ridden and methodical functionary, he had undertaken his task as a duty, and performed it meticulously well, without relish, simply because it was his job. After the war, he escaped to South America, was kidnapped by Israeli agents in Argentina, and tried over a period of months in

Jerusalem without the right of defence. That millions of people had died as a consequence of his acumen was not in dispute. Eichmann claimed that he had not *intended* anyone should die, that what happened to them after he had sent them on their way was not in his control and did not in any meaningful way issue from the exercise of his will. In his final statement to the court, Eichmann said that he had never been an anti-Semite, had never killed anyone or willed that anyone should be killed, and was in fact too squeamish ever to be capable of such an act (this at least was true – he nearly fainted when he was at last confronted with the end-product of his 'transportations'). He said he had obeyed orders as efficiently as he could, and the instructions of Hitler and his disciples had the force of law under the Third Reich. He was tantamount to a scapegoat. 'I am not the monster I am made out to be,' he said. 'I am the victim of a fallacy.'[3] Hannah Arendt wrote mournfully that 'one cannot extract any diabolical or demonic profundity from Eichmann',[4] this ridiculously ordinary little man. Nevertheless, his lack of intent to kill did not excuse him, and he was executed on 15 December, 1961.

The case of Adrian Babb offers an illustration of the same on a much less ghastly scale. Between 1986 and 1988 in the Edgbaston area of Birmingham, seven women in their seventies and eighties were attacked and sexually molested on the roofs of tower blocks, having been first bundled into a lift. Sometimes they were raped, other times subjected to digital exploration (what the *News of the World* used to term 'interfered with'). Certainly, all the women had undergone a traumatic and terrifying experience at the hands of a stranger, and it was pretty clear that the same man had perpetrated the seven attacks. Yet the accounts of the victims indicated that he had not been vicious or brutal, nor had he shown signs of either frustrated anger or a determination to exercise control over another being, both characteristics common in this type of offence. On the contrary, he had been curiously considerate. When the lift would not go as far as the top floor on one occasion, and the weeping lady had protested that she could not walk up the stairs, her attacker had picked her up in his arms and carried her like a baby. Another woman said that she was expecting an ambulance to take her for a regular hospital appointment, and he had assured her that he would see to it she did not miss her appointment. With a third he had brandished a knife, but when she screamed, had run off rather than distress her.

When Babb was caught, the police were understandably mystified by these demonstrations of helpfulness. They reminded him that on occasion his victims had complained that the concrete floor on which they were made to lie naked had been cold, and he had put some clothing underneath them to relieve their discomfort. The police asked him why he had done this. 'There's been one or two like that, says it's cold,' he replied. 'Well, I don't want them to be cold, do I?'

Though undeniably Babb's victims had suffered degradation as the result of his behaviour, it was at least debatable whether degradation had been his intention. He had not wished to hurt or upset the women he abused. Perhaps he was just simple-minded, but the question as to what was in that mind was a worrying one. There was no doubt, however, that he was guilty of the offences with which he was charged, under the law, and his gentle disposition could do nothing to assuage the awfulness of his actions. A lack of specific intent could not help him.

According to a strict Christian view it is possible to be adjudged guilty of sin even if all that exists of the sin is the intention to commit it. We owe this harsh concept to St Augustine, who, mindful of his own youthful dalliance and glorying in self-chastisement, was keen to prevent other people from even thinking about the kind of things he had done. Chastity was a virtue of the mind, he said, which would be terminally corrupted by the mere thought of licentiousness; no act need be performed in order for the intent behind it to be sinful. (This slippery doctrine may logically lead to Peter Abelard's comforting dictum, already quoted, that as long as the mind remains pure, it really doesn't matter what the body gets up to, an idea gleefully adopted by some twentieth-century American cults which permit all manner of excesses in the knowledge that its adherents cannot be guilty in their hearts.) Mercifully, no legal system has seen fit to admit intent to commit an offence as proof of guilt even when no offence has been committed, but, again in America, some states are moving perilously close to precisely this in their efforts to bestow upon everyone the status of a victim. Some years ago there came into the courts a new crime called 'date rape'. Essentially, the offence was deemed to have occurred when a young couple, having decided to spend the evening together, engaged in amorous activities which the girl afterwards regretted. The boy was accused of having taken advantage of her, because she had expected to be out on a date and had not anticipated that a date would include sex. It is not necessary to prove force on the boy's part for a conviction to be obtained in such a case, and it may even be obtained despite the girl's willingness to undergo the experience. Thus the degree of the boy's intent is an *inherent* part of the offence. Even worse, in the matter of 'acquaintance rape' it is the *only* part of the offence. A boy and a girl may share a cup of coffee, fall into conversation, become candid in their talk in the course of which the boy may indicate that he 'fancies' her. He may now be charged with 'acquaintance rape', because he has sullied her imagination with his thoughts. No actual attack need take place – it is all in the intent. St Augustine would have been very pleased with that.

David Mamet's play *Oleanna* illustrated what might happen when intent is elevated to the role of culpable agent. A university lecturer spends the first act trying to console and encourage a female undergraduate who has lost her nerve and fears she will never understand the course he is teaching. He spends the second act fighting for his life, as the previously reserved young woman has become a relentless foe bent on depriving him of his employment and his home, destroying his marriage and reducing him to an imploring wretch. What has been his offence? That he used long words to intimidate her and his professional rank to attract her. Both no more than intentions. She finally has him charged with assault and battery because he had laid a hand on her shoulder when she had been in tears, and had prevented her going through the door with her problems still unsolved. The teacher will therefore find himself accused not so much of an intent on his part, but of an intent which somebody else has ascribed to him.

Nor is it a simple matter to disentangle what exactly is 'intention' from what might be something else. Obviously, if you propose to yourself a certain action and then see that purpose carried through into performance, the degree of your intent is total. But sometimes the progress from intention to performance is curtailed, if you change your mind or lack confidence in the success of your endeavour; then the intent is diluted, and the action might go ahead with but a small degree of willingness on your part. Or you might intend one act and another quite different act ensues; your intent might not then be said to bear upon the result, in the second act, because you intended something else, although the quality of your intent remains robust. You might wish to assist an old lady across a busy road. In the course of doing so, she is hit by a car. Nobody would suggest that you intended she should be killed, but the intensity of your desire to help, your interference in fact, might have promoted an atmosphere of carelessness or exaggerated bravery which resulted in that end. Or perhaps you were coerced, and undertook the risk against your better judgement. Or perhaps you were defective in judgement – not mentally ill but just foolish.

In Iris Murdoch's *The Green Knight* there is a gentle, fey, endearing teenage girl called Moy, whose care and concern for every living creature is boundless. She is a shining example of that empathy, discussed earlier,

189

which is essential if the will is going to be directed towards doing good. She is empathy epitomised. Her determination to do good extends to inanimate objects, at which point even she begins to question whether her intent is justification enough in itself. Could it not be a trifle arrogant?

> But was this not something fruitless or even bad? How did she know what little living creatures, and even *things, wanted* her to do? The whole world was a jumble of mysterious destinies. Did the stones who were picked up by humans and taken into their houses *mind*, did they dislike being inside a house, dry, gathering dust, missing the open air, the rain, perhaps the company of other stones? Why should she think that they must feel privileged because she had, out of a myriad others, discovered them and picked them up? She felt this weird anxiety sometimes as she caressed a rounded sea-worn pebble or peered into the glittering interior of a flint.[5]

Of course, had she been dealing with people, who could articulate their desires, Moy would not have been so confused about the worthiness of her intent. On the other hand, the very *certainty* that what you intend is welcomed by the person to whom you intend to do it, is insufficient ground in law to prepare a defence. In 1988 half a dozen men were brought to trial for actions they had performed with each other to the mutual delight of all. Nobody had anything but the best intent to give pleasure. Unfortunately, the pleasure involved inserting nails into scrotums and pinning penises to walls. The men were variously sadists and masochists, all consenting and all known to each other. They had not presented their peculiar practices to public gaze. Still, the judge found that the purity of their intent was irrelevant, and that they had, in fact if not in heart, inflicted harm upon one another. They were found guilty.

It is because the question of intent can lead one

into tricky debate that the law needs to insist upon the distinction between the *actus reus* – the state of affairs caused by the conduct of the defendant, and the *mens rea* – the state of mind of the defendant at the time of that conduct. Until the Homicide Act of 1957 there existed in English law a notion of 'constructive malice', whereby a charge of murder could be brought even though all sides were agreed that only a felony (e.g. robbery) had been intended and that killing was an accidental consequence. This no longer applies, but there are still some areas where the *mens rea* is either given insufficient weight or is extraordinarily difficult to establish. In no matter is this more problematic than that which goes to the very heart of a person's wish, or will, to inflict intentional harm – the question of legal insanity.

It is a mark of all advanced societies that children and idiots cannot be answerable for their transgressions as if they were responsible sane adults. Whereas the definition of childhood is a purely mathematical one, deciding at what age the transition to adulthood may be said to occur for legal purposes, the definition of sanity has always vexed and confused legislators. For a long time a malefactor had to be visibly and obviously deranged before his state of mind could be introduced as exculpatory evidence, and it was largely hit or miss whether such evidence was allowed. But in the nineteenth century an attempt was finally made to delineate exactly what was meant by 'insanity', the results of which are with us to this day. We owe this far-reaching initiative obliquely to the illness of one monarch and the irritation of another.

In 1800 a man called Hadfield was tried for the attempted assassination of George III. His defence counsel argued that he had shot at the King expressly in order to be executed, having concocted the essentially 'crazy' idea that only by his death would the world be saved. That the defence was successful and Hadfield acquitted was due in some measure to a greater public awareness of madness in the light of the King's own infirmity of mind: sympathy for George III translated into compassion for his demented assailant.

The really crucial date, however, is 1843, when a Scotsman, Daniel M'Naghten, took it into his head to murder the Prime Minister, Sir Robert Peel, thereby unwittingly earning for himself a place in the legal history books. In the days before photography and frequent travel, M'Naghten could have had no idea what Peel looked like, and so it was not altogether surprising that he shot the Prime Minister's secretary, Drummond, by mistake. Drummond died and M'Naghten was tried for murder. It having been established that the defendant believed himself to be persecuted by prime ministers, a number of doctors testified that he was not of sound mind, and he was duly found 'not guilty by reason of insanity'. The public was not pleased and letters poured in to the public prints. *The Times* published a squib which nicely caught the mood of outraged mockery. 'Ye people of England, exult and be glad,' it began. 'For ye're now at the will of the merciless mad ... They're a privileg'd class, whom no statute controls. And their murderous charter exists in their souls.' The piece ended with a principle held dear since biblical times but not much prized by the author, one T. Campbell: 'For crime is no crime – when the mind is unsettled.'[6]

Mr Campbell was in tune not only with the public, but with his sovereign. Queen Victoria was reported to be displeased by the verdict and made it known that she wished the House of Lords to look into the matter. Their lordships obliged with a fierce debate which culminated in the polite suggestion that the judges should get together and define once and for all exactly what they meant by insanity. This they duly did, and Lord Chief Justice Tindal formulated the historic two-limbed directive which has come to be known as the 'M'Naghten Rules'. For a defence of insanity to be made before the jurors, it would have to be demonstrated that, at the time of committing the act, the accused suffered from such defect of reason or disease of the mind that either (a) he did not know the nature and quality of the act, or (b) he did not know that it was wrong. Every ruling since has been a variation on this theme.

The rules were never very satisfactory, as they woefully lacked both precision and a knowledge of psychology. 'Defect of reason' and 'disease of the mind' are, as we reasoned in an earlier chapter, monumental question-beggers which cry out for clarification; they may also be misused by unscrupulous counsel. More importantly, the judges in 1843 took it as self-evident what they meant by the verb 'know'; you either did not know what you were doing, or you did not know that what you were doing was wrong. We live in more sophisticated times and now realise that 'knowledge', in this sense, involves more than a simple cognitive process; it must also involve an emotional element – the ability to appreciate (or feel, or respond to) the wrongness of what you are doing. As Dr Gallwey said in the Nilsen trial, when he was asked by counsel for the prosecution whether Nilsen 'knew exactly what he was doing', 'Leaving aside emotion, yes, but his emotional condition is *vital* . . . The distinction between intellectual and emotional awareness is not a trivial matter. If his emotions were removed, then he would behave like a machine.'[7]

Royal commissions and parliamentary committees have recommended time and again that this anomaly be addressed, the Butler Committee of 1975 specifically proposing the M'Naghten Rules be replaced by more tightly defined examples of a faulty *mens rea*. All legal opinion was in favour, but parliament has never found time to debate the committee's report, lest perhaps members appear 'soft' on crime. Politicians prefer their retribution to be pure. Courts are therefore still relying on the so-called 'diminished' clause of the 1957 Homicide Act, which states that a defendant on a charge of murder may have the charge reduced to one of manslaughter if it is shown, to the jury's satisfaction, that he suffers from an abnormality of mind which may 'sufficiently' diminish his responsibility for his acts. This places upon the jury, after hearing expert witnesses, the burden of deciding what weight to give to the word 'sufficient', for the prosecution may happily argue (and frequently does) that a defendant is certainly mentally abnormal, but not mentally abnormal enough.

In the United States the struggle to measure wilful intent has spawned yet more confusion. For a charge of first-degree murder to stick, the defendant must show premeditation, deliberation, and the harbouring of malice. If he harbours malice without premeditation and deliberation, then the charge is second-degree murder. Should he harbour no malice but still be proven to have had an intent to kill, the charge becomes voluntary manslaughter. When there is no premeditation, no deliberation, no malice and no intent to kill, the only charge possible is involuntary manslaughter with reckless disregard for life. Below that we are left with a mere accidental death. Until fairly recent times, juries were expected to make these distinctions on the evidence of fact before them, in other words to make a judgement as to whether the defendant's actions suggested to them he harboured malice or had intent, and so on. However, with the growth of psychiatric knowledge since about 1950, more and more cases allowed doctors to testify to the jury, not whether a defendant actually harboured malice, but whether he had the mental capacity to harbour malice.

A new standard for measuring how much a murderer 'knew' what he was doing, meanwhile, was introduced by an opinion delivered by Judge David Bazelon in the District of Columbia in 1954. Known as the 'Durham Rule' after the defendant in that case, Monty Durham, it allowed that a man may know right from wrong but still be deficient in emotional appreciation of what he had done, or be unable to control his behaviour, because his act was 'the product of mental disease or defect'. This is a step forward from M'Naghten and has been adopted in some States, though not in Wisconsin, where

194

Jeffrey Dahmer was tried; had the Durham Rule applied, he would likely have been found guilty of voluntary manslaughter. Wisconsin, along with a majority of States, adopted the test for insanity established by the American Law Institute in 1962, according to which (Section 4.01 of the Model Penal Code):

> A person is not responsible for criminal conduct if at the time of such conduct as a result of mental disease or defect he lacks substantial capacity either to appreciate the wrongfulness of his conduct or to conform his conduct to the requirements of law.

The ALI test therefore advances and retreats at one and the same time. In admitting the concept of 'appreciation' it makes clear that 'knowing' right from wrong is an inadequate indication of wilful intent to do one or the other; yet it presents American juries with a similar ticklish problem as that faced by their English counterparts, in having to determine how substantial is 'substantial'.

Notwithstanding all this, sixteen of the United States of America still uphold the M'Naghten Rules of 1843. When they contemplate the muddle into which some other courts hurl themselves in their attempts to quantify capacity and mental disease, they may well consider themselves fortunate. The California Supreme Court, for example, decided in 1964 that a jury had been wrong to convict a teenage boy called Wolff of first-degree murder. The boy had wanted to have group sex with a number of girls at his high school. He went to the house of one of them and tried to climb down the chimney, got stuck, and had to be rescued by the fire brigade. Thereupon he thought he had better stage the orgy at his own home, but he knew full well that his mother would not approve. His solution to the problem was to batter her to death with an axe.

The jury at Wolff's trial, ignoring the testimony of psychiatrists to the effect that the boy was mentally disturbed, found premeditation and deliberation as well as malice to be amply demonstrated and returned a verdict of first-degree murder. The Supreme Court, however, opined that his level of premeditation and deliberation was not 'meaningful and mature' enough to justify such a verdict, and reduced it to second-degree murder.

Seemingly bizarre decisions such as this have led many to lament the involvement of psychiatric testimony in murder trials, which appears to introduce mere opinion, of its nature challengeable, into a tribunal of fact, and to encourage rival psychiatrists, engaged (and paid) by legal adversaries, to squabble in public. The trouble lies in the confluence of separate disciplines. Legal minds and psychiatric experts deal in different languages and often pursue their arguments in opposite directions. The result can be not so much confusion as hostility.

Most repetitive murderers lead dual lives, the one quotidian and visible, the other episodic and concealed. They can catch buses, eat hamburgers, bounce babies on their knees, give to charity, organise office parties and generally manage their lives with competence. This is the man the lawyer sees – logical and purposive. On the other hand, the concealed life of such people may be chaotic, fantastic and absurd, and this is the life the psychiatrist sees – illogical and manic. We here touch upon the dichotomy discussed earlier, Jekyll alternating with Hyde, Frankenstein with his creature, the well man with his diabolically possessed *alter ego*. The courts are prone to see only half the man, the sequential half, and the psychiatrist must battle with abstractions in order to press them to glimpse the hidden half which has been responsible for the crime, and too often he fails because he is in the wrong place. As Professor Canter puts it, the 'inner narratives' which track the murderer's descent into craziness have *only* (my italics) an internal logic. These storylines omit reference to the parallel, more realistic stories that also enabled them to contrive their killings unstopped:

> the reasons for hiding the bodies, the care to make
> contact with their victims without any overt threat,

the change of venue of the murders once people had been alerted. It is the overt logic of the crimes, not the inner narratives, which leads courts to find these murderers fit to plead, sane and guilty.[8]

This seems to me to place the problem back to front. If juries are bound only to consider what is overt, then they are using their logical understanding to set aside the illogical nature of the murderer's inner narrative. Put another way, an act should only be judged according to the *mens rea* of the actor, not of his audience.

Dr Lionel Dahmer was painfully forced to recognise that his son Jeff had for years followed an inner narrative of catastrophic madness, and that he had himself passively encouraged this secret life by his refusal to *look*, by only seeing the overt logic of an ordinary existence as he was bound to see it, because his own *mens rea* was not diseased. It is a situation of irreconcilables, a terrible catch-22:

> He lived in a world behind his eyes . . . had it not been for his murderousness, had his insanity not finally emerged in the insanity of his crimes, I might never have seen it all . . . It was as if I had locked my son in a sound-proof booth, then drawn the curtains so that I could neither hear nor see what he had become.[9]

The inner narrative is driven by delusions of one kind or another, and it is up to the psychiatrist to winkle them out and expose them to scrutiny. Courts are not really interested in delusions, preferring to look at facts. Jeff Dahmer killed people because he felt the warmth of human contact lay in plunging his hands into their open stomachs. Mr Hadfield in 1800 tried to shoot George III in order to be executed and by his sacrifice save the world. Joseph Kallinger, the subject of Flora Rheta Schreiber's seminal study *The Shoemaker* (1983), slaughtered innocents because he thought his penis had been severed by his adoptive parents for its wickedness. Peter Sutcliffe murdered and eviscerated prostitutes to 'clean up the streets' in answer to celestial instruction. The unspeakable crimes of Richard Chase, so-called 'Vampire of Sacramento', owed their origin to his conviction that his body was falling apart, his heart shrinking, his stomach rotting, and that his only salvation was to drink animal blood, which he sometimes mixed in a blender. All these are obvious delusions, yet they follow an *internal* logic, born of a false premiss, which psychiatrists cannot ignore. It is possible, as I have said before, that sane and sequential behaviour may be directed towards an utterly insane and absurd purpose; it is the purpose that must indicate state of mind, not the mechanical means of achieving it.

Albert Fish killed twelve-year-old Grace Budd and used her body to make a stew. He was efficient at it, and deliberate, so the jury decided he was sane and he was executed in 1936. They appear not to have wondered what his purpose was. In Hamilton, Ohio, in 1975, James Ruppert ('one of the kindest human beings I have ever met. He would do anything to help people'[10]) slaughtered eleven members of his family with a shotgun in a few minutes. The jury had to decide whether he did it for the money or could not help himself. They solved this dilemma of outer and inner narratives with a classic compromise: Ruppert was guilty of murder on the first two counts (his mother and brother), but not guilty by reason of insanity on the other nine (his sister-in-law, nephews and nieces).

It must also be admitted that some of the psychiatrists called upon to give evidence do the profession little credit. 'Popular' psychiatry, of the kind found chattering in daily newspapers, has sometimes seeped upwards to infect the minds of those who are supposed to be more subtle. So gullible and immature were most of those psychiatrists who testified in the Hillside Strangler case in Los Angeles in 1978 that one of the defendants, Kenneth Bianchi, was able to hoodwink them for five months on end. He pretended to be hypnotised, going off into a trance in the witness box. He pretended to have multiple personalities and could switch between them at will. He feigned amnesia. When he was eventually found out, the judge had some devastating words for the doctors. 'This action by Mr Bianchi caused confusion and delay in the proceedings,' he said. 'In this, Mr Bianchi was unwittingly aided and abetted by most of the psychiatrists who naively swallowed Mr Bianchi's story hook, line and sinker, almost confounding the criminal justice system.' That 'unwittingly' is crueller than it seems.

One way to avoid this mess would be to adopt the French concept of *démence* as specified in the Napoleonic Code (its English equivalent, 'dementia', is commonly only used with the qualifying adjective 'senile'). Somebody suffering from dementia would be deemed incapable of crime and so no charges would be brought nor any trial take place. That, one feels, would satisfy neither the lawyers nor the doctors in Britain and America, who would both be rendered unnecessary (the examining magistrate in France decides whether a prospective defendant suffers from *la démence*). I have said that, under our system, the jury is inclined to acquit or convict on the basis of the overt logic of the outer narrative (i.e. the *actus reus*), and be little influenced by the inner narrative of madness. There is fair reasoning behind this, for they presumably have undiseased minds and are therefore better placed to 'see' the outer narrative. If a case of dementia came before them, they would have to be as mad as the defendant in order to 'see' the inner narrative which has driven him.

Criminologists tend to try too hard to avoid attributing anti-social behaviour to madness, and will prefer the most extravagantly simple scenarios to any case for dementia. (I heard one witness at the Nilsen trial say, 'There's nothing wrong with him; he just likes killing people.') They want at all costs to deny any validity to the *res ipsa loquitur* argument that a man must be mad to have killed all those people, and are driven to excess in the opposite direction. Levin and Fox offer a fine example. Killers, they say,

> are often evil but not crazy; they recognize the wrongness of their behaviour but don't care. Serial killings generally involve sex and sadism; serial killers are having fun at the expense of their victims. For someone with a sociopathic personality, the act of murder is an end in itself. There is really nothing insane about the deed, except for the fact that the act itself is hideous and inhumane.[11]

This is stuffed with *non sequitur*s. The authors appear to suggest that the hideousness and inhumanity of murder are the only characteristics of it which make it insane, whereas they are in fact the most common characteristics of all types of murder – domestic, military, totalitarian, or punitive. That which adds an element of insanity to one hideous killing and not to another can only be in the state of mind of the killer, in the cause rather than in the effect. There is no insanity in effect.

One will inevitably reach the impossible conclusions of Levin and Fox if one completely discounts the 'inner narrative' of the perpetrator and confuses his deed with his purpose. That is why the question of intent and of the free exercise of autonomous will should always be at the core of any legislation with regard to insanity; it is crucial to ascertain whether an accused man could foresee the harm that would ensue from his acts. If he could not, then he cannot be said to have intended that harm.

Of course, there are different levels of intention, and therewith escalating levels of responsibility. The anti-social personality deplored by Levin and Fox certainly did foresee the consequence of his acts, in the straightforward cognitive sense of knowing that by killing somebody he would make him dead, which is what he wanted to do. However, returning to the earlier point, he may have no emotional understanding of what being dead means. A full-blown psychopath is not a fully formed moral agent; he is a raw child in a man's body, with an infantile level of emotional appreciation. No-one disputes the psychopath's emotional level, and those who would like to see every murderer executed regularly speak of the psychopath's urge for self-gratification, regardless of the cost to others. If they were to talk of the infant's need for self-gratification, regardless of the cost to others, and suggest that the infant be similarly punished when somebody gets hurt, they will recognise the trap into which their anger hurls them. This is self-evidently not to say that the killer should be excused, but that his defective mental (emotional, not intellectual) state be taken into account when assessing his level of responsibility.

This is depicted as the slippery slope towards exonerating every malefactor. Perhaps it is. But I am not so much concerned here with legal penalties as with moral understanding, and have only looked at legal perceptions of moral ineptitude to demonstrate how difficult it is to work out whether a harmful act issues from a wish to inflict harm, or conversely whether a good deed is necessarily born of a good heart. All sorts of temporary mental aberrations may have disastrous consequences. You might be in a rage and behave according to the demands of your fury. You may be terrified, or drunk, or drugged (we saw in Chapter Two that there is medical evidence anger and fear affect the chemical balance of the brain just as demonstrably as drugs). You may be under hypnosis, or chained to a desperate compulsion like claustrophobia, agoraphobia, kleptomania. All these conditions must surely lower the degree of your responsibility for what you do, despite the fact that in every single case you may well have the clear and declared *intention* to do it.

St Augustine wrote that vice was a defect, a deficiency of the will. John the Scot had much the same idea when he said that evil was the privation of good. At every step in life, choices have to be made, and each choice has some moral value — it cannot be neutral. It seems that the will is not always free all of the time, and therefore some choices may be made with a diseased will, or one that is faulty (i.e. deficient in the Augustinian sense), with deleterious results. Is it the case, then, that a good action illustrates the free exercise of free will, and a bad one the misdirected exercise of a rotten, perverted will? As long ago as 1949 Frederic Wertham wrote, in his study of the teenage murderer 'Gino' called *Dark Legend*, that murder was often a way of preventing something worse from happening: 'The act of murder appears to have prevented consequences far more serious for Gino's mental health.'[12] Others agree. 'Usually, the options that lead away from the killing are the most devastating to the killer's psyche,' says Dr Ronald Markman, 'so he chooses the path that takes him in the other direction.'[13] Does that mean that Gino was *right* to kill his father, that what he did was a *good* act? Or was his will defective, and he fought to prevent its further disintegration? How on earth is one to decide what makes a good act if goodness can be sifted even from the ashes of destruction? Or how a bad one if it be executed by an utterly blameless and uncontaminated will?

Hannah Arendt confronted this last problem in her study of Adolf Eichmann. The man who sent millions of Jews to their deaths, she wrote, was 'an average "normal" person, neither feeble-minded, nor indoctrinated, nor cynical, [yet] perfectly incapable of telling right from wrong.' He knew what he was doing. He was medically sane. Even the emotional dimension I have spoken about was intact. Eichmann was no psychopath. Could it be that he was as ordinary as the rest of us, and that extremes of conduct are no more than the reflection, writ large, of the common stuff of humanity?

Given that intention is safe, and that an act has not arisen by fortuitous circumstance or accident, perhaps the will need not be distorted at all for harm to occur. Perhaps it need only be suffocated for a while or deflected while conscience sleeps. And is this not what we all do, every day, to greater or lesser degree?

9

IN THE SAME BOAT

'Chaque homme porte la forme entière de l'humaine condition,' wrote Montaigne.[1]

Within each of us lies the totality of human potential, and no one person, be he extravagantly good or monstrously bad, can ever be entirely foreign to us, because his characteristics reflect ours on a magnified scale. This is a comforting idea when it implies that we each have a little bit of the sanctity of St Francis of Assisi or Jesus of Nazareth in our hearts, but the corollary, that we are also a little like Dennis Nilsen and the Marquis de Sade, causes many people such agonies of surprise that they would be better prepared to see them immolated than admit to brotherhood with them.

The 'problem' of evil, by this argument, is the problem of our acknowledging its presence, latent but sure, within us all. It is the problem which caused Leibnitz sufficient anguish that he formulated an entire philosophical structure bent on dissipating it. There are as many possible worlds, he said, as there are rules of logic, and God created the best of all possible worlds, one that contained an excess of good over evil. He could not have created a world with no evil at all, because one could not have discerned any good without its opposite to set it in relief. That is why free will is a good, but free will could not logically exist if its exercise always resulted in doing good. Therefore God created both free will and the sin of Adam, giving us a world as near perfection as possible, where goodness is normal and badness not our fault but Adam's. Voltaire wickedly mocked the whole concoction in *Candide*.

As Bertrand Russell wrote, 'the world is partly good and partly bad, and no "problem of evil" arises unless this obvious fact is denied.'[2] Jung had gone further with his assertion that the whole energy of mental functioning sprang from the tension between the opposites of sin and saintliness in every person.

The modern equivalent of the Leibnitz conundrum is to dismiss wrong-doing as a manifestation of illness or madness or possession, and nothing to do with us. While there are compelling medical reasons for regarding wrong-doing as sometimes an aberration over which the individual has little control – an aspect of the subject I have tried to examine in previous chapters – the fact remains that the illness or madness is not separate from our *personal* experience, but part of it, though it is generally only active in us in so muted a form that we do not notice it. Moreover, many of the cruelties inflicted by men upon men have not been attributed to madness or illness at all, but to qualities we admire – leadership, conviction, loyalty and so on – and their perpetrators have been regarded less as criminals than as heroes. You will not find many Frenchmen prepared to admit that Napoleon was a dangerous lunatic who brought suffering to millions, or many Englishmen who will allow that Gordon of Khartoum was mentally deranged. It would appear that badness can be transmuted into virtue by some kind of collective conspiracy to delude.

Anything rather than face the unpalatable. Even an experienced forensic psychiatrist like Herschel Prins feels obliged to warn his readers of 'the uncomfortable probability that these apparent extremes of behaviour may be but extensions of conduct that is, in fact, fairly universal.'[3] Very tactful, that. I have had cause to quote Lionel Dahmer more than once already, but he is a tremendously honest witness to a truth which few of us have ever had to face, and none of us want to, and he bears repetition. 'There were areas of my son's mind,' he wrote, 'tendencies and perversities which I had held within myself all my life. Certainly, Jeff had multiplied these tendencies exponentially, his sexual perversion generating acts that were beyond my understanding, and far beyond my capability. Nonetheless, I could see their distinct origins in myself, and slowly, over time, I began to see him truly as my son in far deeper ways that I had previously imagined.' In recognising the similarities between his son and himself, Lionel is bringing Jeff back into the embrace of humankind and, conversely, reminding us all that what Jeff did was not as unfamiliar to us as we should like to pretend. Something, he said, 'could have turned me into the man my son became'.[4]

By implication, something could have turned any one of us into a despot or a murderer by tapping into that potential for wickedness which sleeps unused in all but the most immature. David Canter goes so far as to suggest that criminals are flawed humans, no more, a brave point for a professional man to make. 'It is the distortion of maturing processes, *recognizable in ourselves in a milder form*,' he writes (my italics), 'that are at the heart of all criminal activity.'[5] It should follow that the man who does terrible things must not just *seem* to be innocuous − our neighbour − but is in fact utterly ordinary and commonplace in every other respect. You could have invited Nilsen to dinner and not noticed anything untoward about him. Crippen was a man of impeccable manners and grace. James Ruppert was extremely 'nice'. A poisoner called Armstrong 'was a gentle lawyer from the little town of Hay-on-Wye who not only murdered his wife but attempted to do in a rival solicitor. His manners were so good that when he passed his intended victim a poisoned scone at tea-time he uttered the immortal words, "Excuse fingers."'[6]

Nobody could have been more ordinary than Adolf Eichmann, whose personality was described by his own counsel as 'that of a common mailman'. (Hannah Arendt subtitled her book on his trial, 'A Report on the Banality of Evil'.) He had a gift for consoling himself with clichés, and half a dozen psychiatrists declared their belief that he was 'normal', one of them adding that he was 'more normal, at any rate, than I am after having examined him'.[7] An instance of his normality was afforded by his response when he finally witnessed the fate of the Jews he had transported, an occasion when, as I have said, he was so upset he nearly passed out. 'I hardly looked,' he said, 'I could not; I could not; I had had enough. The shrieking and . . . then I saw the most horrible sight I had thus far seen in my life. The truck was making for an open ditch, the doors were opened, and the corpses were thrown out, as though they were still alive, so smooth were their limbs. They were hurled into a ditch, and I can still see a civilian extracting the teeth with tooth pliers. And then I was off – jumped into my car and did not open my mouth any more.'[8]

It is disturbing, to say the least, that Eichmann reacted to such a sight as I might have done.

Might I have been able to herd people into gas ovens or, just as terrible, mutilate and torture a defeated enemy in wartime? If so, where do I gain the strength to do such things, unless it is already part of my character which I have chosen heretofore to suppress? When Julius Caesar captured the town of Uxellodunum he chopped off both hands of every member of the garrison. William the Conqueror introduced castration as a punishment for adultery in England. Were these men inhuman and unfeeling in their hunger for retaliation and revenge, or would you and I have done the same, given the opportunity and the power?

The history of the human species is stained with the most abominable cruelties, which show no signs of abating. During the Crusades, human heads were used as ammunition for catapulting. A hundred years later Frederick II of Germany was roasting his enemies alive, having first encased them in lead to make the cooking slower. Simon de Montfort, hero of the Inquisition and much applauded by popes, gouged out the eyes and slit the noses of heretics. Tamburlaine the Mongol chieftain once walled up 2,000 prisoners of war, buried alive 400, and impaled another 5,000. The Tudor monarchs in England employed sophisticated gadgets for crushing teeth, fingers and ankles. Ivan the Terrible of Russia had the Archbishop of Novgorod sewn up in bearskins and mauled to death by dogs. On the other side of the world, human viciousness was equally boundless, having no need to be learnt by example from Europe or Asia. The Aztec civilisation allowed hearts to be torn from living people, female dancers to be decapitated as they performed, and children to be forcibly drowned. On one occasion some 70,000 prisoners of war had their hearts cut out in a terrible orgy of delight.

In our own day, Stalin is reputed to have said that 'to choose one's victims, to prepare one's plans minutely, to strike an implacable vengeance and then go to bed, there is nothing sweeter in the world'.[9] A nicely balanced sentence, that, and a not unattractive proposition when put with so beguiling and innocent a manner. It hardly bothers to disguise a horrible greed for death and dominion, but we should pause to consider the insidious sense of satisfaction that it gives us, overriding the sense of dismay and pity, and admit that Stalin's clever sentence brings a smile to our lips.

And why should this be? Because we understand, in the depths of our being, all those vindictive notions of revenge and implacability. They answer to something residual in us. It would be absurd to suggest that we are all little Stalins, but it would be equally blind to deny that we all could be, or to posit Stalin as alien to human nature. The fact is that we are all potentially cruel and sadistic, and are *actually* so in mild or ritualistic ways which we scarcely recognise. 'It is no use pretending that any of us are immune to sadistic feelings,' writes Anthony Storr in characteristic no-nonsense fashion.[10] Stalin, Tamburlaine, Montezuma are exaggerated specimens of common man.

If readers are still sceptical, let them reflect how often common man has delighted in the spectacle of suffering, from the packed audience at the Coliseum in Ancient Rome assembled to watch people torn limb from limb by animals, to the mediaeval habit of dragging traitors through the streets before disembowelling them alive, and the eighteenth-century entertainment of a public execution. Today there is still a waiting list of those who compete for the privilege of witnessing an execution by electric chair in some of the United States of America, an event which frequently involves sparks issuing from the convict's head and his flesh being visibly barbecued so that it falls from his bones like roast chicken; there is also a predictable annual shriek from respectable ladies at the Conservative Party conference for public flogging and punishment by death. One has only to attend a bullfight in Spain to see at first hand what enjoyment the mob derives from heartless cruelty, each member of the audience loudly and dismally excited to virtual orgasm by the sight of suffering. Not one of them needs to be coerced, for the cruelty he feels in his breast finds an outlet legitimised by custom, although, if questioned, he would not consider himself to be cruel at all.

There have always been ready excuses for sadism. The priests of the Inquisition told themselves they were doing God's work, and the mass slaughter of defeated enemies in wartime has been likewise justified as an expression of the righteous wrath of the victorious. Even the trading of human beings as slaves was rationalised until quite recent times. But it is more instructive to examine how, in an era relatively free of war or mass persecution, when sadistic urges are held in check, tiny echoes of their presence may be detected in the most ordinary daily events.

The businessman who mysteriously summons his staff for an unnecessary dressing-down, who fires a respected subordinate without warning or manipulates colleagues into a state of constant apprehension, is quite obviously sadistically inclined and different from Tamburlaine only in degree and opportunity. Political life may attract some sadists for similar reasons, in that the highest authority has unrivalled power to end the career of a rising star from one minute to the next. French politicians are said to be particularly prone to this weakness, and, in literature, Shakespeare's version of King Richard III offers a fine example: there is sadism in his cavalier destruction of his brother the Duke of Clarence; in his brutal despatch of Hastings, who, unsuspecting, hears himself condemned to be beheaded before the King will touch his strawberries; and in his ghastly wooing of the Lady Anne, whom he has just made a widow and whom he dares to lust after beside the very coffin of her late husband. In this audacious scene Shakespeare reveals how dangerously enticing the sadistic impulse can be, and how its attractiveness is tacitly acknowledged in unexpected ways. He also implies that it is omnipresent and may hover in disguise.

Disguise is hardly necessary in the teaching profession, which relies for some of its effect upon the proper harnessing or sublimation of the cruel streak. At Wilson's Grammar School in Camberwell, where Michael Caine and I were both pupils (he a few years ahead of me), we both remember a geography teacher called Min, who epitomised the cool thrust of ritualised sadism better than anyone I have encountered in all the years since. We were never late for his class – indeed we were always early. We sat in absolute utter silence for the terrifying few minutes before he arrived, slithering noiselessly down the corridor to maximise the awe of his arrival. He wore special soft shoes so that we should have no warning at all. To my certain knowledge, no boy was ever caught whispering, but you only had to be looking in the wrong direction for Min (actually Mr Matthews) to haul you out before the class to be mocked, slowly and decisively. He would not bellow at you, but look menacingly and silently, until you realised something was up and you were about to be selected. The sweat trickled on one's hands, neck and buttocks.

Punishment was never swift. One waited for perhaps fifteen minutes, in the corner, while Min pretended to get on with his class, but was all the time working himself up for the thrill of contact and pain. One was thrashed

209

across the palm of the hand with a ruler six times, with pauses in between. The pain was excruciating. Min's eyes glinted. His class was transfixed with hatred and fear. Yet the essence of the cruelty was not so much in the pain as in the anticipation and the humiliation. Proust's Mlle de Vinteuil knew all about that, and she never laid a hand upon anyone.

Min would have served well at Auschwitz. I, on the contrary, would have been useless. I introduce a personal note only to illustrate how the sadistic potential may be so faint as to be virtually undetectable. At Wilson's, discipline was entrusted to the head boy and five school prefects. We had for the purpose our own room, to which boys would be sent by lesser house prefects or occasionally by teachers. After perfunctory questioning the punishment was inflicted, with a rubber-soled slipper on the backside if you were lucky enough to find one of the five drones on duty, or with a vicious cane if you were brought before the head boy. In my year as head boy I recall that miscreants actually rejoiced if they found me in the prefects' room, as word soon got about that my whacks did not hurt. I remember clearly thinking that I ought to be able to bring the arm down with force enough to inflict pain, but unaccountably being perfectly unable to do so. I was not weak; I was unwilling. Some invisible power seemed to stay my hand before the cane reached its object.

The anecdote above is interesting because it suggests that the sadistic impulse may be buried too deep to be of service to warlords or commanders of concentration camps. It belies the notion that anyone could have been conscripted to help run one of the Nazi camps and would have adapted to circumstances; Eichmann could not have done it, for example. On the other hand, it does mean that all those who did run the camps, and there were thousands of such men and women, must have been able to call upon a particularly pronounced sadistic element in their natures, not so far below the surface. Whether or not this is a justified inference, we shall look at later.

To turn to a less noisome aspect of the same phenom-enon, it is undeniable that most of us indulge in some form of mild sadism when we make love. The ubiqui-tous love-bite, with its obvious echoes of vampirism, is intended to hurt in order to heighten the pleasure of intimacy. 'The practice of the love-bite probably stems from the unconscious urge to devour the partner,' opines one study of the Dracula myth, which also points out that our most affectionate language ('I love you so much I could eat you') demonstrates how sex and ingestion are subliminally related. The love-bite may also stem from the conscious urge to dominate and induce submission, as seen in some animals (domestic cats, tigers, etc.). Nor is it without relevance that the dominant partner derives pleasure from the act of intercourse not merely from the sensuality of the experience, but also from the wish to penetrate deeper and further than before, even if that penetration be painful. The pushing is as important as the feeling, an observation which may be made of both heterosexual and homosexual intercourse. Thus vampires, cannibals and sexual sadists indulge in pathological extremes of fairly routine and unremarkable activity.

'I may have smacked a few bottoms,' said the Mar-quis de Sade, 'and he [Lieutenant-General Le Noir] has brought a million souls under threat of death by hunger.' Sade's cruelty was of the ritualistic and feigned kind, an extension of sexual pleasure, so innocuous in the end that the exigent pain-freak Swinburne, when it was explained to him what Sade had done, disappointedly exclaimed, 'Is that all?' His biographer, Donald Thomas, remarks that 'for sheer finesse in sadism, the marquis fell far short of the Victorian public school system'.[11]

Corruption of the sadistic impulse is but one way in which fairly innocent pleasures become 'evil' by exaggeration. There are many others. It is perfectly acceptable that you should wish to gaze upon somebody you are in love with – he or she may well feel your interest is second-rate if you do not; you will also want to show off to the loved one and get him or her to look at you; you will want to telephone frequently, hear the voice and build a lovely fantasy around it; and you will, in moments not of intimacy and nakedness, but of affection in unlikely places, in the kitchen for example, or on a train, feel the wish to rub your body up against his or hers. Nobody will think you odd for doing what everyone else does at some time in his life. But when these activities become distorted, their fantasy element overwhelming the rest to crush inhibition, they are addressed to strangers rather than loved ones and assume special names. The first is called 'voyeurism', the second 'exhibitionism', the third 'telephonic scatalogia' (i.e. making obscene calls), and the last 'frotteurism', or rubbing against a stranger in a public place, such as an underground train, without his or her knowledge.

In each case, the element of consent has been removed, and what the American court psychiatrist Dr Dietz charmingly called 'a titbit of normal courtship behaviour'[12] has become a crime. The term used by psychologists to describe these titbits is 'paraphilia', a great envelope of a word into which can be thrown all manner of aberrations and peculiarities of preference and desire. First coined by I.S. Kraus at the beginning of the century, it was taken up by the now-discredited sexologist Wilhelm Stekel in the 1920s, forgotten, and rediscovered by American courtrooms quite recently. Stekel described a paraphilia as an acting-out of deviant sexual desires, but that is rather begging the question. It is not deviant, as I have said above, to exhibit one's nakedness or make dirty phone-calls; it only becomes deviant when the person expected to look or listen does not want to, and so fantasy smothers fact and you find yourself arrested.

Another form of paraphilia is fetishism. There are people so apprehensive of total mutual desire that they fix upon one object as a substitute and concentrate all their sexual energy upon that. Thus hats, or feet, or leather, or buckles, or red lips, or long legs, a certain make of shoe, a certain kind of sound, a certain whiff

212

of odour, may all stand in place of full sexual ease and excite the libido by themselves. There have been cases of men lumbered with the bizarre fetish of wanting to see a prostitute stand against a wall while they threw cream buns at her (fortunately for them, there are plenty on the game willing to oblige). Other fetishes may be more dangerous and, if indulged, lead to criminal charges, while some are grotesque and 'evil'. Dahmer, for instance, was interested only in the intestines of a partner. As long as his fetish took the form of lying with his ear to a man's stomach and listening to the churnings within, it was harmless enough; when he killed men in order to open the stomach and plunge his hands into its astonishing colours, he was monstrous. But we must not lose sight of the fact that a fetish itself is a widespread and often glorious phenomenon. A whole international industry is devoted to the encouragement of the hair fetish, and there can be few people absolutely immune to it.

Proportion, degree, *mesure*, are the safety-valves of human aberration. It is when these precious values get lost (by whatever agency or influence, and we have looked at many such in previous chapters) that a mere peculiarity of behaviour grows cancerously into a display of sheer vice. It will not do to forget that those whom we designate as 'evil' are but massively overblown models of ourselves. Their surrender to a single fantasy and abandonment of proportion have drawn attention, with the burning precision of a magnifying glass, to one aspect of themselves at the cost of stifling every other. Pope's *Essay on Man* is specific: 'And hence one master-passion in the breast, Like Aaron's serpent, swallows up the rest.'[13] Which is already an echo of Cicero's observation in *De Officiis*: 'When appetites overstep their bounds and, galloping away, so to speak, whether in desire or aversion, are not well held in hand by reason, they clearly overstep all bound and measure.'[14] And Hamlet has something of the same in mind when he tells Horatio that a man may be ruined by some 'complexion' growing to exaggerated form:

213

So, oft it chances in particular men,
That for some vicious mole of nature in them,
As, in their birth – wherein they are not guilty,
Since nature cannot choose his origin –
By the o'ergrowth of some complexion,
Oft breaking down the pales and forts of reason,
Or by some habit that too much o'erleavens
The form of plausive manners; that these men,
Carrying, I say, the stamp of one defect,
Being nature's livery, or fortune's star,
Their virtues else, be they as pure as grace,
As infinite as man may undergo,
Shall in the general censure take corruption
From that particular fault.[15]

To be accurate, Shakespeare here intends more to suggest that a man's reputation in the world is too heavily weighted by his one fault against his several virtues, but the same idea of balance is at the heart of the matter. Likewise, balance and what Molière called *la juste mesure* are at the heart of any discussion about the presence of evil in the world. People can be good, and bad, and frequently are both in quick succession. A little badness is acceptable and may add piquancy to life and social manners; it will not even be recognised as badness. It is when this element is so inflated as to be ungovernable, not disciplined by balance, that real badness may erupt. According to this the Manichean idea, of good and bad existing in separate spheres, unrelated to each other, makes little sense. Good and bad are, on the contrary, co-existent and part of one another, and harmony emerges from the correct and decent balance kept between the two.

A smidgeon of badness (impatience in the temple, cursing a fig tree, neglect of parents) makes Jesus a much more endearing figure than had he been without blemish of any kind, and its absence makes Theresa of Lisieux both implausible and intolerable. Badness should perhaps be welcomed, then kept carefully in its place.

Of course, you cannot welcome and tame badness if you do not recognise it when you see it. One of the curious paradoxes identified by Hannah Arendt in the Eichmann case is that the functionary thought he was being good when he was being bad, for he had lost the ability to tell the difference. When he realised that the whole of the Civil Service was anxious to do Hitler's bidding, he abandoned whatever residual doubts he may have had, on the grounds that he must have been wrong to have them, for who could he be to judge contrary to the whole of the Civil Service. 'Well, he was neither the first nor the last to be ruined by modesty,' is Dr Arendt's acid commentary. She goes so far as to suggest that virtually every German under Hitler had forgotten this ability to distinguish between the opposite poles of their moral compass. 'Evil in the Third Reich has lost the quality by which most people recognize it – the quality of temptation.'[16] Hence, what was good was what Hitler decreed, and to act in opposition to the Führer's wishes would be evil. They were *tempted* not to allow their neighbours to be kidnapped by the authorities, but they resisted temptation, thus turning goodness on its head.

This is the real source of sin – a kind of moral blindness. It permits balance to be upset, overturned, bulldozed, or as a last resort it will allow it to mimic itself, mirror-like, to reflect itself upside-down, as in *Alice's Adventures in Wonderland*. As long as balance can be kept in sight, and as long as we do not allow ourselves to equate goodness with purity – unstained white – and evil with pitch, we shall know that the potential for both is within us and our moral compass will be safe. 'Even the most evil man is human and calls for our compassion,' wrote Erich Fromm.[17] And Victor Gollancz, himself a Jew, deplored the execution of Eichmann for the very fact that it prevented, once and for all, Eichmann's 'divine spark' of goodness from ever shining forth.

10

THE WEB OF LIFE

A worrying consequence of the universality of both good and evil in all men is the presumption that objectivity in ethics and objective assessments of moral behaviour are no longer possible, because there are no absolutes against which to measure good or bad conduct. A torturer is merely an exaggerated nagger, a saint the extreme instance of kindness. If we are all saints and sinners all of the time, praise and blame become redundant. Where on earth are we to find the rules to guide us?

Because the answer is nowhere on earth, men have ever sought it elsewhere. In his thirst for absolutes and certainties, and his dismay at the ungraspability of human nature, he looks to the heavens and to the gods to plug the gap. As far as we know, no other species has come up with such a clever diversion to explain itself to itself. As Aldous Huxley observed, 'Man is so intelligent that he feels impelled to invent theories to account for what happens in the world. Unfortunately, he is not quite intelligent enough, in most cases, to find correct explanations. So that when he acts on his theories, he behaves very often like a lunatic. Thus, no animal is clever enough, when there is a drought, to imagine that the rain is being withheld by evil spirits, or as a punishment for its transgressions. Therefore you never see animals going through the absurd and often horrible fooleries of magic and religion. No horse, for example, would kill one of its foals in order to make the wind change its direction ... asses do not bray a liturgy to cloudless skies.'[1] Nor, he might add, do cats give obeisance to the notion of feline perfectibility and suffer agonies of distress when they fail to attain it. Because humankind is subtle and reflective, are we right to invent models of perfection, and do they sustain and comfort us?

Yet another paragraph ending with a question. The answers, as usual, are in their dozens. Some claim the models are not invented, but 'revealed'. Utilitarians point to their usefulness. Others say they are harmful and literally misleading. So let us first consider whether they are possible, whether there is even room for objectivity and absolute models in a field so fluid.

Obviously, 'subjective' approval of one's conduct is not enough, for that must mean that a man behaves according to his own conscience, and there are potentially as many different consciences as there are men. Genghis Khan probably had as pure a conscience as Little Bo-Peep. We approve of Little Bo-Peep and disapprove of Genghis Khan because we apply measures of 'objective' rightness, by which we mean that the conqueror and the shepherdess must consider the effects of their actions upon the community of which they form part, and not just the satisfaction they personally derive from them. Therefore objective rightness is that which serves the interests of the group, not the individual, and moralities are forged to guide the individual towards the interests of the group and inhibit his own.

The trouble with this is that those interests will vary according to the group and according to the circumstances. Different groups will have conflicting interests. Larger groups will have interests which override those of smaller groups within them. And interests will change even within one group over the years. This is why it is deemed wrong for one man to kill another, but right for him to kill that same other in wartime; right for the government of Great Britain to refuse to pay extra taxes to Brussels, and wrong for the citizens of Great Britain to refuse to pay the poll tax; right to cut off hands as a punishment for theft in Saudi Arabia, wrong to use the same methods in California; right to drive children to an early death in coalmines in 1850, wrong to do the same in 1950. And so on. Objective ethics will not have a long life in any discussion such as this. The dominant group at the advantageous time will impose whatever 'objective' rightness it feels fit.

Herodotus tells how Darius, King of Persia, asked some Greeks how much he would have to pay them to eat their fathers' bodies. They were horrified at the very idea. He then asked some Indian tribe, whose custom it was to consume the deceased, what would induce them to burn their fathers' bodies. Their shock and indignation were overwhelming.[2]

Yet these are, after all, only social habits, and there persists a 'feeling' (for want of a better word) that objective rightness and universal moral probity must surely be possible, and that only its definition eludes us. We tend to say, then, that we have a kind of ethical intuition which permits us to perceive that some acts are *intrinsically* bad even if they are condoned by a particular group (perhaps our own) at a particular time. This comes perilously close to an emotion. By 'feeling' that some conducts are blameworthy and others deserving of praise we admit that the contemplation of these acts makes us either happy or miserable. And that must imply that there is no moral guidance attainable by simply logical, rational means. In the words of David Hume, 'morality is more properly felt than judg'd of'.[3]

In a purely material world, scientifically cold and calculable, consisting only of matter, there would be no right or wrong and no distinction between good or bad actions. The idea would be meaningless. So it must be that the feeling of rightness and wrongness has got to be satisfied one way or another. And if there are no objective measures to be discovered, we must make them up.

The problem is as old as philosophy itself. Aristotle held that we should first define what we mean by the Good, then describe actions which tend to realise the Good as virtuous ones. For him it was simple: the

Good was happiness, and virtuous acts those designed to achieve happiness. The Aristotelian view sees morality therefore as a means towards a procurable end, and not an end in itself. To this extent it is utilitarian and pragmatic. David Hume made a similar point by proposing that a morally good man was actually more useful to himself and to society than a morally reprobate one.

The real flowering of the Utilitarian idea did not come until the nineteenth century with the theories of John Stuart Mill and Jeremy Bentham. Mill held that the right act was the one which tended to produce the greater amount of happiness, both for the actor and for those affected by his action. Hence the maxim now used platitudinously of 'the greatest happiness of the greatest number', happiness being self-evidently a state in which pleasure predominated. There are all manner of objections to this mathematical measure of morality, on grounds of logical flabbiness, of impracticality, and of ethical vacuity.

First, the premisses are intellectually unsound. Mill equated pleasure with the empirical senses, in so far as only things visible are things seen and only things audible are things heard, and he maintained that only things desirable are things desired. Therefore what is desired is conducive to satisfaction in the same way as what is seen satisfies the organs of sight. Bertrand Russell demolished this analogy in one short paragraph, saying that the argument was 'so fallacious that it is hard to understand how he can have thought it valid'. 'He does not notice', continues Russell, 'that a thing is visible if it *can* be seen, but desirable if it *ought* to be desired. Thus "desirable" is a word presupposing an ethical theory; we cannot infer what is desirable from what is desired.'[4] (Incidentally, and irrelevantly of course, Bertrand Russell was John Stuart Mill's godson; when I had the opportunity to discuss these matters with him in 1960, I was talking to somebody who had been held by a man born in 1806.) And what if that which is desired is wicked, and the satisfaction of the desire a further wickedness? The argument from self-interest is naive, to say the least.

Secondly, it is not a very practical way of separating good people from less good ones, for it supposes that a man should actively seek the greater happiness of the greatest number as well as his own, despite the fact that the theory itself recognises man as essentially egotistical. Can we imagine anyone pondering what to do, when faced with a choice, and either refusing to do that which would advance himself if it was harmful to a large number of people, or working out what would be of greater benefit to others irrespective of his own advantage? It is too much to expect the maximisation of the happiness of mankind to be the goal of the individual (though there have been mighty exceptions, like Albert Schweitzer, who nonetheless expressed his goodness in individual acts). Mill recognised the difficulty and came up with the solution that self-regarding acts were all right so long as they did not interfere with the happiness of or inflict harm upon the greater number.

Another objection to the mathematical approach is that it implies some people may be left in misery as long as the greater number are brought to happiness and the satisfaction of their desires. Perhaps even that some people *ought* to be brought into misery in order to achieve this balance of numbers in the happiness chart. By such reasoning, slavery was perfectly all right so long as there were more slave-owners than slaves.

Similarly, Machiavelli advocated the use of cruelty for political purposes in circumstances where its benefits could be measured (though even he felt sufficiently embarrassed to add an apology in parenthesis). There was, he wrote, 'dalle crudeltà male usate o bene usate' (cruelty used well or badly). 'We can say that cruelty is used well (if it is permissible to talk in this way of what is evil) when it is employed once for all, and one's safety depends on it, and then it is not persisted in but as far as possible turned to the good of one's subjects. Cruelty badly used is that which, although infrequent to start with, as time goes on, rather than disappearing, grows in intensity.'[5] I doubt if Mill or Bentham would have been happy to welcome an ally from such a source. In a later chapter Machiavelli advises the Prince to be selective about his virtues and his vices, for some of the former will ruin him and some of the latter may do him rather well. It is difficult to see how a convinced Utilitarian could argue against such pragmatism; he would thereby reduce his own ethical standards to a sort of prudence or expediency shorn of that nobility which should attend a moral precept. There is something withered and cold about the Utilitarians.

Take Bentham's plan for his ideal prison, which he called a panopticon. It would be fashioned like a bicycle wheel with the guard at its hub and the prisoners housed down the length of its spokes. By a clever system of mirrors, the guard would be able to keep watch on all of his charges simultaneously. If a prisoner behaved well, he would be rewarded; if badly, he would be punished. Consequently, thought Bentham, all prisoners would behave well all of the time. The plan did not indicate why it should be assumed that the gaoler at the centre was himself virtuous. And as Russell drily remarked, 'there would still have been people not in prison, and for them other arrangements would have been necessary.'[6]

A system of ethics devoted to maximising pleasure (even supposing for the moment that that be synonymous with happiness) is not attractive or edifying. We do expect and must demand more. One of the reasons Christianity is morally unwholesome is its promise of future benefit in the numbers game – a kind of Utilitarianism in disguise which Jesus would have found repellent. The cynics who dominate political life, many of them nominal Christians, adhere to a moral relativism which is directly descended from the Utilitarians. In his spoof on Machiavelli, the former Tory party treasurer Alastair McAlpine was able to offer the following advice: 'Revenge should not be used against a fallen enemy; in that case generosity is a more certain weapon.'[7] Many of his political contemporaries thought this to be sage counsel.

We live today with the legacy of Utilitarianism in the United Nations Declaration on Human Rights, formulated in 1948, a document openly dedicated to optimum contentment for the greatest possible number of human beings. Its lack of moral muscle and its commitment to the mathematical approach to such concepts as racial equality, freedom, property, education, etc., has enabled the United Nations to reach opposite conclusions on different days of the week depending on circumstances, balance of power, and numbers. This universal declaration is in practice a pragmatist's charter.

If the relativists are descended intellectually from Aristotle, there are those, owing the germ of their thought to Plato, who maintain that ethical absolutes are not only possible but easily discernible. Plato averred that there were indisputable 'facts' in ethics, with as much force as the statements that grass is green, that President Nixon resigned, and that Scotland is north of England. The principal ethical 'fact' is that there is a knowable absolute called the Good, which men strive to interpret correctly. Cicero said this was part of the baggage we carried around with us. If there is a dispute between two people concerning the nature of the Good, then one of them is making an intellectual error, has got it wrong, just as he would have got it wrong if he were to say that Scotland was south of England. It is therefore irrelevant whether or not conduct is useful and leads to happy results; it only matters that it should be right. For Plato the life of the philosopher (and, by extension, that of anyone who thinks, whether it be regularly and painfully, or once for just five minutes) is devoted to ascertaining the Good and applying it to daily needs.

Even more anti-Utilitarian is the ethical system of Immanuel Kant, who would admit of no good acts that were not undertaken as the result of duty and obedience to an exigent moral law. In other words, you would not earn Kant's approval if you were nice to your

222

neighbour because you liked him or her; it would first be necessary for you to dislike the neighbour heartily before being kind for the kindness to be morally good. He thereby scorns the Utilitarian emphasis on pleasure and replaces it with a strong imperative towards virtue *for its own sake*, irrespective of effect. This is what he calls the 'categorical imperative'.

Kant presents us with two sorts of imperative. The hypothetical imperative is that which tells you to perform an act in order to achieve a result, e.g. you must put your hand out at the bus-stop if you want the bus to stop and allow you on. The categorical imperative is that which tells you to perform an act because it is right you should do so, whether you achieve anything by it or not. Ethical understanding and moral behaviour form part of this categorical imperative by which we rule social behaviour and determine what is right and wrong. Kant does not address the problem which would arise if two people interpreted the categorical imperative differently (i.e. if their interests conflicted and their inner moral sense impelled them to diverse courses). Moreover, his system relies upon a very curious view of human nature, or rather makes no allowance for it whatever. As Russell again remarks, mischievously, 'If he really believed what he thinks he believes, he would not regard heaven as a place where the good are happy, but as a place where they have never-ending opportunities of doing kindnesses to people whom they dislike.'[8]

Also, Hegel said that when virtue was equated with conformity to a mere duty, it was reduced to nothing more than rectitude.

Kant's effort to establish a moral absolute which could be acknowledged by all and sundry at all times was laudable, but foolhardy. I have already had cause to point out the huge disparity in what is considered morally desirable by different communities, or by the same communities in different circumstances, none of which would occur if there was a common categorical imperative exhorting them all to behave uniformly. There is not one idea of virtue, but hundreds. The Hindus consider it virtuous to allow a cow to suffer in great pain, and wicked to kill it. Jews thought it quite proper to stone a woman to death if she had been intimate with a man other than her husband. Aztecs considered it their *duty* (not their pleasure) literally to cut out the heart of a living man. Anyone with the stomach for a detailed account of these horrifying rites should seek out José de Acosta's *Natural and Moral History of the Indies* (1590), and then wonder how virtue could demand that such acts be committed. The fact is, it can, and it has done with great frequency.

For virtue is a movable quality. Behaviour which your community approves at the moment will gain you good points, and you must avoid behaviour of which your community disapproves if you do not want your grade to suffer. (It is taken for granted, of course, that behaviour approved by a rival community must necessarily be wrong.) Here we are talking of moral codes, which purport to enshrine in sets of rules and regulations the moral sense of the community. But since moral codes change, since they vary from one community to another, and since they are sometimes demonstrably silly, it must be that ethics contains an element which is less volatile than a moral code. What is it?

The French writers of the Enlightenment did not attempt to deal with this problem. Diderot's *Lettre sur les Aveugles* is concerned wholly with the relativity of moral codes. From pointing out that the blind man's code is different from the orthodox one, he widens the argument to prove that there is no absolute or eternal moral code. The blind man's code is valid for him, because it reflects his needs. The validity of each man's code, according to the conditions in which he finds himself, is relative; there is no universal validity in morals. Though much exercised by moral codes, Diderot and his colleagues did not face the deeper problem of ethics. They were concerned with descriptive statements as to morals, not prescriptive statements as to morality.

Jesus made an attempt to get his community to look beyond their narrow moral codes, much to their annoyance and displeasure. He was something of a moral anarchist, mixing with sinners and even tax-collectors – the lowest of the low – being kind to prostitutes and epileptics. What he should have done was defer to the priests and acknowledge their pre-eminence in moral matters, which were, after all, matters of law. But Jesus was aware of a deeper need in men, and his mission seems to have been to awaken this awareness in others. He might well have spotted the significance of Kant. But we are still no nearer to finding what it is that could be universal and absolute in defiance of the shifting sentiments of men.

We may get closer if we widen the application of our moral codes to encompass the treatment of other sentient creatures apart from mankind. There are two memorable and horrifying scenes in Dostoievsky's *Crime and Punishment.* One is the murder of the old woman by Raskolnikov, described from within his head and heart. The other is not so famous and comes earlier in the novel. Raskolnikov recounts a dream, or perhaps an actual memory resurrected in dream, in which he witnessed the beating to death of a pitiful little mare by a crowd of peasants. The mare, unresisting, helpless, is whipped across the eyes and brought to her knees with a venom which actually flays the reader, so vivid is the writing. And when Raskolnikov embraces her bleeding head he expresses the compassion and desire to console which the reader also feels and needs to have expressed. Why is this scene so harrowing, and why does the reader care so much? Because he knows intuitively that bad behaviour does not become less bad when it is directed against an animal. Artfully, Dostoievsky manoeuvres us into feeling as much horror at this murder as at the other, in which the victim is a human being.

'The time is coming when people will be amazed that the human race existed so long before it recognized that thoughtless injury to life is incompatible with real ethics,' wrote Albert Schweitzer. 'Ethics is in its unqualified form extended responsibility to everything that has life.'[9] There should be no doubt (but unfortunately there still is) that our moral obligations are not just to refrain from causing harm or suffering to another human being, but to refrain from causing harm or suffering. Morality consists in the restraint, not in the status, shape, colour or intelligence of the object benefiting from that restraint. If it were to be so limited, it would be diminished. Thus, it is objectively demonstrable that ethics are not exclusive to intra-specific behaviour, but must include inter-specific behaviour if they are to have wide validity. It is perhaps another step from the concentric circles which start with family, spread to village, to nation, and to species. Ethical behaviour must go beyond one's own species, or it is parochial and self-serving, not ethical at all.

> That I like the flavour of mutton no more entitles me to kill a sheep [writes Brigid Brophy] than a taste for roast leg of human would entitle me to kill you. To argue that we humans are capable of complex, multifarious thought and feeling, whereas the sheep's experience is probably limited by lowly sheepish perceptions, is no more to the point than if I were to slaughter and eat you on the grounds that I am a sophisticated personality able to enjoy Mozart, formal logic and cannibalism, whereas your imaginative world seems confined to *True Romances* and tinned spaghetti. For the point is what your life and perceptions are worth to you, not to me, and what the sheep's life and sheepish perceptions are worth to the sheep.[10]

Alas, for almost the entire run of Western civilisation until the present day, the prevailing view has been entirely the opposite of this, and that is why, I suggest, our ethical notions are still largely in a mess. A moral code which excludes consideration of the vast majority of living creatures cannot be worth much. Nor can it claim to be in touch with those ethical absolutes which we are groping towards. While the followers of Buddha are famously respectful towards all life, believers in a Jewish or Christian God have been notoriously careless about all life save the human. In part this is doctrinal. The Bible makes ample reference to man's 'dominion' over Nature and promulgates the idea that the whole of the Creation is man's larder and dustbin. If it is presumed that all other animals are provided for man's use and nutrient, even his amusement (or 'recreation' as the *Catholic Dictionary* puts it), then, like Greek or Negro slaves, they form no part of the moral universe. A nineteenth-century Jesuit, writing little more than a century ago, and twenty years after Darwin's insights had been published, was able unblushingly to say that 'brute beasts, not having understanding and therefore not being persons, cannot have any rights . . . We have no duties of charity, nor duties of any kind, to the lower animals, as neither to sticks and stones.'[11] In other words, we are not moral (and this from a so-called moral philosopher).

Pope Pius IX, also a contemporary of Darwin, agreed with the Jesuit, for he refused papal assent to the establishment of an animal welfare office in Rome on the blatant grounds that animals did not matter.[12] Quite apart from the noisome quality of these attitudes, their logical implausibility has to be denied by every Catholic, who must avoid the knowledge that other animals preceded the human as tenants on this planet. Henry Salt has fun with this nonsense in a sarcastic verse:

> The Animals, you say, were 'sent'
> For man's free use and nutriment.
> Pray, then, inform me, and be candid,
> Why came they aeons before Man did,
> To spend long centuries on earth
> Awaiting their Devourer's birth?[13]

Whenever Christians talk about the 'sanctity' of human life they mean the 'exclusivity' of human life and immediately disqualify themselves from having any moral view which can be based upon ethical standards. The implication, not always conscious, is that all other forms of life are without value, for they are distinguished by their 'insanctity'. This pernicious doctrine has given rise to the most appalling behaviour towards animals by otherwise intelligent men. The sixteenth-century French philosopher René Descartes is generally regarded as the arch-fiend by defenders of animal welfare, for he it was who first declared in print that animals were no more than machines, or *automata*, but in truth he was only developing the view, accepted since St Thomas Aquinas, that animals were soul-less. When a creature cried in pain as its organs were ripped from it by the curious philosopher, it was equivalent, he thought, to the ticking of a clock.

It is scarcely to be believed that a clever man could be so unobservant. Did he not see the fear in the eyes of the animals he encountered? Did he not recognise the symptoms of alarm and anticipation, which a machine could not possibly simulate? I have myself witnessed the terror of pigs squealing in panic as they entered an abattoir in Canada, fully aware of what was planned for them. The obtuseness of Descartes and the anthropocentric thinkers of the subsequent Enlightenment paved the way for the complete suffocation of moral sense in the practitioners of vivisection, a bland word for the cold dismemberment of living creatures. It is a most terrible paradox that intellectual thought should progress so far in the eighteenth century and be accompanied by a desperate regress in ethical standards; that the one advantage the human may properly boast above the other animals – conceptual thought and the ability to distinguish between right and wrong – should be so carelessly squandered and depraved, so that men no longer knew that what they were doing was ethically monstrous.

Sometimes, they were caught unawares. There was an experimenter in the nineteenth century who suddenly saw the effect of 'an incalculable amount of torture needlessly and iniquitously inflicted'. 'I think the saddest sight I ever witnessed was when the dogs were brought up from the cellar to the laboratory,' he wrote. 'They seemed seized with horror as soon as they smelt the air of the place, divining, apparently, their approaching fate. They would make friendly advances to each of the three or four persons present, and as far as eyes, ears and tail could make a mute appeal for mercy eloquent, they tried it in vain.'[14] They were then murdered.

This is not sentimental sophistry, but a sharp and precise observation of moral doubt. For if ethical precepts (as opposed to moral codes) are universal, and we are straining here to demonstrate that they are, then they must operate in a fully inclusive way. You cannot suggest that certain conduct is right, then qualify your statement by adding that it is *sometimes* right; or that wilfully bad behaviour is wrong, though it can sometimes be right. If it is wrong to cut open a creature who is still alive, or pull out its eyes to see how they work, it remains wrong whether that creature is a human or a dormouse. It is the *quality* of the act that counts, and the quality is constant, not contingent.

There have always been wise and worried men to draw attention to these moral blind spots. Dr Johnson was fierce in his scorn for the so-called professors of medical knowledge who nailed dogs to tables to discover how long life may continue in various stages of mutilation, for he rightly saw that the doctors, in abnegating their moral sense, threw away their status. The knowledge thus derived was not only useless, but tainted, 'and if the knowledge of physiology has been somewhat increased, he surely buys knowledge dear who learns the use of the lacteals at the expense of his own humanity'.[15] Two hundred years later, George Bernard Shaw echoed Johnson's indignation. 'Vivisection is a social evil', he wrote, 'because if it advances human knowledge, it does so at the expense of human character.'[16]

These are not arrows in a campaign for animal welfare, but the pained responses of philosophers who know the

229

potential for human goodness and see, wincingly, the evidence of human badness. Johnson and Shaw are moral universalists who reject the relativist compromise as unworthy of man.

Vivisection is still with us, and there are still some cretins, mostly university-trained, who defend it. But they are a beleaguered minority. Their successors are the battery farmers who condemn their animals to a lifetime of suffering and sensory deprivation without once considering that there is anything morally reprehensible in so doing. They have inherited the comfy prejudices of Aquinas and Descartes, thinking either that animals do not matter or that they cannot be hurt. They have forgotten, if they ever knew, Jeremy Bentham's famous dictum that the important point is not whether an animal can reason or talk, but whether it can suffer. Battery farmers have no ethical understanding and are, *a priori*, immoral.

They can, however, learn. One famous experimenter, the South African pioneering heart-transplanter Dr Christian Barnard, like many of his profession experimented on animals as a matter of course. He once had two male chimpanzees in adjacent cages, where he kept them for months waiting for the day when he could use them. That day came and one of the animals was sedated so that he could be used as a donor. Before the sedation took effect, the chimpanzee chattered and cried incessantly, and after his body had been removed, his companion in the other cage wept bitterly and was inconsolable for days. 'The incident made a deep impression on me,' said the doctor. 'I vowed never again to experiment with such sensitive creatures.'[17]

Barnard realised, in that moment, the universality of the ethical imperative and saw himself diminished if he denied it. It is a hugely important lesson, for it brings us ever closer to the discovery of that essential thread which ties us to right-doing and 'delivers us from evil'. One step is the abandonment of anthropocentrism, and the happy acceptance of humility. 'Man did not weave the web of life, he is merely a strand in it. Whatever he does to the web, he does to himself.' The second step is actively to *pay attention* to ethical imperatives, to listen and heed. There is a passage in which Schweitzer describes the ethically sound man:

> If he goes out into the street after a rainstorm and sees a worm which has strayed there, he reflects that it will certainly dry up in the sunshine if it does not quickly regain the damp soil into which it can creep, and so he helps it back from the deadly paving stone into the lush grass. Should he pass by an insect which has fallen into a pool, he spares the time to reach a leaf or stalk on which it may clamber and save itself.[18]

This is not soppy. It is noble. And what are the crucial words within it? He 'reflects'; he 'spares the time'. He thinks. Return to those other words from Schweitzer which I mentioned earlier, that 'thoughtless injury to life is incompatible with real ethics'. The word here is 'thoughtless'. Anyone who does stop and think about the ethical implications of what he is about to do *will* reach the decision to do right. Most wrong-doing arises from thoughtlessness, hurry, habit, the horrid desire to get on with it and not waste time dreaming. Dreaming, or pondering, is on the contrary an essential part of humanity and a sure route to ethical soundness. And each society's mythology and literature provides the tools for pondering and comparing. The illiterate man is ethically bereft without these models, but he may still learn from myths passed down through oral tradition. The man who is denied even this, ostracised from the rich vein of his culture's ethical history, is likely to be a moral innocent. By this route we come back to our earlier discussion of the Wild Boy of Aveyron and the unblemished but untutored state of nature; the Wild Boy had certainly read no books, heard no myths, and had no ethical perceptions. He had existed for self alone.

The purpose of ethics is to reveal the Good and exhort

us to attain it. The function of morality is to guide us how to attain it. If we all loved our neighbours as ourselves and were never tempted to steal or menace or make somebody unhappy, we should not need the moral codes to keep us from doing these things. Morality is essentially the prevention of our descending to the level of the Wild Boy, indulging only selfish desires while being altruistically deaf. And it can be done by paying attention, thinking clearly, and acting as the result of clear thought. (It is assumed the thought is uncluttered by mental disease or disorder of personality of the kinds I considered in an earlier chapter.) Thus do we resist the limits placed upon our behaviour by selfishness. It is highly significant that the great moral teachers – Confucius, Buddha, Jesus, the Chinese sage Mencius – have all urged men to conquer their self-regard, because they all know that the purity of ethical truth and its elusive, deeply desired objectivity can only be discerned by reflective outward-looking.

They have different words for this process. Some call it meditation. The Christians call it prayer. But it is always hard thinking.

11

ACCURATE VISION

Thinking has always required effort and courage. Effort, because it declines the easy acceptance of dogma and submission to decisions made by others; courage, because the void it reveals is comfortless, the responsibility burdensome.

The human being is frightened by his loneliness and contingent inexplicability. Hence the need to receive tablets, be told what to do, how to earn reward and weigh well in the balance. Hunger for moral code-making is old, profound and exigent, and one of the principal points of worship is to *beg* that some such code be imposed rather than be made to wander wearily on one's own in search of goodness. For we do not trust ourselves to be good if left to our own devices. Once explanations have been ripped from the world and the universe conceived to be without beginning, end, edge, or reason, we tremble at its empty pointlessness. But that is the very launching-pad of wisdom and the discovery of goodness. For when we recognise that we cannot be explained or helped, that all we can do is think as best we are able, on our own, then thinking becomes a purposive companion, a way of going outside oneself and getting rid of self-regard, self-pity, terror. It is the route towards doing right. Smother thought (whether by dogma or some other kind of authority like militarism) and you kill the possibility of doing good.

I once knew a Brahmin in India who inadvertently gave me a fine illustration of the power of positive thought. I was working in Udaipur, writing a history of the ruling family of Maharanas who had founded the State of Mewar 1500 years previously. Most of the documents

I needed to consult in the archives were written in Hindi or Mewari, some engraved on copper, and the court secretary suggested that he send an interpreter to help me sort things out. Thus did Pandit Gahnshyamlal Sharma hike his way up the hill to the palace where I was staying. Fluent in French and English as well as the local languages, Panditji was invaluable, but I worried rather about his long walk up the strenuous hill, the incline never giving pause for a mile or more, for he was well over eighty years old, with a stick in one hand and his other hand held over his hip for support. After four days, I ventured to ask whether I might come down the hill to visit him, rather than the other way around, but he would not hear of it for reasons of honour and respect. 'I know what you are thinking,' he told me, 'you are wondering about my back. Yes, I am in pain, but you know, my pain is my friend, so I do not mind, and if I do not mind, neither should you. You see, when I die, the pain will die too. We shall go together. That is why it is my friend.' I reflected at the time that if a European had made such a statement he would have been laughed to scorn, but I could see the old man meant every syllable, and that he was right. The little episode taught me something about humility and thought. It may seem odd to juxtapose them in this way, but they have much to do with each other, as I hope to show. And they are both necessary to the beneficent life.

One of the worst mistakes of some religious moralists has been to equate evil with the satisfaction of bodily pleasures and good with their eschewal. By this reckoning, the person who denies himself the pleasures of the senses is by definition virtuous. This is a wrong view because it fails to take into account that many of the greatest pleasures as well as the most harmful are mental – residing in thought, not in the senses. Among the most pernicious are envy, jealousy (as we saw in Chapter Four), and the exercise of brutal power. While some popes have been lubricious, there have been not a few, far worse, who have loved the power which their worldly position afforded them. Theirs was a corruption of thought, not of body.

To this extent, then, Kant was perhaps right to say that morality was a matter for reason rather than emotion, that the rational mind alone could discern right from wrong, but his system was too strictly exclusive. In fact, one does *feel* what is right, but the feeling has to be educated by thought. Thoughts are the building bricks of conscience, because thought enables one to see clearly, whereas thoughtlessness places a blindfold across one's eyes.

Plato was on to a similar concept with his assertion that the world of appearances was deceptive and that only by piercing them with the clarity of ideas could one discover reality, and within reality was the Good. For him, the Good was pre-existent, lying in wait to be uncovered and revealed. Thought would peel back the layers of obfuscation. It followed that only a thoughtful man could be a good man. He who was closed to the world of ideas would forever be stuck in a moral no-man's-land, not knowing whither to turn (not *knowing* because knowledge was only attainable through thought).

This kind of knowledge is what Iris Murdoch has termed 'the experience of accurate vision', which she said offered a liberation from the tyranny of self. The individual psyche, she wrote, was relentless in its self-interest, and the will devoted to the pursuit of that interest. By this system, the exercise of will was bound to be self-regarding, and it was only by directing the attention outward that one would be able to free oneself from this arid imprisonment. The word she gave to this outward-attention was love, or sometimes humility, and the only way to achieve it was by looking hard and thinking hard about what one saw. We must keep the attention fixed on the Good and stop it returning surreptitiously to the Self. Goodness is 'the attempt to see the unself', and real humility a kind of firmness of gaze which refuses to be diverted by excuse. 'Freedom', wrote Murdoch, 'is not an inconsequential chucking of one's weight about, it is the disciplined overcoming of self. Humility is not a peculiar habit of self-effacement, rather like having an inaudible voice, it is the selfless respect for reality and one of the most difficult and central of all virtues.'[1]

Let us return again for a moment to Adolf Eichmann. He was not malign. He was not stupid. He had no mental defect. And his emotions were sound. Nobody suggested he was diabolically possessed, or found any evidence of furtive sadism. He did not hate anyone or feel impelled by messianic fervour. He admired Hitler's personal success in rising from nowhere to lead his country, but it was the sort of admiration he might have felt for a scoutmaster. It had nothing to do with Hitler's *ideas*. And that's the crucial point. This perfectly ordinary and perhaps rather pathetic man never bothered to *think*. According to Hannah Arendt, he was unable to think, and therefore to see what was staring him in the face. He was protected from the contemplation of reality by a mental myopia which renders moral blindness inevitable. Had Eichmann been able to place himself in somebody else's shoes and look at the world from beyond his own ridiculously restricted vision, had he been able, in other words, to *think clearly*, he might have been able to grope towards goodness. But without thought, he could not even know what goodness was. Hannah Arendt puts it this way:

> Except for an extraordinary diligence in looking out for his personal advancement, he had no motives at all. And this diligence itself was in no way criminal; he certainly never would have murdered his superior in order to inherit his post. He *merely*, to put the matter colloquially, *never realized what he was doing* . . . It was sheer thoughtlessness – something by no means identical with stupidity – that predisposed him to become one of the greatest criminals of that period . . . such remoteness from reality and such thoughtlessness

can wreak more havoc than all the evil instincts taken together which, perhaps, are inherent in man.[2]

Is it as simple as that? That you cannot do evil if you stop and think about what you are doing? Has one only to follow Socrates' advice to think keenly in order to do right? Yes, in so far as proper reflective thought will reveal things as they really are, and reality is on the contrary smothered and concealed by the various vices which undermine thought or send it reeling. Therefore, you will do good if you think about it, and you will do bad if you stop yourself thinking about it. Indeed, it is usually a prerequisite to bad behaviour that you should *not* think about it, or you couldn't do it; that's the import of the Socratic insight. 'What is needed is a cool, even cold, truthfulness,' wrote Father Damien in *The Green Knight*.[3] One must look at life squarely, unblinkingly, and then one will see.

In the one attested instance of German authorities sabotaging orders from Berlin during the war, when they assisted the escape of Jews from Denmark to Sweden, it is clear that they did not do so under pressure or the influence of example, nor from compassion, but because they stopped to think and suddenly realised that the extermination of people was not to be taken for granted. They changed their minds. Note that it was their minds which needed changing.

Something of the same happened to Oskar Schindler on the hill overlooking the Warsaw ghetto. It happened to Scrooge in Dickens's *Christmas Carol*. It happened to St Francis of Assisi when he encountered the leper. Christians call this sudden switch of gear Revelation, or the hand of God, or the Holy Spirit. I think it is more helpful to call it a thoughtquake. It occurs when the blindfold is removed, the cobwebs and the veils fall away, one sees the brilliance of goodness and is sickened by the ugliness of evil.

This is not a new idea. Rarely is any idea entirely new. Albert Schweitzer was so pained by the relentless blindness of his fellow men that he returned to the theme in book after book, desperately trying to shake people with his words. 'Very little of the great cruelty shown by men can be attributed to cruel instinct,' he wrote in his *Memoirs of Childhood and Youth.* 'Most of it comes from thoughtlessness or inherited habit. The roots of cruelty, therefore, are not so much strong as widespread. But the time must come when inhumanity protected by custom and thoughtlessness will succumb before humanity championed by thought.'[4] The poet Hood expressed a similar conviction: 'Evil is wrought by want of thought/As well as want of heart.'[5]

Clarity of thought is a (dare I say blessed?) release, an opening-up and ready acceptance of one's place off-centre. It ushers in that most liberating kind of humility unfettered by 'the anxious avaricious tentacles of the self' (Murdoch's words)[6] which finally frees the soul to action. Those without this humility simply cannot see. The Good must be first spotted, then grabbed.

One of the most genuinely good people known to history is St Francis of Assisi. He offers a fine example of this kind of humility, which is by no means abject submission or self-chastisement and -deprecation. He was no Uriah Heep, but an intelligent man and a poet, suffused with that love which I have called outward-attention. He was kind to people for their sake, not his own (salvation was not his purpose at all). He loved the warmth and glow of the sun, the rocks and trees, the animals and birds, as well as people who crossed his path. He was utterly uncomplicated and would have proved barren soil for the Freudians. St Francis's greatest asset was his ability to look honestly and act accordingly. It had not always been so. The son of a successful merchant, he might have had every expectation of a comfortable worldly existence. But the thoughtquake intervened, and his intelligence saw where goodness lay. There is no such thing as a holy fool, says one of the incessantly searching Murdoch characters. 'Holiness requires intellect.' St Francis was good because he thought about what he was doing, not because he was some village idiot who chatted to frogs.

Much less attractive is St Theresa of Lisieux, that rather tiresome child who wanted to suffer as much as possible, longed for martyrdom and boldly affirmed her ambition to be a saint. It was not so much clarity of thought which impelled her as self-advancement. Though many of her apologists, the serene Vita Sackville-West among them, have celebrated Theresa's determination to overcome the self by hard training and daily slog, it did not lead to the selflessness which emerges from clear vision and is the beginning of goodness. I think, on the contrary, Theresa never escaped her obsession with herself, and it was ever her own spiritual future that she was tending. While St Francis regarded the self as an interference, St Theresa was so besotted with her imperfections that she thought of little else. She did not have eyes to see.

Neither does Ebenezer Scrooge in the early part of Dickens's story. It is intellectual blindness which prevents him from having any thoughts but the obvious, self-centred ones he has always taken for granted. He does not see the suffering of others, is impervious to their cries, considers their need for pity an intrusion, and appears hard-hearted to all and sundry. In fact, he has to be bone-headed before he is hard-hearted, and when the ghosts force him to look and see clearly for the first time, he changes character dramatically, becomes generous, compassionate, dear and enchanting. The important point is that he was not touched by emotional crisis, at least not first, but by an intellectual awakening. His eyes were opened by clear thinking, and goodness suddenly became available.

'Moral goodness', wrote Cicero, 'depends wholly upon the thought and attention given to it by the mind.' It requires courage and reflection, he points out, not to be reduced to having to say 'I had not thought of that'.[7]

One may even make a similar case for the international financier Jimmy (Sir James) Goldsmith, who from the age of sixteen to his mid-fifties accumulated wives, mistresses and an incredible amount of loot, sued enemies and delighted friends with wit and hospitality, and was unquestionably wedded to the hedonistic, sybaritic life. Though many benefited from his wealth, one could not say it was his purpose that they should; it was a tangential consequence of cleverness and greed. In 1990, however, Sir James retired from business and, under the wise influence of his even cleverer brother Teddy, the ecologist who taught the world about environmental dangers twenty years before governments began to take them seriously, devoted himself to 'green' issues and the advancement of better conditions in the poorest parts of the world.

What happened to Goldsmith was, again, a change of mind, or perhaps an alteration of consciousness. It was an intellectual shift, not an emotional one, which enabled him to see things he had not properly seen before and release that energy to pursue the Good which had previously lain dormant in his gambler's breast. It would be too mischievous, perhaps, to depict Jimmy Goldsmith deep in prayer in the corner of one of his mansions, yet there is much in the quality of his conversion which reminds one of this activity. What, after all, is prayer but concentrated wilful exclusive attention to thought, and especially to outwardly-attentive thought? Of course, there are some forms of prayer which are little more than masturbation of the soul ('Oh God, make me good'), but the best prayer, like the best thinking, is directed away from self and results in a warm humility. Though not a believer myself, I have found this strange unfamiliar humility and invitation to thought in some Catholic churches, and have welcomed it. Whether or not you choose to call it prayer, it does alter one's state of mind and open the route towards beneficence. The longer, the more reflective, the more tenacious the prayer (or the thought which is its essential function), the more likely one is to emerge from it into moral awareness.

There is one serious drawback in this system. What if, after much deep thought and clarity of perception, one were to reach the *wrong* conclusions? How can we be sure that, by facing reality and eclipsing self, we are *bound* to do right? Can a well-considered moral decision be erroneous? Heinrich Himmler is a case in point, and a very worrying one. He agonised over the conflicts, emotional and intellectual, which accompanied the murdering of so many people in Hitler's Germany. He knew it was distasteful, even shocking, and that it would require great courage on the part of himself and his fellow countrymen to carry the unpleasant task through to fruition. But he fought against these difficulties, because his considered view, perhaps (who knows?) after some prayer or meditation, was that he had to steel himself to be firm and resilient precisely in order to *do the right thing*. Himmler's determination to exterminate Jews was, to him, the result of moral responsibility.

We must therefore look at the psychology of 'bad' morality and the concept of sin which has done so much to encourage it, as well as the despicable fanaticisms to which it can lead, before we can be sure that careful thought is inevitably beneficial.

The sense of sin is probably the greatest obstacle to moral decency that mankind has ever devised. It positively hinders clear thinking by its insistence upon certainty on the one hand, which renders thought redundant, and retribution on the other, which encourages cruelty. It must be obvious that real thinking starts from a position of perplexity, so that there is something to think about. Moral problems need to be resolved, not just inherited and passed on. So the sense of sin which precludes inner debate emerging into that clarity of mind which I have suggested is the essential route to good behaviour, can only be harmful. One cannot attain moral probity through ignorance.

Sin did not start with the Christians, but it was refined by them. The idea of being bad and punishable by the gods was present in Egyptian societies and in ancient

Middle Eastern peoples. With the advent of Judaism as chronicled in the Old Testament it became overwhelming. Sinfulness as a state evolved directly from the Jewish belief in their special condition as people chosen by God. It was difficult to explain why, if they were chosen, they should suffer so much. It could not be God's fault – it was not that He had made a mistake, so to speak – so it must be theirs. They did not prosper because they did not deserve to, they were wicked and disobedient, and they would have to mend their ways before God would show favour. But He never did, and it followed that they never had mended their ways. Why? Because they could not. They were, in a word, sinful.

They would, moreover, have to continue to pay the price for this sinfulness by permanent and repeated heavenly rebuke, and must learn to recognise their suffering as part of God's love for them – His way of showing He cares. This element in Jewish psychology has not essentially changed over the millennia. It is important to note that it derives from self-interest (how to earn God's love) and is bathed in self-regard (oh poor we!). For both reasons, the idea of ineradicable sinfulness can have nothing to do with good, outward-looking, moral conduct. The Christian Church inherited these pernicious doctrines, but removed them from the communal level (that of a whole people being tainted) to the individual. Thus the Church itself could not be sinful, only individuals who removed themselves from communion with the Church were sinful. This made things even worse, for it condemned the sinner to solitary pain, ostracism, loneliness, even black fear. No wonder the sense of sin has historically created so much neurosis and self-obsession, and made it virtually impossible to see what is good.

At no time has this neurotic tendency been so prevalent as during the high tide of the ascetics. Since sin explained suffering, suffering was to be endured. Further than that, the really holy person would welcome suffering and even invent it, imposing it upon himself quite unnecessarily.

242

Ugliness, nastiness, filth, personal squalor, all were embraced by the ascetics with mad relish. 'A hideous, sordid and emaciated maniac, without knowledge, without patriotism, without natural affection, passing his life in a long routine of useless and atrocious self-torture, and quailing before the ghastly phantoms of his delirious brain, had become the ideal of the nations which had known the writings of Plato and Cicero and the lives of Socrates and Cato. For about two centuries, the hideous maceration of the body was regarded as the highest proof of excellence.'[8]

Examples of this curious fashion defy belief. One saint is said to have spent three years standing on a rock without food, water or rest, his only nourishment the sacrament on Sundays. Another was proud to have his beard infested. Many lived in tombs or in caves, crawled naked on all fours, refused to find ease for their limbs in sleep but purposefully chose the most uncongenial spot and position. Some ate grass like cattle. St Abraham the hermit declined to wash his face or feet for fifty years. There was a convent of nuns who thought a bath positively devilish, and all stank happily together. There were hundreds of these 'saints of the desert', hermits and holy men, who endeavoured to make life as hard for themselves as they could (note the personal flavour of the penance, all self-regarding and egotistic). The most famous, however, is St Simeon Stylites, whose excesses would today have confined him to Broadmoor.

Simeon had himself tightly bound with a rope which embedded itself in his flesh. The flesh putrefied and he never tended his sores or washed his skin, with the result that he gave off a stench which was intolerable to anyone who came near him. If you got close enough, you would see worms dropping from his body as he moved, his bed filled up with them. He stood on a pillar for thirty years, exposed to the climate and prostrating himself to God every few seconds. For one year he stood on one leg, the other being covered in sores. An accomplice was engaged to pick up the worms which dropped from his

243

body and replace them in the sores, while St Simeon said, 'Eat what God has given you.' And all this to atone for sin and be pleasing to God. 'The cleanliness of the body was regarded as a pollution of the soul, and the saints who were most admired had become one hideous mass of clotted filth.'[9]

It need hardly be said that St Simeon Stylites never did an ounce of good for anyone (not even himself, upon whom all his diseased energies were bent), and that his glory in chastisement betokened the total absence of moral understanding or curiosity.

This relates to the first centuries of the Christian era, but the habit of self-denial has cropped up periodically since then, always with disastrous results. Even St Augustine, who was very keen on sin, punished himself with undue severity for the most trivial of faults. Later saints were most inventive in finding ways to make life miserable. In 1585 St Mary Magdalene dei Pazzi whipped herself and thrashed her body over thorns, tied herself to a post and suffered hot wax to be poured over her. St Margaret Mary Alacoque would only eat fruit that was off and drink water that was filthy from laundry-use, and went so far as to lick other people's vomit. For people such as these, the sense of sin was a kind of stimulant, like a modern-day amphetamine or aphrodisiac, and their psychology was manifestly masochistic and self-absorbed. Once again, not much use morally.

Literature is replete with instances of the damage wrought by morbid self-abasement, from Baudelaire's constantly tortured remorse to Phèdre's moral paralysis in the face of her love for her stepson Hippolyte in Racine's play. Sin permeates and darkens the air of Lorca's play *The House of Bernarda Alba*, in which a harsh and penitent mother plunges the lives of her five daughters into sin-poisoned frustration and gloom. Spanish friends tell me this is the most accurate depiction of rural Spanish life ever seen on the stage; if they are right, then sin yet holds the power to infect the soul and divert the moral sense from benevolence.

That it does so in reality is all too clear from dozens of case histories. Charles Manson, having been taken from his mother, was brought up in the stern household of an obsessive grandmother who rebuked her husband, Manson's grandfather, as a wicked sinner whenever he tried to show her some human warmth. Manson said that owing to this he never once witnessed a display of affection between them. While it would be grotesque to hold them partially responsible for the terrible crimes their grandson inspired, it must nonetheless be true that any incipient moral sense he may have been holding on to would have been conquered by the atmosphere of sin, hopelessness and selfishness which surrounded his childhood. Dr Alice Miller has made a cogent case to show that the notion of sin may have so infiltrated the consciousness of Christian societies that even non-believing parents can corrupt the moral development of their children by punishing them with the words that it is 'for their own good'. These words instil the belief (not a belief, really, so much as a subconscious certainty) that what hurts emotionally and physically is to be welcomed because pain is inevitably deserved. Such an attitude encourages self-obsession, masochism, asceticism (figurative mostly, but in the sad cases of *anorexia nervosa* or wilful starvation quite actual, and reminiscent of St Simeon Stylites), and moral inertia.

The uncomfortable irony is that Jesus would have recognised nothing in any of it. His remarkable inno-vation, which identified him as a maverick among traditional wandering Jewish teachers, was to extend forgiveness even to sinners, to keep company with them and heal their misery. To his contemporaries this was rank irresponsibility, scarcely credible theologically and socially subversive. To the Church which was founded in his memory, his teaching on the matter of sin remains an embarrassment and is usually avoided (though not by individual priests – see Father John Arnold's *The Quality of Mercy*[10]). Certainly in Latin America the Vatican continues to promulgate a vicious doctrine of sin of which Jesus would have heartily disapproved. An acute psychiatrist, he knew that the concept of perpetually damaging sin was inimical to a moral outlook on life and one's duties within it, and so he constantly sought to assuage and give solace rather than blame. The Gospels are full of examples of his forgiveness offering renewal to frightened souls, who then, released from their burden of worry and egotism, suddenly look outwards and see human life with the eyes of responsible morality. Jesus's enlightened teaching awakened the moral sense; the Roman Church's doctrine tends to suffocate it.

If the sense of sin has encouraged hopelessness in the individual contemplating his own fate, and prevented him from developing that clarity of thought from which moral decision-making may emerge, its effects upon the individual contemplating the destiny of others is still more catastrophic. When you see sin in other people, be they family, the neighbouring community, or a foreign country, and you feel a concomitant duty towards God to root it out, all manner of unspeakable acts may result. Better, I suppose, to be introspectively clogged up, standing on a pillar and stroking wriggly worms, than to be fired by the vindictive fuel of holy retribution. Again, certainty is at the core; clear thinking is vanquished; the route to efficient morality dammed; and fanaticism flourishes. The fanatic is perhaps the most pernicious of moralists, for he has no idea that he has abnegated morality and surrendered it to dogma.

The fanatic is essentially a moral coward. Faced with the difficult choices involved in careful thought he prefers to avoid them altogether by not thinking at all. All that uncertainty and doubt de-anchors him, all that responsibility worries him. Better to hitch his wagon to an already thundering train and allow the wheels to carry him and the noise to infect him.

It is an historical fact that the first instances of mass cruelty were accompanied by the first emergence of moral certainty as a creed, and so little have we changed across the generations and through the different civilisations and cultures that to this day it is advisable to steer well clear of anyone who professes zealous commitment to a moral cause. As soon as the voice adopts that tone of righteous fervour one may be sure it is the prelude to some outrageous prejudice or, worse, to some act of brutal unreflective force. For men to overcome what may be an innate repugnance to doing wrong, they must first prevent themselves from thinking about it or, if that fails, turn the thought inside-out and pretend instead that their moral duty imposes a harsh burden upon them for which they deserve some pity (this was Himmler's line). Nearly all the worst atrocities committed by men against other humans have derived their energy from a powerful sense of moral duty. Idealism, said Jung, was a narcotic as addictive as alcohol.

The number of idealisms and idealists that have poisoned human history is legion, and we have already had cause to look at some of them in other contexts. They have in common a contrived self-attribution of moral superiority. In the fifteenth and sixteenth centuries about 200,000 women were mercilessly tortured and put to death for no other reason than that the Book of Exodus declared 'Thou shalt not suffer a witch to live'. The same sacred text enjoined the murder of anyone who sacrificed to any god but the Lord, an obligation happily adopted by some Christians (one is reminded of the lady who, on learning of the repellent sights discovered by the liberators of Belsen, responded, 'After all, they did kill Our Lord'). The vileness of the Crusades in the eleventh century, the massive slaughter of Albigensians in the thirteenth, the horrors of the Inquisition, were all undertaken with papal blessing to save souls. Similarly superior in moral tone was Senator McCarthy's single-minded hunting down of dissidents in the 1950s, not to save souls but to preserve the American 'way of life', and no-one can doubt he would have been as ruthless as Stalin in liquidating his perceived 'enemies' had he had the power. The Jews annihilated the Amelekites in biblical times, and would dearly love to get rid of the Palestinians today (the former foreign minister Ariel Sharon came close to suggesting as much). The Iraqis who support Saddam Hussein would extinguish the Kurds, the Serbs would wipe out the Muslims in Bosnia, all in the name of righteousness and moral duty.

How plaintive and useless, in the face of all this, does the caution of a Cicero sound. What is morally wrong can never be expedient, he says, even if it achieves its object. 'For the mere act of thinking a course expedient, when it is morally wrong, is demoralizing.'[11]

Fanaticism is a relentless innovator. It appears that once the doubt which should attend all moral choice has been neutralised, nothing is left to inhibit the invention of yet more refined cruelties. St Cyril, Patriarch of Alexandria, sanctioned the horrible murder of Hypatia by a gang of his zealous supporters on the dubious grounds that she read philosophy – she was a learned and decent gentlewoman who had the temerity to value thought for its own sake. The mob dragged her from her chariot, stripped her naked, marched her to the church, and there scraped the flesh from her bones with sharp oyster-shells, hurling her quivering limbs to the flames.[12] Gibbon adds a footnote to inform us that 'oyster-shells were plentifully strewed on the sea-beach before the Caesareum' and that he believes the manner of Hypatia's torment to be literally, and not just metaphorically, true. 'I am ignorant, and the assassins were probably regardless, whether their victim was yet alive.'

The Huguenot merchant Jean Calas was taken to the scaffold; his arms, legs, thighs and loins were systematically smashed; his nose was pinched while great quantities of water were poured through a funnel into his mouth; and his still-living body was stretched upon the wheel beneath the skies, the spokes mingling with his splintered bones; all because the Catholics of Toulouse were convinced he had murdered his own son to prevent apostasy (he hadn't).[13] In England, Margaret Clitheroe was crushed between millstones for having harboured a Catholic priest, and Dr Storey was disembowelled in excruciating agony for having spoken against the Protestant cause.

Such is the obtuseness of the fanatical mind that even the victims of persecution, when they are themselves fanatics, welcome their torment as a sign of superior moral virtue. St Laurence, roasted upon a spit, declared that this was one banquet he had long been looking forward to (the hagiographer Jacobus de Voragine suggested that love of Christ, in this case, acted as 'a refrigerant'). St Ignatius begged to be thrown to the lions ('O salutary beasts that are being readied for me, when will they come? When will they be turned loose? When will they be allowed to feast on my flesh? I shall invite them to devour me.'). And St James the Dismembered uttered cries of joy as each of his fingers, then his toes, then his limbs, were hacked off to leave a triumphant torso.[14]

These peculiar events are partly explained by the ancient belief that death did not matter, a belief shared by the Crusaders as by twentieth-century Islamic suicide-bombers. But it is the air of certainty and lack of any thought processes which, for the present discussion, are most noteworthy. When the Spanish *conquistadores* pulled babies from their mothers' teats in sixteenth-century Cuba and smashed their heads against the rock, they did not consider death, for the infidel, to be a gift, but rather a duty towards *their* God – they praised Jesus of Nazareth and his apostles as the infant brains stained the earth. And in our own century the Croatian friar Miroslav Filipovic habitually tied Serbs to haystacks and watched them burn alive as he shouted at them to say whether or not they believed in God.[15] The most one can say for such people is that they have lost the power to reflect; like Eichmann, they simply do not *realise*, conceptualise, what they are doing.

The propaganda of nations and armies is specifically tuned to help them go dead in the head, in the knowledge, as I pointed out earlier, that a man would find it far more difficult to do wrong if it was not disguised. His moral sense must be smothered, a function regularly undertaken by hymns and exhortations. Mark Twain's iconoclastic 'War Prayer', in which the truth for once is told, would be unbearable to listen to and would dispel that fanaticism with which the uniformed killer must be armed:

O Lord our Father, our young patriots, idols of our hearts, go forth into battle – be Thou near them. Help us to tear their soldiers to bloody shreds with our shells; help us to drown the thunder of their guns with the shrieks of their wounded, writhing in pain; help us to lay waste their humble homes with a hurricane of fire; help us to wring the hearts of their unoffending widows with unavailing grief; help us to turn them out roofless with their little children to wander unfriended the wastes of their desolate land.

This kind of candour is deeply inimical to the frame of mind necessary for brutal action, since it introduces thought into the equation, and is most resented by those who want to stir the pot of fanaticism for idealistic purposes. This is why the Prime Minister of Great Britain, Margaret Thatcher, was so irate when the Archbishop of Canterbury, Robert Runcie, said prayers for all who suffered in the Falklands conflict, Argentine as well as British, at the memorial service in St Paul's; he should not have been so honest or clear-sighted. No doubt she would have deplored the poems of Wilfred Owen ('I am the enemy you killed, my friend'), had she been around for the First World War, and would have boycotted Benjamin Britten's majestic setting of these poems to music in his *War Requiem* when it was first performed, with painful symbolic power, at Coventry Cathedral on 30 May, 1962. (The original cathedral had been bombed out of existence by the Germans, and the baritone solo at this performance was Dietrich Fischer-Dieskau.)

Far from recognising the humanity of the person or persons to be slaughtered, it is important for the survival of fanaticism and triumph of thoughtlessness that the enemy be stigmatised as non-human or sub-human, alien and possibly even insentient. This is easily achieved by the use of nicknames, usually with an insulting edge to them, which manages to objectify – reduce to an object – the person you are about to hurt, a phenomenon we looked at in an earlier chapter. In the First World War, the Germans were called Huns by the British and Boches by the French. The Vietnamese were called gooks by the Americans, Jews are referred to as yids and almost any dark-skinned person is a wog to many Englishmen. While it may not be acceptable, except to a sadist, to tear a peasant lady's head off as her children watch, the feat can be accomplished with ease if she is only a gook, a wog, or a yid.

Another characteristic of fanaticism is that it thrives in a mob and often withers in the individual. Again, this has much to do with the encouragement or prohibition of clear thinking. Left alone, a man has a better chance of sorting out his moral decisions than when he is swept up in the intoxication of the crowd. He may even welcome the release from decision-making and enjoy freedom from conscience by submitting himself to the group. This is why it is important to put soldiers in uniform, to remind them that they no longer exist as individuals and will act in concert as one. It also helps with schoolboys and football fans. The observation echoes a theme at the very beginning of this book, that of the prehistoric animal source of group behaviour. Horrid thought, but it may be that when we are at our most fanatical, most blind, and most amoral, we are at our most ineradicably human. As Robert Ardrey puts it, a trifle floridly as usual:

> The hot symbol of a cross, a swastika, a dummy hanged in effigy. A mob transcends its leaders, becomes a single wild happy thing satisfying identity, stimulation, the following response, xenophobia, australopithecine joys of the hunt and the kill, a thing that through delirious social self-approval

discards all neocortical inhibition. To describe a
mob as sub-human is incorrect; it simply ceases to
behave like individuals. To regard it as a storm of
disorder is equally incorrect, for a mob is as orderly
a human phenomenon as one will ever encounter; let
a single voice of rational dissent be raised within it,
and observe what happens to the dissenter.[16]

We are approaching the most delicate, not to say
intractable, stage of our enquiry, namely the problem
of Adolf Hitler and the German people over whom he
ruled. Does everything said so far stand up to examination when we apply it to what happened in Germany
between 1933 and 1945? Is it possible to explain that
nauseous time by reference to lack of clear thinking and
temporary abandonment of moral identity? Was it only
refuge in group mentality and reversal to basic human
indifference? It seems too simplistic, too insulting, to say
so. Of the eleven and a half thousand judges working in
Germany before Hitler, five thousand went on to do his
vicious work for him in the courts of the Third Reich.
Were they not decent people? When I was a boy, I used
to think there had been four or five extermination camps
in Germany and German-occupied Europe – the ones
we had all heard of (Dachau, Buchenwald, Auschwitz,
Belsen). There were scores of them, manned and run
by thousands of people, served by yet more thousands.
There could scarcely have been a village not involved
in the business of murder when the policy of genocide
was in full swing, and ordinary folk, shop-owners and
teachers, must have participated in this worst squalor of
all. Yet 'the flames and the stench did not distract them
from their daily lives'.[17] Almost the whole of Germany
believed in Hitler and supported him to the hilt (although,
to be fair, up to 150,000 Germans were imprisoned for
disobedience, dishonesty, or resistance to the Reich). The
degree of culpable complicity, to say the very least, in one
of the worst examples of moral madness in the history of
mankind, was overwhelming. A few of those involved

were sadists; some were probably mentally ill; some could have been genetically unstable (an irony Hitler and Heydrich would not have appreciated); some may have meekly followed the crowd.

None of this is enough.

Despite the apologists who point to the crimes of Stalin and Mao Tse-Tung and claim comparison (they think only in mathematical terms), the Holocaust rightly stands out as unique. 'The wickedness of the "final solution" was that it combined in one wickedness every wickedness the human mind can conceive,' wrote Victor Gollancz.[18] It was beyond anything in cruelty and moral degradation. Our analysis thus far has tried to show how wrong-doing may result from an inability to think. And I intend in the last chapter to look at those people who by means of careful thought have found their moral compass and do right and beautiful things. Here we have wrong-doing which emerged from proper political *decision*, and applauded by people who thought that the decision was *right*.

This was not immorality by default, but by design, and it is terrible to contemplate. 'Totalitarian domination tried to establish those holes of oblivion into which all deeds, good and evil, would disappear.'[19] It almost succeeded.

12

THE LOSS OF SHAME

Those shop-owners and teachers may simply have been trained to be obedient and unquestioning. We saw in Chapter One how Stanley Milgram's famous experiments with volunteers who were instructed to administer potentially lethal electric shocks to patients demonstrated the fearsome propensity of people to submit to higher authority. Once personal responsibility is placed in abeyance, *and somebody else can be blamed*, there is seemingly no limit to the amount of wickedness man may wilfully perform. No, that 'seemingly' is misplaced; the Nazi experience finally proves that there is no limit. When human beings are taught to regard other human beings as obstacles or vermin, and accept that teaching as authoritative, clear moral judgement is no longer possible. This must account for the complicity of a large part of the German people in addition to those (proportionately) few sadists who relished the opportunities which were offered.

There are those who cannot bear the indictment of a whole nation, and blame Hitler personally and alone for what happened. There is some justification for this, since it was from Hitler's diseased personality that emerged the virus which eventually infected the German people. Many of the potentially dangerous character defects which we considered early on in this book were manifest in Adolf Hitler to a florid degree. Both Alan Bullock's solid biography and Erich Fromm's more contentious study[1] make it clear that Hitler was almost autistic as a child, incapable of forging any links with other human beings, and that this emotional isolation remained with him throughout life. He was an extreme narcissist, measuring every event and opinion according to how it affected him, and a wild fantasist. He never showed any sustained interest in anything, not even painting, which he had ostensibly studied in Vienna with a view to becoming an artist. Later, architecture engaged his attentions, but only in a superficial way. He was over-zealous in his personal cleanliness, forever frightened of germs and contamination, a disorder of personality which fed his hatred of Jews, gypsies and homosexuals. He had a schizoid tendency to see everything in black and white terms with no redeeming subtleties – the obvious source of his predilection to hatred of the excluded.

Hitler was also a necrophile, with necrophilic habits and fascination with death. That death involved people was a concept which could not penetrate his frighteningly closed mind. Add to all this a fierce lust for power, continually frustrated by his own failures and combined with a total absence of affection, and one may well allow that Adolf Hitler was predestined never to have the smallest hope of moral wisdom.

In a sense, he was the victim of a collision of circumstances and adverse influences. He was also the cause of unparalleled misery. The two are not incompatible. The whole of Europe paid for the deficiencies of this one man, and the price was the lives of millions upon millions of men, women and children, and the devastation of cities (in his fury in defeat, Hitler demanded the destruction of Paris, but his order was for once disobeyed). But it was not only Hitler's personality which was attainted – it was his mind. Were it only the personality, one might well see that all these elements combined to make it impossible for him to think morally, that he was constitutionally deprived of the ability to work things out. This will not do, however, since Hitler was not stupid. He did think. It is the thinking itself which was misdirected.

The clichés engendered by post-Darwinian social theorists ('survival of the fittest', 'war is a biological necessity', etc.) were eagerly swallowed by young Adolf as he trawled the libraries in Vienna following his failure at art college and his brief period as a tramp living on charity. He was humiliated and he was angry. Partially digested Darwin focused his anger and explained his humiliation, and he devoured books on eugenics, racial distinctions, the purity of race and racial hygiene. He would certainly have been familiar with the ideas of Cesare Lombroso (1836–1909), Professor of Criminal Anthropology at Turin University, who sought to demonstrate that genius on the one hand and criminal types on the other were both visible and identifiable in biology. These notions had influence; even within the terms of a novel Joseph Conrad felt the need to ridicule Lombroso as 'this imbecile who has made his way in this world of gorged fools by looking at the ears and teeth of a lot of poor luckless devils'.[2]

Thus, Hitler adopted the fashionable view, widespread in quasi-scientific circles in Britain and the United States as well as Germany, that compulsory sterilisation should be imposed on those people who risked breeding feeble-minded or degenerate specimens, in order to assure that only the best should procreate. His first call to organised murder was that imperfect infants should be eliminated. His schizoid character easily assimilated the idea that Aryans were perfect and non-Aryans defective (in fact, Aryan was not an anthropological definition but a linguistic term with no application to racial distinction), and from this it was but a short step to the doctrine of the master race and the liquidation of the rest.

It is a vicious and cruel irony that Hitler was wrong even on his premisses. We now know far more about genetics, and could have told him that humans, having evolved only recently as comparative upstarts in the world, are a much more homogeneous species than most others, and that there is much more difference between two snails from different valleys in the Pyrenees or between an orang-utan from Borneo and an orang-utan from Sumatra than there could ever be between a black man and a pink one. 'For a snail or an orang-utan it makes good biological sense to be a racist,' writes Steve Jones, 'but humans have to accept the fact that they belong to a tediously uniform species.'[3]

The point is that Hitler's wrong-doing evolved out of wrong conclusions, not from the inability to reach conclusions at all. It was not that he did not ponder, but that his ruminations were sterile, coldly scientific, unrelieved by imagination. He had enough of a mind to think clearly, but the shortcomings of his personality directed his clear thinking along lines totally bereft of the human dimension. The moral sense was not permitted to intrude, and he would not have understood its urgings if it had. For him, it was morally right that he should further the logical aims of scientific knowledge, and that led, in theory, to the death of eleven million individuals in circumstances of unprecedented horror.

The tragedy of the European Jews was not the first genocide in history, nor, alas, is it likely to be the last. Indeed, there have been others since, including the Indonesian determination to wipe out the people of East Timor and the Khmer Rouge policy of obliterating Cambodians. Genocide is not a peculiarly German invention. The Australian settlers had systematically exterminated all the inhabitants of Tasmania, and nearly succeeded in doing the same to the Aboriginal natives of Australia proper. The Spaniards, need we say it again, destroyed everyone living in what is now Latin America, on purpose and with conviction. Those who invaded North America had to develop genocidal policies of astonishing thoroughness and enormity. Nobody knows for certain, but it has been reliably estimated that the population of North America before the European arrived was about eighteen million, in mostly village-based agricultural communities. The last twenty members of the Susquehanna people were murdered by white men in 1763 *because* they were the last twenty. The final 'wild' Indian in America died as recently as 1916. Not only are these numbers greater than those of the victims of the Nazi holocaust, but the reasons given by politicians for their destruction sound grimly familiar.

'Established in the midst of another and a superior race, and without appreciating the causes of their inferiority or seeking to control them,' said President Andrew Jackson, 'they must necessarily yield to the force of circumstances and ere long disappear.' George Washington blatantly declared that his immediate objectives were 'the total destruction and devastation of their settlements. It will be essential to ruin their crops in the ground and prevent their planting more'.[4] Both these gentlemen could now be tried for war crimes, and would probably be found guilty. Theirs are racial comments of the fiercest kind, and they resemble Nazi philosophy both in their intellectual props (the assumption that 'inferior' races must be liquidated) and ruthless methods.

Yet still these genocidal policies fall short of the Nazi experience in two major respects. Hitler's inspiration was first of all obsessive, manic, the product of a disordered personality and not merely the outcome of political determination; and secondly, the arrangements put in place by Germans to realise the Führer's aims were necrophilic in character – mechanical, harsh, efficient and absolute.

The degree of obsessiveness involved was staggering. Though Germany was at war on several fronts, the extermination of the Jews took precedence over everything, and to achieve its success whole areas of land had to be requisitioned, camps built, trains adapted for transport and made to run in preference to ordinary commercial services, medical and engineering manpower turned away from other tasks, a huge bureaucracy established with this one purpose in view, and none of it for military gain but to satisfy a philosophical idea. Even towards the end of the war, when army supplies were desperately short, the transport of Jews to their death was deemed more important, and puppet governments in occupied countries were urged to be more vigorous in their efforts to get rid of Jews. Germany's whole national effort and energy were bent to the purpose, and soldiers were educated to hold Jews responsible for the First World War, for syphilis and typhus, for filthy infection of the human race, blamed for their cleverness and despised for their success. They were taught also not to imagine that a Jewish woman or child could be innocent simply because they were unarmed and helpless; on the contrary, they represented a permanent cultural threat, because germs could multiply exponentially.

Fomented by such a degree of obsession, it is less surprising that individual Germans could be heard to boast that up to 9,000 people could be gassed in one day at a concentration camp, without a shred of suspicion that they were uttering something heinous. (Actually, they could get through 20,000.) 'History itself seemed to have gone malignant' when the systematic murder of masses of people at once was taken as a matter of course, a question only of efficiency, 'scheduled, habitual, industrial'.[5]

The word 'holocaust' has lamentably lost some of its power through frequent use. Like 'unemployment' or 'child abuse' it has been reduced to a collection of syllables representing a specific idea and paradoxically concealing the reality behind it. Not many people who talk of the 'holocaust' have a graphic and vivid image of what they are saying, though they might offer some generalities when challenged. Since we are dealing here with the human potential for kind and for wicked behaviour, it is as well we should understand, through just a few examples taken from Martin Gilbert's documentary account *The Holocaust*, of what the wickedness of the Nazi plague consisted.

At the gates of the Warsaw ghetto, German guards relieved their boredom by devising entertainments for themselves. They would choose a Jew at random and order him to throw himself into the snow with his face down. 'If he is a Jew who wears a beard, they tear it off together with the skin until the snow is red with blood.'

In Lodz, Poland, Jewish girls were ordered to clean

lavatories by removing excrement. They were given nothing to do the job with, and were told to use their blouses. The Germans then wrapped their faces in the blouses, still filthy with excrement, and laughed uproariously. They were much given to laughter, as they inflicted humiliation, pain, finally death, upon their hapless victims, and would invite passers-by to join in the fun. Countless eye-witness accounts of such conduct exist. After a while, it ceased to make much impression. 'Gradually entire populations became immune to feelings of outrage, and learned to shun compassion.'

The murders accelerated as the war progressed. People would be lined up in trenches or on the edge of huge pits they had themselves dug, then shot, covered with lime by the next batch of victims, who would then be shot on top of them. Many did not die from wounds, but from suffocation beneath corpses. 'Only the children were not shot. They were caught by the legs, their heads hit against stones and they were thereupon buried alive.' The most appalling torment was reserved for mothers, who were made to watch the pitiless destruction of their offspring and to grieve for them before they were themselves despatched. Here is one event among many, in Lithuania:

> The infant fell out of her arms. One of the two, the one with the flashlight, I believe, took the infant, raised him into the air, grabbed him by the leg. The woman crawled on the earth, took hold of his boot and pleaded for mercy. But the soldier took the boy and hit him with his head against the wall, once, twice, smashed him against the wall.

Whole communities were obliterated in a single day, entire villages disappeared. The Germans would round up the inhabitants, torture them, herd them into a barn and burn them alive. This they did not only to Jews but to Russian civilians (whom they thought of as 'degenerate Slavs') and to anyone who dared oppose them. Sometimes they encouraged spectators to enjoy the sport. One witness has described a ditch filled with corpses, in which there were some bodies visibly still breathing:

> At the top of the embankment stood German policemen in bloodstained uniforms. German soldiers were congregating in groups. It was a hot day, and some of the soldiers were wearing bathing shorts. Civilians, too, were watching, together with their wives and children.

One despairs to think what those children, who would now be roughly my age, became, or how they survived this kind of education. There are instances, too, of Hitler youth, handsome healthy boys in their teens, dragging women to the floor, spreading their legs apart, and shooting them through the vagina.

All this slaughter, before the extermination camps were multiplied and improved, was tiring. The SS commanders charged with the ordeal would pause for sandwiches and beer, their dogs at their feet, before continuing to kill. The executioners complained of fatigue, that their arms ached from so much shooting, and economised on effort by not bothering to finish off the wounded but let them be buried alive. Less trouble all round, and the sooner they could get to lunch. Once again, children were not worth killing; it saved time to throw them into the pit alive. When the task was complete for the day, the Germans would go down into the pit, walking over the bodies to search for gold rings and the like. If a ring could not easily be removed, they would amputate the finger.

Those male prisoners deemed fit to work, at least until they dropped, were sterilised immediately, and all pregnant women executed. An SS man was seen to isolate a woman in the last stages of pregnancy, throw her to the ground and stamp on her with his boots until the birth was forced. 'In blood and pain the woman died wretchedly.'

'We are in the presence of a crime without a name,' said Winston Churchill, for once shocked out of his eloquence. His awkwardness with words in the face of Nazi wickedness adequately conveys the sense that this was, despite mankind's terrible history, something worse, something more sinister.[6]

Here is an account, to stand for many, of extermination in the Ukraine:

> ... people undressed, stood around in family groups, kissed each other, said farewells, and waited for a sign from another SS man, who stood near the pit, also with a whip in his hand. During the fifteen minutes that I stood near I heard no complaint or plea for mercy. I watched a family of about eight persons, a man and a woman, both about fifty, with their children aged about one, eight and ten, and two grown-up daughters of about twenty to twenty-four. An old woman with snow-white hair was holding the one-year-old child in her arms and singing to it and tickling it. The child was cooing with delight. The couple were looking on with tears in their eyes. The father was holding the hand of a boy about ten years old and speaking to him softly, the boy was fighting his tears. The father pointed to the sky, stroked his head and seemed to explain something to him. At that moment the SS man at the pit shouted something to his comrade. The latter counted about twenty persons and instructed them to go behind the earth mound. Among them was the family which I have mentioned. I well remember a girl, slim with black hair, who as she passed close to me pointed to herself and said, 'Twenty-three.' I walked around the mound and found myself confronted by a tremendous grave. People were closely wedged together and lying on top of each other so that only their heads were visible. Nearly all had blood running over their shoulders from their heads. Some of the people shot were still moving. Some were lifting their arms and turning their heads to

show that they were still alive. The pit was already two-thirds full. I estimated that it already contained about 1000 people. I looked for the man who did the shooting. He was an SS man, who sat at the edge of the narrow end of the pit, his feet dangling into the pit. He had a tommy-gun on his knees and was smoking a cigarette. The people, completely naked, went down some steps which were cut in the clay wall of the pit and clambered over the heads of the people lying there, to the place to which the SS man directed them. They lay down in front of the dead or injured people; some caressed those who were still alive and spoke to them in a low voice. Then I heard a series of shots. I looked into the pit and saw that the bodies were twitching or the heads lying motionless on top of the bodies which lay before them. Blood was running away from their necks.[7]

Conditions in the concentration camps, where people were either gassed, worked, or starved to death, were indescribable. Adjectives are useless – too feeble and familiar – to deal with such sights. Plain facts suffice. When the British entered Belsen, for instance, they found a situation more horrific than Dante had imagined for any of his circles in Hell. Thousands of naked corpses lay rotting. Those prisoners who were yet alive were as thin as skeletons, teeming with lice, covered in excrement. 'Both inside and outside the huts was an almost continuous carpet of dead bodies, human excreta, rags and filth.' In the huts, where people slept several to a bunk and the bunks were piled six high, skeletons were used as makeshift pillows. The people in the lowest bunk, too weak to move, drowned in the urine and faeces which fell from the bunks above. The smell was overpowering. Guards were indifferent to what they had lived with, in some cases for years. Outside the gates of Belsen lay some of the richest and most fertile fields in Germany, where fresh vegetables grew in abundance.[8]

Further away, in the fashionable restaurants and

posh homes of occupied Paris, French hostesses had been entertaining Nazi guests at happy dinner-parties, discussing the outcome of the war and the solution of the Jewish 'problem'.

The solution had been nicely under way at Birkenau, or 'Auschwitz II', where the gas ovens worked to capacity:

> They succeeded in locking the doors. One heard cries and shouts and they started to fight against each other, knocking on the walls ... When the doors were opened a crowd of bodies fell out because they were compressed so much. They were quite contracted, and it was almost impossible to separate one from the other. One got the impression that they fought terribly against death. Anybody who has ever seen a gas chamber filled to the height of one and a half metres with corpses will never forget it. At this point the proper work of the Sonderkommandos starts. They have to drag out the bodies which are still warm and covered with blood, but before they are thrown into the ditches they have still to pass through the hands of the barber and the dentist, because the barber cuts the hair off and the dentist has to take out all the teeth. Now it is proper hell which is starting. The Sonderkommando tries to work as fast as possible. They drag the corpses by their wrists in furious haste. People who had human faces before, I cannot recognize again.[9]

Some of these accounts have an uncanny ring. They resemble the frantic struggle of a population against a fearsome encroaching disease and are reminiscent of campaigns against plague. It is no accident that the attitude of these men and women towards Jews, homosexuals, gypsies and dissidents was like the attitude you or I might adopt if faced with an invasion of rats, because Hitler's régime did precisely inculcate the notion that such people were vermin, to be eradicated at all costs. The only way we might spare a rat would be to use it for experiment, as did scores, perhaps hundreds, of medical men use the inmates of concentration camps to satisfy scientific curiosity. They appear to have acted without qualm or doubt. The experiments of Joseph Mengele with twins have seeped into public consciousness, but there were other commonplace exercises performed daily, with chilling indifference. At Dachau, for example, Dr Sigismund Rascher wanted to discover the effects of changing air pressure:

As many as twenty-five persons were put at one time into a specially constructed van in which pressure could be increased or decreased as required. The purpose was to find out the effects of high altitude and of rapid parachute descents on human beings ... Most of the prisoners who were made use of died as a result of these experiments, from internal haemorrhages of the lungs or brain. The rest coughed blood when taken out ... Rascher also conducted experiments on the effects of cold water on human beings. This was done to find a way for reviving aviators who had fallen into the ocean. The subject was placed in ice-cold water and kept there until he was unconscious. Blood was taken from his neck and tested each time his body temperature dropped one degree. This drop was determined by a rectal thermometer. Urine was also periodically tested. Some men lasted as long as 24 to 36 hours. The lowest body temperature reached was 19 degrees C., but most men died at 25 degrees C., or 26 degrees C. When the men were removed from the ice water attempts were made to revive them by warmth from the sun, from hot water, from electrotherapy or by animal warmth. For this last experiment prostitutes were used and the body of the unconscious man was placed between the bodies of two women.

Those who survived this treatment were sent to the 'invalid' block and there liquidated.[10]

Although I have been to Munich a dozen times over the last forty years, it was not until two years ago that I had the courage to visit Dachau. The silence there is sadness itself, and I felt lonely. It was not the loneliness of being alone, but the loneliness of fear in the presence of intangible evil.

Writing about such things, one is driven to leave the keyboard and turn away to weep. That Martin Gilbert should have imposed upon himself the agony of minutely documenting this solemn and sickening episode of the derangement of human morality in *The Holocaust*, a volume of over 800 pages, makes one wonder at his sheer strength. But then, of course, he would see it as his duty. Not the oft-quoted duty never to forget, but the more subtle duty of opening the door to the sun, of allowing people to ponder and shiver, then replenish with light. If you turn your back on wickedness you forfeit the joy of contemplating the good, the kind and the worthy for what they really are – not accidents of fate or character, but big, bold choices.

What happened to the Germans between 1933 and 1945 was an unparalleled surge of nastiness, without disguise and without shame. The perpetrators of deeds such as those mentioned above (a tiny fraction, alas, of the whole) had lost the sense of shame without which the moral sense cannot flourish. They had been given permission, by the State, to plumb the depths of their potential and were forbidden, also by the State, to soar to the heights. It was no longer a question of thinking clearly, because the necessity for thought had been removed, all the thinking having been done by Hitler and his henchmen; it was a question of thinking wrongly. Heaven knows, the thought was clear enough. But it was untinged by imagination, by emotion. It was logical, mathematical, direct, unflinching thought, iron-clad and untroubled. And ultimately inhuman. This kind of imperturbable straight-arrow thinking is not the end to which our species has evolved. It has nothing to do with character, whether derived from animal inheritance or DNA structure or prehistoric hunting packs. It is free of mental disease and personality disorder, despite overwhelming evidence to suggest insanity. It is an intellectual aberration, a freezing of the process of moral thought which induces a sort of paralysis. Instead of the result of thinking clearly, an activity akin to prayer, the tragedy of the Jews and the Germans in our time was the result of thinking coldly, an activity only neurologically distinguishable from death.

The essential character of the saint or good person, on the contrary, is the ability to think warmly, that is to combine firm clarity of thought with equally firm emotional honesty. Escape from self, from disease, from determinist strategies, from obedience, from moral codes, are all prerequisites of the benevolent life. Having struggled with all these influences, one may emerge into the sweet-smelling day of humanity at its most radiant.

13

SAINTS

In spite of everything I still believe that people are
really good at heart.
>   – *Anne Frank, who died in Belsen
>   within a year of this entry in her journal.*

By now it must be obvious that many of those saints who
are meant to be God's messengers and examples on earth
would not pass our test of saintliness. Ours is more exact-
ing, for it demands active thoughtfulness, that is action
full of thought, as well as selflessness, kindness, maturity
and sanity in abundant measure. There are dozens, perhaps even hundreds, of saints who cannot measure up.

Iñigo Lopez de Recalde, more famously known as
Ignatius de Loyola, the founder of the Jesuit movement
in 1534, is a case in point. Canonised in 1622, a mere
sixty-six years after his death, his single-mindedness and
ferocity of purpose were admirable, but his character
was not good. He was brutal to his subordinates and
cruelly indifferent to the loyalty of his secretary, Juan
Pelanco, whom he treated with disdain. So harsh was
he that many of his colleagues openly wondered why
they should suffer such indignities, but they resisted
the clear conclusion, namely that Ignatius was malign.
There was an arrogance and blindness about him which
prevented him ever being a real saint, devoted to the cheer
of people. On the contrary, his closed mind and iron heart
made it impossible for him to think compassionately,
and, though he undeniably ranks high in influence, he
must lie low in goodness.

Nor can St Catherine of Siena (1347–1480) count for much by our measurements, as she was quite obviously ill, suffering from what we should now term a 'mental disease or defect'. One of twenty-five offspring of a prosperous wool dyer and his wife, Catherine first showed signs of aberration at the age of sixteen, an age when some modern young ladies fall into the dangerous trap of anorexia nervosa or bulimia. Catherine's trouble might well nowadays have been diagnosed anorexic, for she forced herself to live on a couple of spoonfuls of herbs per day, and to sleep no more than two hours a night. She stayed in her room and spoke to nobody. This continued for three years until, her mind presumably weakened by starvation, she had hallucinations. A pageant of dazzling light and colour came towards her, with dozens of angels, Jesus, Mary his mother, St John, St Paul and quite a few more, all sumptuously dressed and accompanied by the sort of heavenly music that would have been totally unfamiliar to them in the eastern Mediterranean, to assure her that the Lord would be with her throughout life. She then walked into the kitchen and startled her long-suffering family in the middle of dinner.

Catherine became famous for her bullying of popes and town councillors to do as she bade them, and for her spectacular fainting fits. She would pass into a trance at the drop of a hat, be quite unreachable on a human level, mumble and tremble and offer vulgar entertainment for the crowd, who thought she was blessed with holy visions. Her favourite word was 'blood', with which she seems to have been almost obsessed, with psychiatric implications a modern doctor might find interesting. She died at the age of thirty-three, not surprisingly from a stroke, and was canonised eighty-one years later.

For our purposes, however, St Catherine appears to have done not an ounce of good for anyone, and cannot enter our list of the morally admirable. There was little thought in her posturings and, despite her belabouring of the powerful, no truly outward-directed attention. She was as imprisoned in self as are the clinically mad, and her private joy, which no-one must begrudge her, was to be married to Christ.

She was not the only one, of course. That perfect hysteric St Theresa of Lisieux (1873–1897) was embarrassingly ecstatic about giving her life to Jesus. 'Ah, how sweet was the first kiss of Jesus to my soul,' she wrote. 'Yes, it was a kiss of love! I felt that I was loved, and I said also, "I love you, I give myself to you forever." Jesus asked nothing of me. He required no sacrifice. He and the little Thérèse had long since looked at one another and had understood. That day, our meeting could no longer be called a simple look, but a *fusion*. We were no longer two.'[1] That was a description of her first communion, but in her mind it represented the giving of herself, body and all, in a grand dynastic marriage. Without a trace of self-consciousness this pubescent girl was able to write, 'God Almighty, Creator of heaven and earth, sovereign Dominator of the world, and the Most Glorious Virgin Mary, Queen of her celestial court, are pleased to inform you of the spiritual marriage of their august Son, Jesus, King of Kings and Lord of Lords, to little Thérèse Martin, now Lady and Princess of the realms brought her as her dowry by her divine Spouse.' She ought to have been spanked.

Still more objectionable was Theresa's self-serving ambition. There was only one thing she wanted in life, and moreover was determined to get, and that was to be recognised as a saint. In her own words, not just any old saint, but a 'great saint'. To this end, her visions of the mother of Jesus, usually evoked after having worked herself into a state of fever and excitement with the statue of Mary in front of her, were deliberate attempts to mimic sanctity and divine ecstasy, and would have been diagnosed pathological self-induced erotic mania by a wary and informed doctor. (Contrast the infinitely more beguiling St Theresa of Avila, who never took herself seriously and was amused when somebody told her that, though she may be a saint, she didn't look much like one.)

Pope Pius XI described Theresa of Lisieux as 'an exquisitely delicate miniature of perfect saintliness'. We should prefer a tediously morbid example of hysterical egotism. She is mentioned only because there are many still today who would agree with Pius XI, and because her fame and reputation are not supported by any evidence of escape from self-obsession. Again, one can find nothing of any good that she ever did.

Mother Teresa of Calcutta, on the other hand, has done some good for poor, diseased and abandoned children in India, but she has also done a great deal of harm along the way. Famously picked out by Germaine Greer as the one person in the world she would unhesitatingly call a villain, and by Christopher Hitchens as 'dangerously sinister', Mother Teresa nonetheless has the Nobel Prize. The answer to this riddle lies, I think, in the occasional disparity between goodness and effectiveness. Public opinion, of the barely informed variety, reveres Mother Teresa as a saint on the assumption that she has devoted her life to saving children from degradation or death. It is true that the Sisters of Mercy who work in her name bring the sweetest compassion to their dreadful task. The children they rescue are either girls or crippled boys, thrown out because useless in Hindu culture, and they are cared for selflessly until somebody adopts them. The aged nun who takes all the credit, and is rarely in Calcutta herself, must originally have been moved by just such pity and the urge to help the human débris of life. But that is long since past, and she now adds to the débris by her proselytising example.

Mother Teresa is before all else a sincere committed ambassador for the Vatican. When she says that the greatest single threat to world peace is the practice of contraception and abortion, she believes it, and cannot see, because she does not think, that she is talking bunk. Though she sees all around her the disastrous effects of unchecked population, the misery and wretchedness which result from the denial of contraceptive possibilities, she encourages these evils, even rejoices in them. She has applauded the world's most wicked life-poisoning dictators, such as Haiti's Duvalier and Albania's Hoxha, because they welcome increase in population and express their love for the poor by rewarding prolific mothers and punishing sensible ones. In short, she is not a charitable force so much as a dogmatic one. She is perhaps the best living exemplar of the dangers of an empty head allied to a decent heart. Thoughts are not her friends, and so she can do little that is positively good in the long term. Mother Teresa is a public relations officer for the Vatican, not a saint, but doubtless the Roman Catholic Church will beatify her one day.

The Church's favourite English saint, Edmund Campion, likewise falls short of the standards we have set, for he relished the fight against the Protestant establishment too much, revealing a degree of vanity and self-satisfaction which militate against true outward-looking thoughtfulness. So, too, did Thomas More; they suffered from what the Church has often called (though not in relation to them) the sin of pride. On the other hand, it was a sin which enabled them to withstand interrogation in court, in the face of much legal sophistry, with tremendous courage and dignity, qualities that would be manifested in similar circumstances three centuries later by Oscar Wilde, likewise taunted and pilloried in the dock. None of the three – Campion, More, Wilde – was saintly, however. Theirs was the victory of intellectual stubbornness, not benign disposition, and they were all three too pleased with themselves for true saintliness.

John Henry Newman, probably the most famous Catholic convert, had the same trouble, measuring every incident and opinion according to how it affected himself. If humility be an essential ingredient of beneficence, as I suggested in Chapter Eleven, then Cardinal Newman hardly qualifies for sanctity. The sufferings of the disadvantaged in society, to which Mother Teresa at least responds in her way, left him indifferent, even occasionally hostile. The Jewish teacher whose goodness his religion nominally celebrated would not have recognised him. 'He seemed continually to fail to come to grips with the concept of forgiveness as well as its practice,' wrote Newman's biographer. 'He nourished resentment far too deeply; he refused to take efforts at reconciliation at their face value; and a trust once broken was a trust destroyed.'[2]

Newman was fond of saying that it was the imperfections of saints that made them endearing. I suggest, rather, that it makes them suspect. Of course, as I said earlier, the true measure of moral goodness lies in the struggle to attain such a state against the myriad adverse influences which constantly assail it, but saints who tend to pat themselves on the back for having triumphed are still stuck in the mud of self-regard. The struggle must not be advertised, or it risks being simple pretence – egotism in mufti. Cato in Iris Murdoch's *Henry and Cato* forsakes the priesthood in order to devote himself to the care of Beautiful Joe, his beguiling protégé, but Joe sees through his sacrifice, recognising it as self-serving pursuit of sanctity[3] (recalling Hobbes's dictum that generosity and disinterestedness could be subtle forms of the will-to-power). Wilde confronted the problem squarely in his *Picture of Dorian Gray* (1890), which sought to discover whether one could be moved by 'that passion to act a part that sometimes makes us do things finer than we are ourselves'. Dorian gave a grimly pessimistic answer to his own question. 'Through vanity he had spared her [Hetty Merton]. In hypocrisy he had worn the mask of goodness. For curiosity's sake he had tried the denial of self.'[4]

This is an arresting expression of the moral danger inherent in thoughtfulness without heart.

And yet the very presence of the hypocrite in our midst indicates that there must be real virtue for him to ape; hypocrisy is impossible without genuine goodness as its model. 'The existence of fake rescuers and benefactors, far from disproving the existence of the real thing, actually establishes it.'[5]

On the other hand, one hardly needs to be a cynic or hypocrite in order to avoid doing good. Cowardice or inertia are equally effective. By cowardice I mean nothing more fundamentally reprehensible than apprehension, the fear that choosing to do the right thing for its own sake might upset the fragile balance of daily desires and duties, throw in a heavy unexpected weight which sends tumbling all the other ingredients which render life pleasurable or at least familiar. 'The burden of genuine goodness is instinctively appreciated as intolerable.'[6] Well, difficult, certainly, and liable to jostle one out of comfortable routines. Liable, also, to uncover a potential for heart-informed thoughtfulness that one may not have noticed hiding in a corner of one's being. To keep it unbidden for fear of its revolutionary effects might make for tranquillity, but it must also make for non-humanity, a kind of deadness of the soul. 'The man whose desires are limited within the circle of his own experiences will find, as he grows older and his future becomes more circumscribed, that life grows continually narrower and less interesting, until nothing remains but to sit by the fire and keep warm.'[7]

Thus it is that the outward-directed, thought-inspired, wilfully good act is an enrichment as well as a Kantian duty, a rejoicing in that element of life which courses through us and makes us, whether we inherit it in genetic form from our animal forebears or not, utterly and distinctively human. Goodness can be a celebration of humankind and a discovery of the human within the individual. It is akin to the Hindu concept of *ahimsa*, which Mahatma Gandhi elevated into his strategy of non-violence. 'Ahimsa is not just a negative state of harmlessness, but also a positive state of love or good-will even to evil-doers.'[8]

In literature, this state of love is best presented by Myshkin in *The Idiot*. 'My intention is to portray a truly beautiful soul,' said Dostoievsky. Myshkin is depicted as deeply innocent (not just harmless, as the word literally implies, but incapable of thinking harm), pure and benign. His goodness is based not on any theory or analytical thought, but upon love of people, and therefore on *personal* thought. The result of his attitude is to create harmony, completeness, a feeling of proportion and ease, all those attributes we have been struggling in these pages to define and rediscover. He is moral goodness made into flesh.

However, Dostoievsky is too canny a writer not to recognise the obverse of the coin. Aglaya, who pays tribute to Myshkin's 'beautiful and kind-hearted simplicity', is aware of the unwelcome burden this goodness places upon all those around him, who are tired of being constantly forgiven and thereby made subtly to detest themselves. 'You have no tenderness,' she says, 'nothing but truth, and so you judge unjustly.' They are also weary of Myshkin's self-abasement, his insistence on his own shortcomings, which they guiltily interpret as a veiled accusation against themselves. Personally, I think Aglaya's stricture unfair; Myshkin does have tenderness, but it is unlikely to be discerned as such by people for whom truthfulness – that is, honest thought – is an unpleasant interference. Tom Pinch in *Martin Chuzzlewit*, Dickens's depiction of a man who can only think well, similarly comes up against this wary obtuseness, and there are still critics who distrust him. No doubt Jesus of Nazareth was much bothered by folk like these.

Of all the people who have walked into and out of these pages, none is more vivid than this obscure, little-known, much mythologised wandering prophet. We have no idea what he looked like, how tall he was, how his voice was pitched, who his mother was (apart from her name), when he was born, whether he fathered any children. In contemporary history there is but one fleeting mention of him, barely half a sentence. Yet his example of goodness is overwhelming, and if half the stories in the Gospels are true, he was a man rare in his compassion, almost unique in his wisdom. The conclusions I have been edging towards are all illuminated by him.

I say Jesus is 'almost' unique because to make him without parallel of any kind would be to fall into the trap of god-creation. Francis of Assisi surpassed him in compassion and humility (Jesus could be quite proud at times); Dr Johnson surpassed him in creative wisdom; Theresa of Avila was more humorous, less solemn, and Aelred of Rievaulx more friendly. Grand Duchess Ella had more courage, and even Audrey Hepburn more spunk. Sometimes Jesus's goodness seems to flow out of him and eddy round him, his presence having much the same effect as that of St Francis. This could be due to exaggeration by the writers of the Gospels, but I suspect not, given the sense of authentic astonishment in their narrative. (The one thing we cannot doubt about the Gospels is their tone of voice.) And if it is true of St Francis, a much more recent and historically attested character, then why cannot it be true for Jesus?

Jesus's purpose was not just passive – the careful avoidance of wrong-doing – writes Father John Arnold, it was 'filled with the unpredictable activity of responding to the needs of others'.[9] In this he echoed the Hindu concept of *ahimsa*, mentioned above, as he did also in his remarkable willingness to forgive wrong-doers and openly associate with them, which did not make him popular with the authorities (and indeed, would not make him popular now with the Roman Catholic Church). John Arnold rightly calls his forbearance 'lavish':

> This attitude to forgiveness which shines through the whole of Jesus's ministry can well be described as lavish. It reaches in all directions, touching all types of people in every sort of circumstance. It was never refused.[10]

The Pharisees and the Essenes, who held that forgiveness could only be bestowed upon the pure, were scandalised. Their representative in the nineteenth century was Cardinal Newman. Jesus knew, intuitively one supposes, that it was not easy to do the right thing and that those who did wrong were often too lazy or weak or unsure of themselves to think clearly. Even those who did think and came to immoral decisions Jesus was willing to understand. He recognised that the potential for goodness in every person had to be nourished, not flattened by condemnation, vengeance and retribution. The most vociferous and vindictive Conservative politicians now busy in Britain, those who delight in punishment for the wicked, would have flung Jesus of Nazareth from their midst in disgust. He would certainly have been evicted from the party conference.

It is even more important, in the light of all I have said before, that we do not diminish Jesus by loading him with the apparel of a deity. In the first place, he was a pious Jew who would have been horrified to be accused of blasphemy; to claim he was God would have made him the grossest blasphemer possible. In the second place, and far more significantly, it is in his condition as a human being, a person of goodness and positive pure thought, that his greatness lies. To suggest that he was an incarnate divinity 'threatens to deprive the central figure in the Gospels of his moral seriousness', writes A.N. Wilson. He goes on, '[Jesus] is depicted as a fully human being. But it was in the richness of that humanity that those who knew him felt close to heaven.'[11]

Nobody would pretend today that Jesus of Nazareth was an historically isolated figure. There had been teachers like him before, and teachers who were his contemporaries. Much of what he had to say was inherited in Jewish tradition, and much of the mythology which grew around him had grown around other prophets, likewise credited with virgin mothers and martyred deaths. Yet his honest, frank vision and his gentleness marked him out as an original, and after his death attempts were made by those who had known him to perpetuate his memory. They were led by his brother James, who carried on his teaching with some success until he, too, was crucified and the incipient religious movement in honour of Jesus was hijacked by St Paul. Had this not happened, there might have evolved a true 'Jesus church' ('Christ' only means 'anointed', and thus 'Christian' is not very specific), dedicated to the promulgation of the man's voice and views. Instead we had the Roman Catholic Church, wherein he is unrecognisable.

St Francis of Assisi was another who humanised by his presence, whose humanity brought one 'close to heaven'. He said, 'Not to hurt our humble brethren is our first duty to them, but to stop there is not enough. We have a higher mission – to be of service to them wherever they require it.' St Vincent de Paul was similarly disposed to devote his energies to the poor – Frank Longford calls him 'the saint of the outcasts' – but nobody apart from Jesus himself has ever been able to match Francis's astonishing, genuine goodness. He disdained nobody, forswore possessions, and lived upon whatever people would give him. A leper, a poisoner, an adulterer, would all be swept into his embrace and ennobled thereby. Were he alive today, he would befriend the child-abuser and the serial killer. Incapable of hatred, vindictiveness, pomposity or self-righteousness, Francis was the supreme reconciler. His famous poem was read to the cameras by Margaret Thatcher as she arrived at 10 Downing Street on the eve of her premiership in 1979:

> Where there is hatred, let me sow love;
> Where there is injury, pardon;
> Where there is discord, union;
> Where there is doubt, faith;
> Where there is despair, hope;
> Where there is darkness, light;
> Where there is sadness, joy;
> For your mercy and truth's sake.
> O Divine Master, grant that I may not so much seek
> To be consoled as to console,
> To be understood as to understand,
> To be loved as to love,
> For it is in giving that we receive,

278

It is in pardoning that we are pardoned,
It is in dying that we are born to eternal life.

The last sentiment, taken figuratively, is as valid as the rest, and may be re-stated as 'It is in subordination of self that our humanity is revealed'. Those who prefer to interpret it literally do no harm thereby.

Francis also taught that the accumulation of wealth was a major spiritual menace, but Mrs Thatcher did not quote that part of his message. Nor have his heirs, the Franciscans, paid much heed to it. They began to demolish his legacy of humility and self-abnegation almost the day after his death. Anyone who passes a beggar on the streets and wilfully avoids the opportunity of doing good should pause to ponder the man from Assisi.

If goodness resides in the positive bestowal of love, informed by clarity of thought, then the number of true saints who adorn the history of mankind far exceeds that of the ravagers we considered in the last chapter. It may not always seem so, for the actions of wicked men are more florid and conspicuous than the quiet decencies of ordinary beneficence, and their effects are obviously more dramatic. They also unsettle, and we tend to respond to unsettling knowledge with great noise and anguish. Goodness, creating harmony and the full flowering of human character, trickles quietly beside us, unnoticed and unexplored. There are dozens of St Francises in all our lives.

Aelred of Rievaulx, another hero of this book, likewise celebrated the positive power of friendship and loyalty in realising what is fully human. Aelred is the enemy of all cynicism. It is a commonplace in our passionless times to believe that the moment you give, either materially or emotionally, you establish an indebtedness which will destroy whatever friendship you enjoyed with the beneficiary of your kindness. Alastair McAlpine, in his brilliant parody of Machiavelli, caught the misanthropic spirit of this deadly caution in his couplet, 'The man who would do you a favour is your friend for life. The one who would ask a favour will one day be your enemy.'[12] This is truly the level of public-house wisdom, and is absolutely false. But it requires an Aelred or a Cicero or a Montaigne to tell us that it is false, for we are easily seduced by such paradoxes, and it takes an Aelred to demonstrate its falsity in life and example. The cynics and the destroyers would have watched their spleen and ire evaporate in the atmosphere of Rievaulx Abbey in Aelred's day, and even Himmler might have been subdued. Aelred showed conclusively that goodness in demeanour and behaviour towards one's fellows cannot be mere inhibition – the subjugating of disintegrating forces within the psyche – but must be positively benign. Oddly enough, Lord McAlpine followed his cynical observation with a gentler reflection: 'The giving of true friendship is the greatest gift that one man can give another, and he that would give this friendship can always be relied upon.'

Many of the finest monks and nuns have, like Aelred, encouraged the free flow of affection within their walls. Theresa of Avila had countless friends, and her convent was a place of mirth and enjoyment as well as worship. It could hardly be otherwise when she implored God to save her and her sisters 'from fleas, ghosts, and bad roads'; when she told Him that He had so few friends because He treated them all so badly; and when she could utter the most mischievous prayer, 'God deliver me from sullen saints!'[13] She also possessed to an extraordinary degree that capacity for forgiveness which is the essence of benign thought.

I know of no more exuberant example of forgiveness, however, than that displayed by Grand Duchess Ella of Russia, whose story is epic in scale, whose sweetness of disposition disarmed the fiercest men.

Her real name was Elizabeth and her proper title was Grand Duchess Serge, but it is as Ella that she was known to all. She was born in 1864, daughter of Grand Duke Louis IV of Hesse-Darmstadt and his wife, Princess Alice of England. She started life, therefore, as Princess

Elizabeth of Hesse, one of Queen Victoria's favourite grand-daughters. She grew into an exceedingly pretty adolescent, fairly bright, fluent in English as well as German, an accomplished ballroom dancer and considerable flirt. It was quite clear that Princess Elizabeth was one of the most eligible young ladies in Europe, a jewel for any prince. Shortly before her twentieth birthday, she married Grand Duke Serge of Russia, uncle to the Tsar. (Her sister Alexandra married the Tsar himself, which made Ella her own sister's aunt.)

The wedding was one of the most lavish and spectacular to adorn that age of extravagance – the late nineteenth-century aristocratic illusion. Carriages, horses, glitter, gold and pomp brought the ravishing princess to St Petersburg, and Russian society was entranced by her. Not only was she a brilliant dancer, but her conversation was attractive, her laughter infectious, her friendliness beguiling. She took a great interest in her clothes and jewellery and made her husband Serge proud. She grew to love him passionately. But she also secretly suffered at the plight of the poor, whom her Romanov relations appeared not to notice. And she was deeply religious.

There was much resentment in the country against the Romanovs, and against Ella on account of her 'foreignness'. The war with Japan exacerbated tensions, although few noticed that Ella herself worked on the ambulance trains; dressed in plain grey she passed unremarked.

Inside her palace one day in February, 1905, Ella heard a shattering explosion in the street and knew it was a bomb. Without waiting to put on a coat, she ran down the ornate staircase and into her carriage, which had been ready to take her to an appointment. She and the coachman approached a crowd not a hundred yards away. Peasant women tried to stop the Grand Duchess getting out, for fear she might be alarmed by what she saw. But she would not heed them.

Stepping into the blood-stained snow, Ella picked up pieces of clothing, fingers, a severed hand, a severed foot, a whole leg. She could not handle the torso, which was an indescribable mess, but she was able to recover part of the shattered skull. The face, reduced to red sponge, was no longer identifiable, but she knew, as did everyone else present, that it was her beloved husband Serge.

Ella, kneeling in the snow, her dress stained with blood, gave directions for the wounded coachman to be carried off to hospital, then organised the placing of her husband's remains on a stretcher. She did it alone, the crowd stunned into silence by awe, pity and respect. Only when men carried the stretcher off did she rise to her feet and walk calmly behind it. Meanwhile, the police had arrested the assassin at the back of the crowd.

In the palace, Ella wrote several telegrams imparting the shocking news, then went straight to the hospital to see the dying coachman, whose only concern was the welfare of Grand Duke Serge. 'All is well with him,' she told the man, 'it is he who sent me to see you.' Thus was he able to die with a peaceful heart. Next she went to Taganka Prison and asked to see the murderer, Kaliaev. Shown into his cell, she stayed alone with him. He asked who she was. 'I am the wife of the man you have killed,' she said. 'Why did you do it?' Kaliaev said he had acted in accordance with high principle. She left him with a small holy picture and said she would pray for him. She wondered whether he would keep it or throw it away, but she said she left it because she had to – he could not go to his fate so burdened with bad conscience. Later she found out that the assassin had treasured her little gift.

Ella explained that 'zuerst muss sie verstehen alles verziehen können' (that she must understand all in order to be able to forgive all), a worthy ambition much derided by societies stale with vengeance. Her brother described her goodness in a phrase which recalls some of the conclusions we have been edging towards in these pages. 'Wie ihr Ausseres, so war auch ihr Inneres.' (Her exterior conduct was in harmony with her interior self.) In other words, the integrity of Ella's character was not splintered or fractured in any way; she was at ease and secure in her soul, and therefore able to behave well. Everyone was afraid that her apparently incredible self-control would lead to a nervous breakdown. Not so; she did not have to force herself into conduct which was not natural to her. She continued to pray for the man who had stolen from her everything she loved in a few seconds one February afternoon.

Ella changed in one respect. She decided to ignore the world's description of her as the most beautiful and wealthiest Grand Duchess in Russia, and re-invent herself as she wished to be. In this sense she was one of the most striking examples of existentialist woman. She divided her jewellery, one of the most famous collections in the world, into three piles: a small pile to be returned to the crown jewels; another small pile to be distributed to nieces and nephews; and the greater part to be sold off. She got rid of all her luxurious furniture and reduced her room to a bare cell. Finally she left the palace altogether and became a nun.

Without hysterics or trances or visible drama, Ella exchanged the grand possessions she had been used to for a peasant's cart. She must be one of the quietest saints ever.

Ella went into the slimiest and most dangerous slums of Moscow, incognito but privately watched by the police who deemed it their duty still to protect her. When the police themselves became frightened and told her they could do no more for her safety, she thanked them for their kindness but asked them not to worry, for she was in God's hands and not theirs. She cared for the vermin-infested and the disease-ridden, cooked for them, washed their dishes, scrubbed their floors to improve hygiene. She comforted the bereaved and the desperate. One story tells of Ella's visits to the home for incurables. Sitting with a dying woman as she lay in bed, and realising that the moments left to her were few, she sent for the woman's husband, a communist revolutionary, who was also a devoted husband. When he arrived, he found Ella holding his wife's hand, and he quietly took the other hand. The Grand Duchess and the terrorist together saw her leave the world. To be in the same room with her was peace, he said.

With the advent of the Great War, hostility against the good nun's German accent as well as her Romanov marriage and exalted status grew bitter, and Ella was in constant danger. Known as *matushka* (little mother) by the street urchins of Moscow, and as The German by her detractors, Ella went quietly about her business of rescuing the poor and unlamented. Prisons and lunatic asylums were emptied, their inmates set loose in Moscow. One day a group of violent prisoners, drunk and filthy, accosted her. One of them knew who she was.'You're not an Imperial Highness any more. What are you?' he shouted. 'Your servant,' Ella replied. 'Then dress my sore,' he said. Smelling abominably, his skin caked with grime, the man thrust himself at her. There was an ulcer on his groin. Without saying a word, Ella fetched hot water, ointment and bandages, carefully cleaned and dressed the ulcer and told the man to come back next day. 'You should not neglect it. You might get gangrene and that is not pleasant,' she said. The man was dumbfounded, only managing to stumble out the words, 'Who the hell are you?' 'I've already told you,' said Ella. 'I am your servant.'

Even when she was arrested, as she was bound to be, by the Bolsheviks, Ella retained this natural, undramatic dignity. She was not like an ascetic bent upon self-flagellation, but a simple and direct exponent of goodness. She was like the expression of goodness itself, its definition and delineation. The guards took her and those arrested with her, including another Romanov grand duke and one of her faithful sister nuns, to a disused mineshaft. The grand duke resisted them, so they shot him, and threw his body down the shaft. He was not yet dead. Ella knelt at the side of the pit as the guards clutched her shoulders. 'God forgive them,' she said, 'they don't know what they are doing.' Having toppled her in, they threw a hand-grenade after her. Still the shaft was not deep enough to despatch her.

When the guards had departed, peasants gathered round. They heard chanting from the bottom of the mineshaft all night and throughout the next day. It grew dimmer and fainter and eventually ceased.

Some time later the White Army brought their bodies to the surface. Ella's fingers were folded in preparation for the sign of the cross. They had all died of starvation.[14]

I like Ella's story for its bravery and calm distinction in facing up to human nature and finding within it that kernel of goodness which makes real life possible. She did not flinch. She did not lie to herself. She did not protect herself with ecstasies and imaginings and visions, or claim supernatural guidance (though she was a believer). She demonstrated that good action evolves from good thought.

So, too, did Audrey Hepburn. It may seem odd, to some people even impertinent, to speak of a filmstar in juxtaposition to a nun, and within the same chapter as a prophet, but that would be to misunderstand the nature of human goodness. It knows no measure or status. It is revealed in unexpected places and in unlikely people. This is not to imply that Audrey Hepburn was in any way a convert from wickedness, but only that there had been nothing in her life to predict that it would end in a sort of martyrdom. She was a world-famous, successful, beautiful and wealthy actress, with a modicum of talent and a great deal of luck. True, her childhood had been troubled, with a father suspected of Nazi connections, but she overcame that and never spoke about it publicly. Her early memories as a refugee did not appear to have infected her personality, which was sunny and carefree, warm but slightly reserved, and enticingly elegant.

At the end of her career Miss Hepburn retreated from the limelight and devoted herself to working for UNICEF. This did not occur as the result of a sudden revelation, but rather did she slide into it following a personal appearance at a fund-raising event. Thereafter she saw it as her 'mission' to help destitute children by direct action rather than glamorous name-lending.

She joined the staff. The position was unsalaried and she had to meet her own expenses, and she made a point of discouraging attention to herself. Her first assignment was to Ethiopia, where she told reporters, 'I am not here to be seen but so that the rest of the world may see others.' Then, like Grand Duchess Ella, she swapped the limousine for a peasant cart and went into the depth of the famine-struck hinterland, leaving press and photographers behind her for good. Audrey Hepburn spent months travelling through danger and disease, wiping flies from the eyes of dying children, giving comfort and love and paying scant regard for her own welfare on what was to become a total of over fifty journeys into squalor. Each time she returned, she would give press conferences only to talk about the work, deflecting any enquiry as to herself. There was a sob from the back of the press room as she spoke.

The scale of Audrey Hepburn's involvement in her work told visibly on her health. She began to look like the stricken children she was succouring, her face gaunt and pained, her previous elegance wrapped in sorrow. When it was discovered that she had a galloping cancer, she was advised to curtail her trips. She retorted that there was not time. Someone suggested she was sacrificing herself. 'It's not a sacrifice,' she said, 'because a sacrifice means that you give up something you want for something you don't want. This is no sacrifice; it's a gift I'm receiving.' The thousands of children who stood in wonder at her devotion to their well-being looked upon her as a visitation of goodness, but they had no idea who she was or that she had been known throughout the world for her beauty.

She died at home in Switzerland. The crowds lining the streets for her funeral came not to goggle at the last journey of a filmstar but to honour a good woman, and there was no pushing or shoving. The UN commissioner Prince Sadruddin Aga Khan commented that Audrey Hepburn had endured more hardship and hazards in her work than most diplomats would be prepared to

286

accept. The film director Fred Zinneman said that she had gone way beyond being an actress. 'I would say she achieved a kind of wisdom.'[15]

Wisdom is the recognition of human worth, the rejection of human wickedness. It is clear-headed and brave, aware of the perils inherent in human character but determined to make flourish the delights. It does not vaunt itself or claim attention. And it may achieve nothing heroic – the Oskar Schindlers of our world are not the only celebrants of humankind; it is significant, too, that Schindler did not seek to be noticed, whereas Goeth, his brother and contrast, his evil double, heralded his every wicked deed with bombast. No, wisdom is frequently tranquil and obscure. Let us finish with an example known to barely half a dozen readers at the most, a person who may serve to illustrate in miniature many of the themes we have tried to adumbrate.

Mabel Sophia Charlotte Ingledew was born in Surrey during the Great War, the daughter of a regular soldier, Albert Ingledew, and his wife, Mabel Court. The Ingledews were self-evidently of old Anglo-Saxon stock, but untraceable, for they had never had property or influence; they were indeed only just literate and only just beyond the reach of poverty. The Courts came from Chichester, a Victorian artisan family, prolific with their children and somewhat cavalier as to their children's parentage. There were seven sisters and three brothers, the sisters giving birth to legitimate and illegitimate offspring with dizzying regularity, the fathers of the bastards usually the mothers' brothers-in-law. Thus Mabel Ingledew was born into a confusing kaleidoscope of cousins who may have been half-sisters and aunts who were most certainly cousins.

Her parents died before her second birthday. Only in their twenties, they succumbed to tuberculosis, then known as consumption. Albert probably contracted the disease on service in India, and his wife may have caught it from him. Not much is known in detail, for they were not worth post mortems or elaborate analysis, and consumption was rife. Mabel had to be passed on to one of her aunts, Lotte, who was married to Nobby Clark. But Lotte had a daughter already, not by Nobby her husband but by one of her sisters' husbands, and Nobby agreed to take Mabel in on condition that Lotte get rid of the other girl. So Bertha (as was her name) went to another aunt, and Mabel was brought up as Mabel Clark. No documents of adoption were ever made and no record of the switch existed. Nor was Mabel told.

She was soon told, however, that she was a wretched nuisance. She had inherited her parents' weak lungs and might even have been mildly consumptive herself, with the result that she coughed uncontrollably for two hours every morning. Lotte told her to 'shut up that noise', so Mabel would go out to the streets to cough (they then lived in Brixton, South London) or shut herself in her room and bury her head between her knees to muffle the sound. She gradually became hunch-backed with routine bending, and was frequently sent to hospital when the coughing fits became dangerously persistent. There she would stay under observation for weeks on end, sometimes months, to the relief of Lotte who was glad to be shot of her. When she came home after one of these interludes, there was no welcome, rather a stony resignation. Lotte and Nobby did not interrupt their lives to make way for Mabel's return; they went to the pub as usual and she stood outside until closing time.

Mabel's schooling was severely disrupted by constant illness and weakness. Her hearing began to suffer (she would be stone deaf by the time she was in her forties). As soon as she caught up on lessons, she was sent to hospital again and fell hopelessly behind. She was inevitably bottom of the class, was teased and mocked. She did not complain. There was nobody to complain to, and Lotte would not have listened with a sympathetic ear. Nor did she feel disposed to blame. She knew perfectly well there were people worse off than herself, or she could imagine it to be so. She was not beaten or abused or treated with real cruelty, although she was aware that

Lotte and Nobby did not behave well and showed no love. She saw the badness in human nature, but was never deflected from looking for the goodness.

By the time she was seventeen the doctors had despaired of her. They told Lotte that she was unlikely to survive until her twentieth birthday. Lotte decided that she should be told (reasoning, no doubt, that she had been a bloody nuisance all these years and now she was about to die on them, which was the last straw). 'You might as well know,' said Lotte, 'we're not your parents anyway. And, by the way, you've got a brother.' Whereupon a strange young man of twenty was brought in from the kitchen. The Ingledews had had a son before Mabel had been born. Nobody had ever mentioned him before.

Mabel's response to this double set of astonishing news was telling and pertinent. She at last realised that she had indeed been a dreadful burden upon people who were not obliged by duty or blood to care for her, and she felt an enormous swell of gratitude for their sacrifice. At the same time, she was rapturously grateful to discover a big brother about whom she could boast and with whom she could look forward to a future. A less biophilic person would have cursed the Clarks for having made her life such a misery of self-abasement, and bewailed the lost years when she had not known her brother.

The doctors said she could not live to twenty. She did. They then said that she was lucky, but she must never marry. In her twenty-first year she met a quiet and hesitant man with a stutter, himself the product of unorthodox upbringing (mother promiscuous and father unknown) and married him. They said that whatever happened, she would never be strong enough to bear children. She went on to have two sons and nearly died after the birth of the second. I know, because I remember it well; I am her elder son.

My brother Colin was born just before the end of the Second World War, and I remember my mother leaving for hospital in one ambulance as I left in another (I had measles or chicken pox – I can't remember which – and had to be isolated). My father asked me to pray for her. I did not quite realise why it should be necessary, but I did as I was bidden. A photograph of my mother holding her new baby shows her to have shrunk to a weight of six stone, with the hunch-back more prominent than ever. It was then that I dimly recognised she had suffered. Later still, I remembered with shame (though I was hardly at fault) that I had learnt to cough before I learned to speak. Since the eternal, racking cough was the first and most repeated sound I encountered in infancy, I had naturally copied it. My mother must have been mortified, but I do not recall her ever chastising me for it.

We had been bombed out of our modest room in Herne Hill during the war, then out of another in Crystal Palace and another in Penge. So had thousands of Londoners, and I do not wish to suggest that our experience was in any way uncommon. Others died, and others were smitten with frail health. I mention it only because the example my mother proffered me (without overt teaching, for she was not articulate and would not have attempted to impose a view anyway) was a perfect illustration of positive thinking, of emergence from self and inward-directed sorrow, of non-religious prayer and non-denominational charity, of giving attention to goodness and caring about its survival in a world stained by war. I never heard her say anything bitter, recriminatory or unkind. I do not recall her ever being selfish. She was completely free from self-pity, even when my father's six-month bout of insane jealousy, referred to in an earlier chapter, drove her to the very edge of tolerance. She was always encouraging and patient, and when I entered the dark, secretive world of early adolescence, she did not remonstrate with me for my sulkiness and obsessive privacy, but gently told me later, when it was all over, 'You know, you didn't speak to me for two years.' She said it without chiding, almost with wry amusement, but tacitly suggesting I would do well to think it over.

Describing his grandmother, the narrator of *A la*

recherche du temps perdu says she was 'so humble and so sweet that her gentleness towards others, and her continual subordination of herself and of her own troubles, appeared on her face blended in a smile which, unlike those seen on the majority of human faces, had no trace in it of irony, save for herself.'[16]

Mabel outwitted the doctors and outlived her husband. When she was about seventy she developed breast cancer. In another woman the doctors might have been able to operate, either to remove the lumps or to take the breast off completely, but they said that her weak chest would not tolerate the anaesthetic and she might die on the table. So she was only able to take hormone pills and, eventually, radiotherapy. She said they were working and that she was comfortable, not in pain and free at last from anxiety. Her deafness was now virtually total, and though I could watch her thinking, and chewing her bottom lip, I had been used to these withdrawn ruminations since my childhood and assumed it was better for her to think quietly rather than force herself to hear in snatches or lip-read. When she died, the first night she was admitted to a hospice for cancer patients, I noticed that her lip had been almost bitten away. The cancer had obviously spread and she had been munching on her lip to beat the pain. What she had been thinking was that she must not protest her discomfort and cause me worry.

I have introduced my mother because she offers an instance of modest benevolence, one that I happen to know well. You do not have to be heroic to discover the good in human nature, or saintly, or bold. You do not need the stigmata of the cross to advertise your credentials, nor does your body have to lie incorruptibly in the earth unless relic-hunters have hacked off bits of it to worship. You do not need fame to support you or power to promote you.

Neither do fame and power disqualify you from the discovery of good. It seems too obvious to merit stating, but the disadvantaged are apt sometimes to assume that

291

fame and power necessarily corrupt. A bus conductor and a cabinet minister have equal chances of being good, just as they have equal chances of stoking gas ovens. But the one quality they must share is alertness. The moral antennae must be alive and receptive, the eyes must be open, the mind free and unencumbered. Constant attention is the conduit of fine conduct. Father John Arnold writes, 'My life becomes guided by something far more challenging than just "keeping the rules". Because I am trying to imitate the goodness and creative love of Jesus, I have the invitation to see everything that I do as an opportunity; and opportunities require reflection and deliberation. Being Christian really does require a lot of careful attention and hard work.'[17]

So does being human.

NOTES

1. The Ashes in the Bread

1. Victor Gollancz, *The Case of Adolf Eichmann*, Gollancz, 1961, p15.
2. *Independent on Sunday*, July 10, 1994.
3. 'Le crime est originellement naturel. La vertu, au contraire, est artificielle, surnaturelle.' *Art Romantique*.
4. Iris Murdoch, *Nuns and Soldiers*, Chatto & Windus, 1980, p69.
5. Christopher Marlowe, *Faustus*, Act I.
6. Quoted in John Julius Norwich, *Christmas Crackers*, Allen Lane, 1980, p178.
7. Stanley Milgram, *Obedience to Authority*, Harper & Row, 1974, pp3–10. A. H. Buss, *The Psychology of Aggression*, Wiley, New York, 1961.
8. Filson Young, *The Trial of Hawley Harvey Crippen*, Hodge, 1920, pxxxii.
9. *ibid.*, ppxiii, xxxiii.
10. Jack Levin and James Alan Fox, *Mass Murder*, Plenum Press, 1985, pp69–70.
11. Thomas Keneally, *Schindler's Ark*, Hodder & Stoughton, 1982, p188.
12. There lies within the breast of every man, at every minute, two simultaneous impulses, one towards God, the other towards Satan.
13. Brian Masters, *Killing for Company*, Cape, 1985, pp25–26.
14. Seneca, *Letters*, XC.
15. Quoted in Oliver Thomson, *A History of Sin*, Canongate, 1993, p103.
16. *The Letter of Paul to the Romans*, XII, 21.

17. Brian Masters, *The Shrine of Jeffrey Dahmer*, Hodder, 1993, p87.
18. Lawrence Kohlberg, 'Stage & Sequence: the Cognitive-Developmental Approach to Socialization', in *Handbook of Socialization Theory and Research*, ed. David Goslin, Rand McNally, 1969.
19. William Shakespeare, *Richard III*, Act I.
20. Iris Murdoch, *Henry and Cato*, Chatto, 1976, p295.
21. Iris Murdoch, *The Time of the Angels*, Chatto, 1966, p185.
22. Mary Midgley, *Wickedness*, Routledge & Kegan Paul, 1984, p4.
23. Mikal Gilmore, *Shot in the Heart*, Viking, 1994, p194.
24. Bruno Bettelheim, *Surviving and Other Essays*, Knopf, 1979, p270.
25. Anthony Storr, *Human Destructiveness*, Routledge, 1972, 1991, p138.

2. Foregone Conclusions

1. Michel de Montaigne, *Essais*, Book II, Chapter 11, 'On Cruelty'.
2. Anthony Storr, *Human Aggression*, Allen Lane, 1968, p26.
3. Niko Tinbergen, *Social Behaviour in Animals*, Methuen, 1953.
4. Recent research suggests that the praying mantis pair may well end up with a pleasant fox-trot instead of ritual slaughter; scientists have been guilty in the past of not giving them enough to eat. See Marina Warner, *Managing Monsters*, Vintage, 1994, p16.
5. Quoted in John Julius Norwich, *Christmas Crackers*, p166.
6. Jared Diamond, *The Rise and Fall of the Third Chimpanzee*, Radius, 1991, p64.
7. Anthony Storr, *Human Destructiveness*, p21.
8. Ismond Rosen (ed.), *The Pathology and Treatment of Sexual Deviation*, Oxford University Press, 1964, p316.
9. David Canter, *Criminal Shadows*, HarperCollins, 1994, p58.
10. Jared Diamond, *The Rise and Fall of the Third Chimpanzee*, p81.
11. Bruce Chatwin, *The Songlines*, Cape, 1987, p228.

12. Robert Ardrey, *African Genesis*, Collins, 1961, p29 *et passim*.
13. Sigmund Freud, *Beyond the Pleasure Principle*, Hogarth Press, 1955, pp36–38.
14. Melanie Klein, *Envy and Gratitude*, Tavistock Clinic, 1957, pp4–5.
15. Steve Jones, *The Language of the Genes*, HarperCollins, 1993, p84.
16. Roger Shattuck, *The Forbidden Experiment*, Secker & Warburg, 1980, p27.
17. Brian Masters, *Gary*, Cape, 1990, *passim*.
18. M.F. Ashley Montagu, *Culture and the Evolution of Man*, Oxford University Press, 1962.
19. Elizabeth Burford, *Representations of the Self using Spatial Ideas*, unpublished, p113.
20. *Spectator*, June 25, 1994.
21. H. Cleckley, *The Mask of Sanity*, C.V. Mosby, 1976.
22. Mary Midgley, *Beast and Man*, Harvester, 1979, p336.
23. Jared Diamond, *The Rise and Fall of the Third Chimpanzee*, p98.
24. Steve Jones, *The Language of the Genes*, p69.
25. *ibid.*, pp185, 197.
26. *ibid.*, p178.
27. Richard Dawkins, *The Selfish Gene*, Oxford University Press, 1976, p37.
28. *ibid.*, p64.
29. Jared Diamond, *The Rise and Fall of the Third Chimpanzee*, p83.
30. Herschel Prins, *Dangerous Behaviour, the Law, and Mental Disorder*, Tavistock, 1986, p147.
31. Mary Midgley, *Beast and Man*, p172.
32. Oliver Sacks, *The Man Who Mistook His Wife for a Hat*, Duckworth, 1985, pp154–157.
33. From the very vileness of a germ or an atom, vile was I born. I am a wretch because I am a man, and I feel within me the primeval slime. Act II, Sc 1, libretto by Arrigo Boito.
34. In *History of Western Philosophy*, Allen & Unwin, 1946, p362, and in *Human Society in Ethics and Politics*, Allen & Unwin, 1954, p93.

35. Rosalind Miles, *The Children We Deserve*, HarperCollins, 1994, p130.
36. Charles Hampden-Turner, *Maps of the Mind*, Mitchell Beazley, 1981, p32.
37. Brian Masters, *The Shrine of Jeffrey Dahmer*.
38. B.F. Skinner, *Beyond Freedom and Dignity*.
39. Leon Radzinowicz and Joan King, *The Growth of Crime*, Hamish Hamilton, 1977, p92.
40. Steve Jones, *The Language of the Genes*, p225.

3. Beastly Behaviour

1. Richard Dawkins, *The Selfish Gene*, p150.
2. Charles Darwin, *The Origin of Species*, Murray, 1959 (p116 in Penguin edition).
3. Charles Darwin, *The Descent of Man and Selection in Relation to Sex*, Murray, 1871.
4. Richard Dawkins, *The Selfish Gene*, p185.
5. D.O. Hebb, *Organization of Behaviour* (New York, 1949), quoted in Oliver Thomson, *A History of Sin*, p3.
6. Robert Ardrey, *African Genesis*, p78.
7. Eugène Marais, *My Friends the Baboons*, 1939.
8. Konrad Lorenz, *On Aggression*, Methuen, 1966, p94.
9. Frank Longford, *Saints*, Hutchinson, 1987, pp129–136.
10. Bertrand Russell, *Human Society in Ethics and Politics*, Allen & Unwin, 1954, p124.
11. Bruce Chatwin, *The Songlines*, p247.
12. Anthony Storr, *Human Destructiveness*, p72.
13. Iris Murdoch, *The Green Knight*, Chatto, 1993, p46.
14. Jean-Jacques Rousseau, *Deuxième Discours*, and *Emile*, Book II.
15. M.A. Amiel, *Ethics and Legality in Jewish Law*, 1992.
16. Robert Ardrey, *African Genesis*, pp149–150.
17. In fairness it should be noted that some studies of so-called innocent primitives, by R.B. Lee and Melvin Konner for example, have indicated a possible murder rate higher than in the United States of America. See the latter's *The Tangled Wing*, 1982.
18. Bruce Chatwin, *The Songlines*, pp18, 21, 218.

19. Marina Warner, *Managing Monsters*, p33.
20. Roger Shattuck, *The Forbidden Experiment*, pp28, 52, 182.
21. *ibid.*, p83.
22. *ibid.*, p127.
23. Jared Diamond, *The Rise and Fall of the Third Chimpanzee*, p34.
24. Bruce Chatwin, *The Songlines*, pp259–260.
25. *ibid.*, pp199–200.

4. Out of Order

1. Cicero, *De Finibus*, Loeb Classical Library, Book I, Chapter X.
2. D.J. West, *Murder Followed by Suicide*, Heinemann, 1965.
3. Herschel Prins, *Bizarre Behaviours*, Tavistock, 1990, pp11–14.
4. Herschel Prins, *Dangerous Behaviour, the Law, and Mental Disorder*, p40; and the *Guardian*, June 30, 1984.
5. R.D. Laing, *The Divided Self*, Tavistock, 1960, Chapter 11.
6. Anthony Trollope, *He Knew He Was Right*, 1869, Trollope Society edition, p325.
7. Herschel Prins, *Dangerous Behaviour, the Law, and Mental Disorder*, p97.
8. J.C. Pritchard, *A Treatise on Insanity and Other Disorders Affecting the Mind*, 1835.
9. D. Henderson, *Psychopathic States*, 1939.
10. Ed Gein, Dennis Nilson, Edward Paisnel.
11. Tim Clark and John Penycate, *Psychopath*, Routledge, 1976.
12. *Independent*, September 26, 1987 (quoted from Herschel Prins).

5. Tics and Demons

1. Brian McConnell and William Tatum, *Multiple Murder and Demonic Possession*, Book Guild, 1993, p73.
2. J.L. Mackie, *Ethics*, Penguin, 1977, pp213–214.
3. Charles Baudelaire, Preface to *Les Fleurs du Mal*.

4. 'The devil's most cunning device is to persuade us that he does not exist.' Charles Baudelaire, *Petits poèmes en Prose*.

5. Charles Baudelaire, *Les Fleurs du Mal*, 'Avis au lecteur'.

6. Rev. Carl Vogel, *Begone Satan*, Tan Books, Rockford, Ill., 1973, pp10, 18, 30.

7. McConnell and Tatum, *Multiple Murder and Demonic Possession*, pp. 159–163, 180–185.

8. Brian Masters, *The Shrine of Jeffrey Dahmer*, pp111–112.

9. Stephen G. Michaud and Hugh Aynesworth, *The Only Living Witness*, p288.

10. Joel Norris, *Serial Killers*, Arrow, 1990, p265.

11. Joel Norris, *The Killer Next Door*, Arrow, 1992, pp126, 125, 114.

12. McConnell and Tatum, *Multiple Murder and Demonic Possession*, pp51–53, 82–84.

13. A. Hyatt Williams, 'The Psychopathology and Treatment of Sexual Murderers', in *The Pathology and Treatment of Sexual Deviation*, ed. Ismond Rosen.

14. *Mail on Sunday*, April 26, 1987.

15. St Augustine, *Confessions*, Book V.

16. Quoted in Frank Longford, *Saints*, p94.

17. Mary Midgley, *Wickedness*, p103.

18. Oliver Sacks, *The Man Who Mistook His Wife for a Hat*, p109.

19. Oliver Sacks, *An Anthropologist on Mars*, Picador, 1995, pp73–101.

20. Oliver Sacks, *The Man Who Mistook His Wife for a Hat*, pp117–118.

21. J.G. Frazer, *The Golden Bough*, Papermac, 1987, pp542, 543, 546, 554–557.

22. A.N. Wilson, *Jesus*, Sinclair-Stevenson, 1992, p112.

23. McConnell and Tatum, *Multiple Murder and Demonic Possession*, Chapter 4.

6. To Do or Not to Do

1. Lionel Dahmer, *A Father's Story*, Morrow, 1994, p140.

2. Iris Murdoch, *The Time of the Angels*, p147.

3. 'Virtue refuses facility as a companion . . . it demands a harsh and thorny road,' *Essais*, Book II, Chapter 11 'On Cruelty'.

4. Brian Keenan, *An Evil Cradling*, Hutchinson, 1992, p223.

5. Jean-Paul Sartre, *Le Sursis*, Gallimard, 1945, p419.

6. Jean-Paul Sartre, *Les Mouches*, Gallimard, 1943.

7. Maurice Cranston, *Sartre*, Oliver & Boyd, 1962, p11.

8. Jean-Paul Sartre, *Les Mots*, Gallimard, 1963, p71.

9. Iris Murdoch, *The Sovereignty of Good*, Routledge, 1970, p97.

10. See Jean-Paul Sartre, *Baudelaire*, Gallimard, 1947, *passim*.

11. Sartre, *Saint Genet, Comédien et Martyr*, Gallimard, 1962.

12. *Independent*, April 9, 1994.

13. *Daily Mirror*, October 1, 1992.

14. V. Sackville-West, *Saint Joan of Arc*, Cobden-Sanderson, 1936, p382.

15. *ibid.*, p383.

16. *ibid.*, p387.

17. Colin Wilson, *New Pathways in Psychology*, Gollancz, 1979, p236.

18. Anthony Storr, *Human Aggression*, p24.

19. David Canter, *Criminal Shadows*, p158.

20. Jack Levin and James Alan Fox, *Mass Murder*, p68.

21. Colin Wilson, *Serial Killers*, W.H. Allen, 1990, pp139–146.

22. Alexander Artley, *Murder in the Heart*, Hamish Hamilton, 1993, *passim*.

7. Looking Out

1. Iris Murdoch, *The Sovereignty of Good, p59.*

2. Brian Keenan, *An Evil Cradling*, p287.

3. Cicero, *De Officiis*, Book I, Chapter IX; Book III, Chapter VI.

4. Lionel Dahmer, *A Father's Story*, pp183–184.

5. Oliver Sacks, *The Man Who Mistook His Wife for a Hat*, p188.

6. Joel Norris, *The Killer Next Door*, pp136–137.

7. Muriel Gardiner, *The Deadly Innocents*, Hogarth, 1977, pp95*ff.*
8. David Canter, *Criminal Shadows*, p213.
9. Dom David Knowles, *The Monastic Order in England*, p242.
10. Lionel Dahmer, *A Father's Story*, pp222–224.
11. *ibid.*, p193.

8. Avowed Intent

1. II Samuel 6, lines 6–7.
2. Peter Abelard, *Commentary on the Epistle to the Romans.*
3. Hannah Arendt, *Eichmann in Jerusalem*, Penguin, 1977, pp247–248.
4. *ibid.*, p288.
5. Iris Murdoch, *The Green Knight*, p109.
6. 'On a Late Acquittal', *The Times*, March 8, 1843.
7. Brian Masters, *Killing for Company*, p217.
8. David Canter, *Criminal Shadows*, p260.
9. Lionel Dahmer, *A Father's Story*, pp186–187.
10. Levin and Fox, *Mass Murder*, p107.
11. *ibid.*, p210.
12. Frederic Wertham, *Dark Legend*, p99.
13. Ronald Markman and Dominick Bosco, *Alone With the Devil*, Piatkus, 1989, p43.

9. In the Same Boat

1. Michel de Montaigne, *Essais*, Book III, Chapter 2, 'Du repentir'.
2. Bertrand Russell, *A History of Western Philosophy*, p571.
3. Herschel Prins, *Bizarre Behaviours*, p2.
4. Lionel Dahmer, *A Father's Story*, pp212, 228.
5. David Canter, *Criminal Shadows*, p271.
6. John Mortimer, *Villains*, Oxford University Press, 1992, p ix. A recent book posits a convincing case for Armstrong's innocence.

7. Hannah Arendt, *Eichmann in Jerusalem*, pp25, 55, 145.
8. *ibid.*, pp87–8.
9. Taken from Isaac Deutscher's biography. I am indebted for this and previous examples to Oliver Thomson's *History of Sin*, pp100, 125, 135, 140, 141, 147, 153, 154, 168, 231.
10. Anthony Storr, *Human Aggression*, pp98–99.
11. Donald Thomas, *The Marquis de Sade*, Allison & Busby, 1992, pp159, 296.
12. Brian Masters, *The Shrine of Jeffrey Dahmer*, p262.
13. Alexander Pope, *Essay on Man*, Epistle 2, line 131.
14. Cicero, *De Officiis*, Book I, Chapter XXIX.
15. William Shakespeare, *Hamlet*, Act I.
16. Hannah Arendt, *Eichmann in Jerusalem*, pp114, 150.
17. Erich Fromm, *Anatomy of Human Destructiveness*, p573.

10. The Web of Life

1. Aldous Huxley, *Texts and Pretexts*.
2. Quoted in *Ethics*, ed. Peter Singer, Oxford University Press, p57.
3. David Hume, *A Treatise on Human Nature*, Clarendon Press, p470.
4. Bertrand Russell, *A History of Western Philosophy*, p744.
5. Niccolò Macchiavelli, *Il Principe*, Chapter VIII.
6. Bertrand Russell, *Human Society in Ethics and Politics*, p147.
7. Alastair McAlpine, *The Servant*, Faber, 1992, p78.
8. Bertrand Russell, *Human Society in Ethics and Politics*, p49.
9. Albert Schweitzer, *Civilization and Ethics*.
10. Brigid Brophy, *Animals, Men and Morals*.
11. Joseph Rickaby SJ, *Moral Philosophy*, Longmans, 1889, p248.
12. *Animals' Rights: A Symposium*, ed. Ryder & Paterson, Centaur Press, 1979, p36.
13. *Cum Grano*, in *The Extended Circle*, ed. Wynne-Tyson, Centaur press, 1985, p305.
14. Frances Power Cobbe, in *The Extended Circle*, p55.

15. *The Idler*, August 5, 1758.
16. G.B. Shaw, Preface to *The Doctors' Dilemma*.
17. Christian Barnard, in *The Extended Circle*, p9.
18. Albert Schweitzer, *Civilization and Ethics*.

11. Accurate Vision

1. Iris Murdoch, *The Sovereignty of Good*, pp67, 69, 78, 85, 91, 93, 95, 103.
2. Hannah Arendt, *Eichmann in Jerusalem*, pp286–287.
3. Iris Murdoch, *The Green Knight*, p39.
4. Albert Schweitzer, *Memoirs of Childhood and Youth*, p230.
5. Thomas Hood, 'The Lady's Dream'.
6. Iris Murdoch, *The Sovereignty of Good*, p103.
7. Cicero, *De Officiis*, Book I, Chapter XXIII.
8. W.E.H. Lecky, *History of European Morals*, Longmans, Green, 1892, Vol. II, p107.
9. *ibid.*, p111.
10. John Arnold, *The Quality of Mercy*, St Paul's, 1993.
11. Cicero, *De Officiis*, Book III, Chapter XII.
12. Edward Gibbon, *Decline and Fall of the Roman Empire*, Chapter 47.
13. Voltaire, *Traité sur la Tolérance*, 1762.
14. *The Golden Legend.*
15. Robert Fisk, *Independent on Sunday*, June 19, 1994.
16. Robert Ardrey, *The Social Contract*, Collins, 1970, pp358–359.
17. Thomas Keneally, *Schindler's Ark,*, p275.
18. Victor Gollancz, *The Case of Adolf Eichmann*, Gollancz, 1961, p14.
19. Hannah Arendt, *Eichmann in Jerusalem*, p232.

12. The Loss of Shame

1. In the final chapter of his *Anatomy of Human Destructiveness*.
2. Joseph Conrad, *The Secret Agent*, p43.
3. Steve Jones, *The Language of the Genes*, p193.

4. Taken from Jared Diamond, *The Rise and Fall of the Third Chimpanzee*, p277.
5. Thomas Keneally, *Schindler's Ark*, pp193, 157.
6. Martin Gilbert, *The Holocaust*, Collins, 1986, pp105, 64, 145, 137, 155, 159, 170, 188, 178, 194, 198, 204, 796.
7. *The Trial of the Major German War Criminals, Proceedings of the International Military Tribunal at Nuremberg*, Her Majesty's Stationery Office, 1949.
8. Martin Gilbert, *The Holocaust* p795, and *Independent on Sunday*, January 15, 1995.
9. *The Trial of Joseph Kramer*, quoted in *The Faber Book of Reportage*, ed. John Carey, 1987, p604.
10. *The Trial of the Major German War Criminals*, HMSO.

13. Saints

1. St Thérèse de l'Enfant Jésus, *Histoire d'une Ame*, quoted in V. Sackville-West, *The Eagle and the Dove*, Michael Joseph, 1943, p113.
2. David Newsome, *The Convert Cardinals*, John Murray, 1993, p371.
3. Iris Murdoch, *Henry and Cato*, pp190–195.
4. Oscar Wilde, *The Picture of Dorian Gray*, 1890.
5. Mary Midgley, *Beast and Man*, p124.
6. Iris Murdoch, *The Black Prince*, Chatto, 1973, p149.
7. Bertrand Russell, *Human Society in Ethics and Politics*, p64.
8. G. Ashe, *Mahatma Gandhi*, 1968, quoted in Oliver Thomson, *A History of Sin*, p240.
9. John Arnold, *The Quality of Mercy*, p31.
10. *ibid.*, p39.
11. A.N. Wilson, *Jesus*, p158.
12. Alastair McAlpine, *The Servant*, p74.
13. V. Sackville-West, *The Eagle and The Dove*, pp68, 71, 76.
14. E.M. Almedingen, *An Unbroken Unity*, Bodley Head, 1964, pp29, 52–58, 65, 75, 107, 110, 128.
15. Alexander Walker, *Audrey*, Weidenfeld & Nicolson, 1994, pp266–291.

16. Marcel Proust, *A la recherche du temps perdu*, Vol. I, p24 in Gallimard edition, p13 in Scott-Moncrieffe translation (Chatto & Windus).
17. John Arnold, *The Quality of Mercy*, p58.

INDEX

Abelard, Peter 185, 188
aborigines, Australian 82
achieve, need to 177, 178–9, 180–1
Acosta José de 224
actors representing conflict in human nature 25–6
actus reus 191
Adam and Eve 56
Adler, Alfred 156
  on need for achievement 179–80
Aelred of Rievaulx, St 13, 78, 176–7, 276, 280
Africa and demons 40, 133
African Genesis (Ardrey) 40
Aga Khan, Prince Sadruddin 286
aggression
  channelling of 46–7
  in children 43–4, 46–7
  and death wish 42–3
  defensive 32–3
  disrupted into destruction 39
  as expression of being 34
  fear of displaying 92–3
  and gender 34–5
  innate human 32
  lack of healthy 38
  as life force 32–3
  natural 38, 40–1, 86, 167
  unassuaged 37–8
  useful 32–3
aggressiveness
  benign 35–6
  definition of 35–6
  in display 35

proper nurturing of 48–9
  result of frustration 46
ahimsa, Hindu 274, 276
Albee, Edward 130
Albigensians, slaughter of 247
Alice's Adventures in Wonderland (Carroll) 215
Allitt, Beverly 97
alter ego 117
altruism 62
  in animals 64–6
Amelekites 247
American Law Institute 195
Amiel, M. A. 81
amity–enmity complex 74
amnesia
  feigned 199
  in Korsakov's syndrome 124, 125
  organic 55
anarchy engendered by absolute licence 46
animal behaviour
  beneficial 64–6
  pre-existent 63
animal superiority 89
animals
  and aggression 38
  cruelty to 39, 172, 227–30
  human relationship with 69–72, 79–80, 227–31
  natural aggression of 41
  negative instincts of 80
anorexia nervosa 46, 245, 269
Anthony of Padua, St 11–12, 13, 14, 29, 155
anthropocentrism 230

313

314